当代国外语言学与应用语言学文库（升级版）

# 认知语言学和语言教学

Cognitive Linguistics and Language Teaching

Randal Holme 著
蓝纯 导读

外语教学与研究出版社
FOREIGN LANGUAGE TEACHING AND RESEARCH PRESS
北京 BEIJING

京权图字：01-2010-6500

First published in English under the title
Cognitive Linguistics and Language Teaching
by R. Holme, edition:1
Copyright © Randal Holme, 2009
This edition has been reprinted and published under licence from
Springer Nature Limited.
For copyright reasons this edition is not for sales outside of China's mainland.

## 图书在版编目 (CIP) 数据

认知语言学和语言教学 = Cognitive Linguistics and Language Teaching：英文／（英）兰德尔·霍姆（Randal Holme）著；蓝纯导读. —— 北京：外语教学与研究出版社，2021.9
（当代国外语言学与应用语言学文库：升级版）
ISBN 978-7-5213-2870-7

Ⅰ. ①认… Ⅱ. ①兰… ②蓝… Ⅲ. ①认知语言学－应用－语言教学－研究－英文 Ⅳ. ①H09

中国版本图书馆 CIP 数据核字 (2021) 第 155337 号

出 版 人　徐建忠
项目负责　姚　虹　李亚琦
责任编辑　李亚琦
责任校对　都楠楠
装帧设计　李　高
出版发行　外语教学与研究出版社
社　　址　北京市西三环北路 19 号（100089）
网　　址　http://www.fltrp.com
印　　刷　唐山市润丰印务有限公司
开　　本　650×980　1/16
印　　张　18.5
版　　次　2021 年 9 月第 1 版　2021 年 9 月第 1 次印刷
书　　号　ISBN 978-7-5213-2870-7
定　　价　46.00 元

购书咨询：(010) 88819926　电子邮箱：club@fltrp.com
外研书店：https://waiyants.tmall.com
凡印刷、装订质量问题，请联系我社印制部
联系电话：(010) 61207896　电子邮箱：zhijian@fltrp.com
凡侵权、盗版书籍线索，请联系我社法律事务部
举报电话：(010) 88817519　电子邮箱：banquan@fltrp.com
物料号：328700001

# 当代国外语言学与应用语言学文库

（升级版）

## 学术委员会
（按姓氏拼音排列）

| 蔡金亭 | 陈新仁 | 程　工 | 程晓堂 | 戴曼纯 | 丁建新 |
| --- | --- | --- | --- | --- | --- |
| 丁言仁 | 董　洁 | 董燕萍 | 范　琳 | 封宗信 | 高　远 |
| 顾永琦 | 韩宝成 | 何莲珍 | 何　伟 | 胡建华 | 胡旭辉 |
| 胡壮麟 | 黄国文 | 黄友义 | 贾玉新 | 姜望琪 | 金　艳 |
| 蓝　纯 | 李　兵 | 李福印 | 李战子 | 梁晓晖 | 刘立华 |
| 刘润清 | 刘世生 | 马秋武 | 苗兴伟 | 宁春岩 | 冉永平 |
| 申　丹 | 施　旭 | 束定芳 | 宋　莉 | 苏　祺 | 田贵森 |
| 田海龙 | 王初明 | 王海啸 | 王克非 | 王文斌 | 王　寅 |
| 文秋芳 | 文　旭 | 吴　霞 | 吴一安 | 武尊民 | 徐　浩 |
| 杨信彰 | 杨延宁 | 姚小平 | 于书林 | 余国兴 | 张　辉 |
| 张绍杰 | 周晓林 | | | | |

# 出版前言

"当代国外语言学与应用语言学文库"（以下简称"文库"）从2000年至今已出版近200个品种，深受语言学与应用语言学专业师生和研究者的欢迎，大家既把"文库"视为进入语言学与应用语言学百花园的引路人，又把"文库"视为知识更新的源泉，还把"文库"当成点亮科研之路的明灯。

为了追踪相关领域的研究进程，并满足广大读者的需求，外语教学与研究出版社从2020年开始启动了"文库"的更新升级工作，与牛津大学出版社、剑桥大学出版社、劳特利奇出版社等世界知名出版机构合作，推出"文库"（升级版）。

"文库"升级的原则如下：

1. 对原有经典图书，若无新版，则予以保留，并予以必要修订；若有新版，则以新版代替旧版，并请相关领域学者撰写新版中文导读。

2. 引进语言学与应用语言学领域的新锐力作，进一步拓展学科领域。

3. 用二维码代替CD-ROM，帮助读者更加快捷地获取内容。

"文库"（升级版）定位为一套大型的、开放性的系列丛书，希望它能对我国语言学教学与研究和外语教学与研究起到积极的推动作用。外语教学与研究出版社亦将继续努力，力争把国外最新、最具影响力的语言学与应用语言学著作奉献给广大读者。

外语教学与研究出版社
2021年8月

# 当代国外语言学与应用语言学文库（升级版）
## 2021年出版书目

—— **Cognitive Linguistics 认知语言学**

*Cognitive Linguistics and Language Teaching*
《认知语言学和语言教学》
　　Randal Holme

*An Introduction to Cognitive Linguistics (Second Edition)*
《认知语言学入门（第二版）》
　　F. Ungerer & H.-J. Schmid

—— **First Language Acquisition 第一语言习得**

*An Introduction to Child Language Development*
《儿童语言发展引论》
　　Susan H. Foster-Cohen

—— **Functional Linguistics 功能语言学**

*Genre Relations: Mapping Culture*
《语类关系与文化映射》
　　J. R. Martin & David Rose

*An Introduction to Functional Grammar (Third Edition)*
《功能语法导论（第三版）》
　　M. A. K. Halliday, revised by Christian Matthiessen

—— **General Linguistics 普通语言学**

*Course in General Linguistics*
《普通语言学教程》
　　F. de Saussure

*General Linguistics (Fourth Edition)*
《普通语言学概论（第四版）》
　　R. H. Robins

*An Introduction to Linguistics*
《语言学入门》
　　Stuart C. Poole

—— **History of Linguistics** 语言学史

*A Short History of Linguistics (Fourth Edition)*
《语言学简史（第四版）》
  R. H. Robins

—— **Intercultural Communication** 跨文化交际

*Intercultural Interaction: A Multidisciplinary Approach to Intercultural Communication*
《跨文化互动：跨文化交际的多学科研究》
  Helen Spencer-Oatey & Peter Franklin

—— **Lexicography** 词典学

*Dictionary of Lexicography*
《词典学词典》
  R. R. K. Hartmann & Gregory James

—— **Philosophy of Language** 语言哲学

*How to Do Things with Words*
《如何以言行事》
  J. L. Austin

—— **Pragmatics** 语用学

*Meaning in Interaction: An Introduction to Pragmatics*
《言谈互动中的意义：语用学引论》
  Jenny Thomas

—— **Psycholinguistics** 心理语言学

*The Articulate Mammal: An Introduction to Psycholinguistics (Fourth Edition)*
《会说话的哺乳动物：心理语言学入门（第四版）》
  Jean Aitchison

—— **Research Method** 研究方法

*Research Perspectives on English for Academic Purposes*
《学术英语的多维研究视角》
  John Flowerdew & Matthew Peacock

—— **Second Language Acquisition** 第二语言习得

*Fossilization in Adult Second Language Acquisition*
《成人二语习得中的僵化现象》
  韩照红（Zhaohong Han）

*Linguistics and Second Language Acquisition*
《语言学和第二语言习得》
  Vivian Cook

*Strategies in Learning and Using a Second Language*
《学习和运用第二语言的策略》
  Andrew D. Cohen

*Tasks in Second Language Learning*
《第二语言学习中的任务》
  Virginia Samuda & Martin Bygate

## ——Semantics 语义学

*Meaning in Language: An Introduction to Semantics and Pragmatics (Third Edition)*
《语言的意义：语义学与语用学导论（第三版）》
  Alan Cruse

*Semantics (Fourth Edition)*
《语义学（第四版）》
  John I. Saeed

## ——Sociolinguistics 社会语言学

*The Handbook of Sociolinguistics*
《社会语言学通览》
  Florian Coulmas

*An Introduction to Sociolinguistics (Seventh Edition)*
《社会语言学引论（第七版）》
  Ronald Wardhaugh & Janet M. Fuller

## ——Stylistics 文体学

*A Linguistic Guide to English Poetry*
《英诗学习指南：语言学的分析方法》
  Geoffrey N. Leech

*Patterns in Language: Stylistics for Students of Language and Literature*
《语言模式：文体学入门》
  Joanna Thornborrow & Shân Wareing

*Style in Fiction: A Linguistic Introduction to English Fictional Prose*
《小说文体论：英语小说的语言学入门》
  Geoffrey N. Leech & Michael H. Short

*Stylistics: A Practical Coursebook*
《实用文体学教程》
  Laura Wright & Jonathan Hope

——Syntax 句法学

*Chomsky's Universal Grammar: An Introduction (Third Edition)*
《乔姆斯基的普遍语法教程（第三版）》
  V. J. Cook & Mark Newson

——Testing 语言测试

*Language Testing and Validation: An Evidence-Based Approach*
《语言测试与效度验证：基于证据的研究方法》
  Cyril J. Weir

——Text Linguistics 语篇语言学

*The Language of Evaluation: Appraisal in English*
《评估语言：英语评价系统》
  J. R. Martin & P. R. R. White

*Metadiscourse*
《元话语》
  Ken Hyland

# 导　　读

蓝纯

## 1. 总述

　　自1980年Lakoff & Johnson的 *Metaphors We Live By* 出版，认知语言学作为语言学领域里一种新的研究路径已经经历了四十余年的蓬勃发展。进入二十一世纪后，认知语言学研究表现出的一个比较明显的趋势是与其他学科相结合，产生了新的研究视角。比如，认知语言学与文学评论相结合，产生了认知诗学（cognitive poetics）；与文体学相结合，产生了认知文体学（cognitive stylistics）；与语言教学相结合，产生了新的教学理念和方法。Randal Holme的这本《认知语言学和语言教学》便是将认知语言学理论运用于语言教学实践的一个有益尝试。

　　全书分九章四个部分。第一章是序论。第二到第四章为第一部分，讲述认知语言学关于人类认知的体验性的基本观点，即认知源于人类在跟外部世界打交道的过程中所产生的身体经验和社会文化经验，并探讨这一观点对于语言教学的启示。第五、六章构成第二部分，讲述认知语言学的概念观（conceptualisation）和范畴观（categorisation），并尝试从语言所承载的认知视角和认知方式出发，探讨语言教师如何能善加利用来有效地讲解目标语的形式和意义。第七、八章构成第三部分，分别阐述教师如何帮助学习者习得语词所激活的百科意义（encyclopaedic meaning）和语言中不同级别的构式（construction）。第九章是结论部分，作者提出了开发认知语言学大纲（cognitive linguistics syllabus）的构想，并对其指导原则、教学理念和运作方式进行了尝试性的梳理。

## 2. 分章介绍

### 第一章: 序论

本章简要介绍本书的理论背景和整体框架。作者首先分析了生成语言学（generative linguistics）和系统功能语言学（systemic functional linguistics）理论对二语教学的影响：前者引领了理论指导型教学法（linguistics applied approach，LA），后者引领了实用理论型教学法（applied linguistics approach，AL）。在以生成语言学为主导的LA模式中，语言被视为"理想的说者–听者关系中的恒定的实体"（a stable entity within… an 'ideal speaker-hearer relationship'，p. 2），被剥离了社会和文化背景，甚至被与大脑所从事的其他认知活动分离开来。据此，二语习得（SLA）不过是存在于理想的说者–听者大脑中的普遍语法（universal grammar，UG）与作为一个抽象的逻辑系统而运作的目标语之间的一种互动。这一模式弊端很多，往大了说，语言不能脱离具体的社会和文化背景，也无法与人类的其他认知

• 导读 •

活动分开；往小了说，它也无法解释二语习得与母语习得的差别，无法解释为什么成人在习得母语之后还能不同程度地习得二语。

与生成语言学不同，系统功能语言学强调语言的根本目的是交流，而交流是一种社会活动。在这一理论的指导下，二语学习的目的向培养学习者的交际能力（communicative competence）倾斜，而这意味着在语言形式与语言形式所承载的交际意图和所表达的意义之间建立起很强的关联。不过AL模式同样存在不少短板：理论上，它把语言视为一个存在于人类社会中（而不是人类大脑里）的"外在的物体"（extraneous object, p. 5）；实践中，语言被简化为固定的表达法与这些表达法所承载的交际功能之间的对应关系。

认知语言学的兴起最初与语言教学研究无关，而主要源于学者们对生成语言学的诸多假设的质疑。比如，生成语言学致力于从不同语言中抽象出普遍语法规则，但迄今这方面的研究仍没有实质性进展；生成语言学将句法研究视为语言研究的核心，而忽视了意义的表达，但有越来越多的证据表明句法并不能独立于意义而存在；生成语言学认为语言能力独立于人类的其他认知能力，但随着认知科学的发展，越来越多的学者对此也提出了质疑。

认知语言学的产生和发展与两个名字紧密相连：George Lakoff 和 Mark Johnson。二者在1980年出版的 *Metaphors We Live By* 中对隐喻（metaphor）和转喻（metonymy）的开拓性研究奠定了认知语言学的基础。他们认为，隐喻和转喻都不是单纯的语言现象，而是体现了人类的隐喻认知方式和转喻认知方式。由此生发，认知语言学家们逐渐提出了认知语言学的一些核心观点：

1）意义是认知的产物；

2）认知来源于人类的各种物理经验和社会经验；

3）人体（the human body）在人类与外部世界打交道的各种

物理经验和社会经验上都打下了自己的烙印。

认知语言学原本无心插手语言教学研究，但在其发展过程中，越来越多的学者注意到它对语言教学的价值。从学习语言的角度来看，生成语言学的误区在于它过于强调语言是一个抽象的、自主的逻辑系统，存在于理想的说者-听者大脑中，而忽视了语言是为人使用的这一基本事实；系统功能语言学的不足则在于它过于强调语言的社会性和功能性，而忽视了语言是遵循一定的规则而运作的符号系统。认知语言学则因其认知性和社会-文化性有望解决语言教学领域LA和AL之间的矛盾：认知语言学认为，语言既是认知的（它源于人类认知世界的方式），也是社会的和文化的（它存在于人类社会中，是文化的载体，并且在代代相传中不断演变）。因此，语言既不是作为一个自主的逻辑系统而存在，也不是作为一个外在的物体而存在，它所记录和表达的是人类社会在岁月的流逝中如何将集体经验规约化。

本章最后一节简述作者写作此书的目的是向一线教师介绍认知语言学的基本原理，希望能在此基础之上生发出一种新的教学理念，来跨越LA和AL模式之间的鸿沟。

## 第二章 关于语言的意义的难题

传统的语言教学建立在这样一条假设之上，即二语学习就是拿一种新的语言形式去套母语中的旧的意义，而这又是建立在传统的语义学研究对意义的认识上，即意义就是语言与外部世界之间一种直接的对应关系。比如，snow这个单词之所以有意义，就在于它指称外部世界里一种客观存在的自然现象，而"Snow is white"这个断言之所以有意义，就在于它真实地描述了外部世界这种客观存在的自然现象。

认知语言学对此提出了质疑。认知语言学认为意义不是简单地再现外部世界的物体、事件或关系，而是将人类对外部世界的主动认知用语言表述出来，因此存在模糊性和规约性，存在跨文化的差异。比如，英语中的brother一词并不等同于汉语中的"兄弟"一词；brother一词在英语中也并非只有单一的释义，而是拥有多个彼此相关的释义，这些释义通过隐喻拓展或转喻拓展相互关联，形成一个网络体系。

Holme对认知语言学关于意义的观点作了如下总结：

1）意义是复杂的、可以延展的；

2）不同的语言表达的意义也不尽相同；

3）意义不是直接取自人类共享的、普遍的感知经验的恒定实体。（p. 20）

认知语言学将意义视为"范畴"或"概念"（meanings are generally referred to as categories，p. 20）。比如，tree指称的是由各种各样的树组成的一个TREE范畴，love指称的是由各种不同的情感状态组成的一个LOVE范畴，等等。不难看出，英语的TREE范畴不一定等同于汉语的"树"范畴，而英语的LOVE范畴也不一定等同于汉语的"爱"范畴。因此，二语学习的关键不是拿二语所提供的新的语言形式去套学习者用母语能够熟练表达的旧的意义，而是去掌握二语中的新的概念和范畴，以及这些新概念、新范畴所形成的错综复杂的网络体系。

Holme据此提出了"语言学习即范畴学习"（language learning as category learning）的观点，并以stand一词为例作了详尽的解释，说明stand可细分为三个子范畴，表达的意义分别是：achieving a vertical posture、retaining a vertical posture和becoming prominent through a vertical posture（p. 21）。本章的最大亮点是Holme从认知语言学的意义观出发，为二语课堂里的词汇教学设计了生动有趣的活动。比如，通过让两个学生互相推搡、彼此支撑的活动，来体会"stand your ground"的意思；通过让学生把一本厚书放在手背上,然后高高地举过头顶的活动,来体会"what I can't stand"的意思,等等。这些活动的可操作性和实际的效果还有待教学实践来检验,但作者的这种尝试是有益且值得鼓励的。

## 第三章 概念化、体验性和意义的起源

本章围绕概念化过程（conceptualisation）、体验性认知（embodied cognition）和意义的起源（origins of meaning）进一步论述认知语言学关于语言和认知的理念,并探讨这些理念对二语教学的启示。作者首先简述了西方知识界关于认知的两个传统的二分观念：首先是人作为认知的主体和外部世界作为认知的客体的二分；其次是人的肉体和心智的二分,前者被视为后者的物质载体,后者被视为前者的指令和操控系统。这两个二分观念自二十世纪初叶起受到越来越多的挑战。比如,哲学家Merleau-Ponty提出,在作为认知主体的人和作为认知客体的外部世界之间应该加入作为媒介的人类的身体,因为一方面我们对身体的感知是主观认知过程的延续,另一方面我们通过身体与外部世界的接触和交往来感知外部世界。进一步说,人类的认知经验是身体和心智共同的产物。人类的身体,"通过它的能动性和它的实际动作及体姿",引导并塑造了人类的"认知"（The body, 'through its motor abilities, its actual movements and its posture', informed and shaped 'cognition', p.30）。认知语言学对这一观点有一个简洁而贴切的表达,那就是"embodied mind"（p.30）。

本章的重点是从下述六个方面证明embodied mind这一观点：

1）人类的本体感受能力（proprioception）,即我们都知道身体的各个部位在空间中的位置。这一能力并不因我们看不见身体的各个部位（比如,在暗室里,或者视力丧失）而受到影响,

甚至两三周大的新生儿也表现出这一能力。这很可能说明人脑中储存有关于身体构造的图式，并通过在这些图式上不断映射身体的动作来及时定位身体各部分所处的空间方位。

2）人类的物体感知能力：我们在感知物体的时候，并不仅仅是判断该物体的客观大小、颜色、形状等，而是同时在判断我们操控该物体（比如，拿起它、挪动它、抓住它的一部分等）的可能性、难易度等。换言之，我们不是简单地在看（seeing）一件物体，而是在概念化（conceptualising）该物体。

3）认知能力的发展与婴儿运动能力的发展之间的关联：不少研究表明，婴儿的爬行等运动能力的发展与婴儿的认知能力的发展有着密切的关系。

4）幻觉肢体症（phantom limb syndrome）：医学研究发现，有些截肢病人或先天缺少某部分肢体的病人仍会感知到缺失肢体的存在。这可能像人类的本体感受能力一样，说明人脑对身体的认知更多地受控于人脑中储存的关于身体的意象图式，而较少受控于个体的身体实际拥有的形状。

5）镜像神经元（mirror neurons）：对短尾猴的实验发现，不仅短尾猴自身的动作能够激发短尾猴的腹腔前运动皮质（ventral pre-motor cortex）作出反应，看别的短尾猴的动作也能产生同样的引发作用。有间接证据表明，人脑也存在同样的"镜像"现象。更耐人寻味的是，这些镜像神经元在人脑中恰恰位于布罗卡区（Broca's area），而布罗卡区一直被认为与人的语言能力密切相关。

6）意象图式（image schemas）：意象图式是存在于我们的感知和身体运作程序中一种反复出现的动态模式，它使我们的身体经验具有结构和连贯性。意象图式有着固有的内在空间结构，它们对于人类来说是直接有意义的，因为人类的身体构造以及在地球这个大环境中的运作模式决定了我们每天反复地、直接地体验各种意象图式。例如，我们无数次地接触到一件物体置于另一件物体之上，由此我们很自然地获取了OVER这一意象图式，并且可以用这一意象图式去理解其他类似的空间关系。同样，UP、DOWN、FRONT、BACK等意象图式也都是从我们的身体经验中自然而然地产生的，均可被用于描述或者构筑其他空间关系甚至是非空间关系。

本章最后当然落足在认知语言学的embodied mind观念对于教育，尤其是二语教学，有什么影响。Holme认为，教师可以设计一些课堂活动，让学生身体和大脑并用，以帮助他们更有效地习得语言。比如，中国学生学习英语的一个难点是如何把握英语的节奏和韵律，为此，Holme设计了"feeling the stress"（pp. 41-42）的活动，让学生在行进中操练单词和句子，用重的步伐配合重读音节，用轻的步伐配合弱读音节。再比如，在教授表示方位和动作的词语时，可以蒙上一个学生的眼睛，藏起一个物体，待藏妥后，让该学生在其他同学给出的指令下找到该物体。

## 第四章 手势

第四章篇幅很短，内容也相对单薄。作者的主要观点是语言交流总是伴随着肢体动作或手势——甚至在对方看不见这些动作或手势（比如电话交谈）时说话人仍会不自觉地比画——因此，在语言教学中，如果能有意识地调动学生运用肢体动作或手势，应该有助于语言的习得。

Holme以介词教学和冠词教学为例来证明自己这一提议的可行性。比如，across、over和through这三个介词的意思有重叠之处，不少学生掌握起来觉得困难。Holme建议用下列伴随动作来辅助讲解和操练这三个词的异同：

across: 手平放，掌心向下，模仿拖地的动作划过地面；

over: 手平伸，胳膊向上做跨越某个物体的动作；

through: 双手做用力前推的动作。（p. 59）

不过，正如Holme自己承认的，这样的练习可能更适合儿童，成人学习者未必会接受或喜欢。但是，这样的练习的确能在潜移默化中帮助学习者悟出介词背后的意象图式结构，而这会在未来的学习中帮助他们更好地掌握介词的各种拓展意义。

总之，贯穿整个第一部分"Embodied Experience"（第二至四章）的主题是人类的认知是体验性的，语言作为人类认知的一部分也是体验性的，而语言学习是一种认知过程，因此也可以是体验性的。

## 第五章 语言、文化和语言相对性

本章重在探讨语言与文化的关系，以及跨语言和跨文化的差异对于二语学习的影响。这就涉及语言学研究里非常著名的"语言相对性"（linguistic relativity）假说。

关于语言和语言之间、文化和文化之间可能存在的异同历来有两种观点：一种是感知观（the perceptual view），另一种是认知观（the conceptual view）。前者认为人类的认知像镜子一样映射外部世界，因此，一种语言所再现的世界与其他语言所再现的世界应该存在根本的相似性。后者认为人类所认知到的世界并不是那个客观存在的外部世界，而是人类的心智和身体所体验到的世界，这就给跨语言和跨文化的差异提供了较大的可能性。

认知观促使语言教育者思考下述问题：

1）如果不同的语言承载着不同的认知世界的概念系统，那么学习一门外语就意味着学习者必须对自己从母语那里继承来的概念系统作出或多或少的调整。语言教师该如何帮助学习者完成这样的调整？

2）如果每一种语言的背后都有一种独特的文化体系，那么这是否意味着成功地习得一门外语必定伴随一定程度的异族文化的渗透？

3）如果外语学习意味着一定程度的认知方式的调整和异族文化的渗透，对于成人学习者来说，这两点都很难，这是否就是成人学习者很难完全掌握一门外语的根本原因？（p. 67）

不少研究证实，二语学习者在学习过程中所犯的错误很多都可以归为母语思维方式和文化体系的影响，这些错误又可分为以下三类：

1）把母语中存在而二语中缺失的语言形式和意义移植到二语中；

2）把二语中存在而母语中缺失的语言形式和意义扩大化；

3）把母语和二语中看似相同实则不同的语言形式和意义混用。（p. 83）

从认知观出发，Holme提出了语言学习的新理念，即"语言学习应该完成于同目标语的文化实践的长期和系统的接触中"（learning a language should be completed by a sustained and ethnographically structured encounter with the practices of the language's culture, p. 95）。为了有效地帮助学习者的语言学习，教师应该有意识地培养学生的文化敏感性和参与度。为此，Holme设计了一些课堂实践作为抛砖引玉的尝试。比如，在名为"culture game"的活动里，Holme建议将学生分为两组，每组设计出自己的文化传统（包括信仰、礼仪、禁忌等），然后双方互派使者进行访问。在名为"collecting a culture as language"的活动里，Holme建议教师与学生一起对目标语中一些重要的概念隐喻（比如：Life is a journey. Business is war. Machines are living things.）进行考察和拓展。

在本章的结尾，Holme对语言教学的目的进行了重新定位：

我们的目的不是培养在单一文化环境中生存的学习者，而是在各种文化群体之间能自如地交流和沟通的学习者。

## 第六章 建构和概念化

人类认知的一个核心能力是能够从不同的视角、用不同的方式来认知同一事物或事件。这种建构能力在语言的词汇和语法上都体现出来。本章的重点就是从那些不同的认知视角和认知方式出发，探讨语言教师如何能对其善加利用来有效地讲解目标语的形式和意义，并通过有针对性的课堂活动来帮助学生更好地掌握。

本章所考察的认知视角和方式包括：

1）注意力（attention）和突显度（salience）：人可以有意识地把注意力集中到某个重要的物体或事件的某个重要环节上而忽视其他物体或环节。承受了最多注意力的物体或环节因此得以从环境中突显出来。

2）判断（judgement）和比较（comparison）：人类总是在不断地对外部世界所存在的物体或所发生的事件作出判断和比较，比如，判断某个物体是否属于某个范畴，这涉及范畴化能力（categorisation competence）；比较两个物体或事件的异同，这涉及隐喻能力（metaphorical competence）；判断两个物体之间的关系（可以是物理空间关系，也可以是更抽象的关系），这涉及角色–背景的分离（figure-ground segregation）。

3）视角（perspective）和场景感（situatedness）：一般说来，说话人习惯于从自己的视角来看待和定位某个物体或事件，但说话人也可以有意识地转换视角，从听话人甚至第三者的角度来看待和定位某个物体或事件。这种认知能力在语言中最明显的体现就是指示词（deixis）的运用。此外，主动语态和被动语态的选择、不同的介词的选择等也都体现了说话人的视角和从特定的视角出发对场景的把握。

4）整合（constitution）和完形（gestalt）：人类在观察周围环境时，通常倾向于把物体或事件作为一个完形的整体来看待，而不是作为支离破碎的零部件来看待。比如，如果屋子里摆放着一张桌子，一般说来我们看到的会是作为整体的桌子（反映在语言表达上就是"屋子当中放着一张桌子"），而不是作为桌子的组成部分的桌面和桌腿（我们不太可能说"屋子当中放着一张桌面和四条桌腿"）。

5）结构性图式化（structural schematisation）：人类能够从日常生活中反复出现或反复体验的物体、现象或事件中抽象出意象图式结构，然后用这些意象图式结构去理解其他类似的物体、现象或事件。

Holme在本章设计了13项课堂活动，尝试将上述认知方式运用于语言教学，其中比较新颖的包括通过肢体语言的运用帮助学生把注意力集中在名词复数的词缀上，从而更好地习得英语名词的复数形式；通过画图帮助学生更好地理解英语的TIME概念；通过头脑风暴帮助学生探索不同隐喻表达背后共同的概念隐喻，以及该概念隐喻可能生成的更多的隐喻表达等等。

# 第七章 百科意义的教学

生成语言学强调的是语言的结构，而认知语言学更看重语言的意义，并且认为每一个语词所表达的意义都既是概念性的（conceptual），又是百科性的（encyclopaedic）。前者指的是一个语词所指示的不是一个简单的、孤立的词，而是一个有着丰富庞杂的网络结构的概念，比如，mother这个词并不是简单地指示a female parent，而是以此为原型意义，通过隐喻、转喻、意象图式结构的投射等往不同的方向拓展而形成的一个复杂概念，涵盖了从原型意义出发，到a woman who acts as the parent of a child to whom she has not given birth，a woman regarded as the creator, instigator, or founder of something，直至the cause, source, or origin of something等各种不同的意义。后者指的是一个语词所表达的意义包含了一系列相关的百科知识，比如，table这个词不是简单地表达a piece of furniture with a flat top and one or more legs，而是会在使用者头脑中激活一系列百科知识，包括：在英语文化中，桌子通常是木制的，但也可以是玻璃的或塑料的；通常是长方形的，但也可以是圆形、椭圆形、正方形的；通常有四条腿，但也可以少于或多于四条腿；通常是供人们围坐吃饭用的，但也可以有其他用途，等等。

Holme认为，意义的概念性和百科性对二语课堂的词汇教学有以下两点启示：

1）语词的意义存在于一定的框架（frame）或知识域（knowledge domain）中，因此，在进行词汇教学时，教师可以有意识地帮助学生构筑相关的框架或知识域。比如，在教授buy、sell、goods等单词时，可以提醒学生，一个典型的商业活动的框架通常包括卖主、买主、商品、货币等要素。

2）不同语词的意义交织成复杂的网络体系，彼此相连，因此，在词汇教学中，教师可以有意识地帮助学生构建词语的上下义关系（比如：animal-dog-poodle, plant-tree-pine等）或部分–整体关系（比如：tree-branch-leaf, body-head-neck-arm-leg等）。

Holme在倒数第二节里还特别介绍了语词的音和意之间可能的关联。比如，英语中有一系列以gl-开头的单词，其意义都与"light"相关，如：glance、glare、glass、glaze、gleam、glimmer。

虽然人类语言的规约性决定了绝大多数词语的发音与其所表达的意义之间没有必然的联系，但是我们也不可否认每种语言中都有少量词语的发音与意义之间残留了原始的拟声成分。了解这一点至少可以增加二语课堂教学的趣味性。

## 第八章 语言的使用和语法的意义

在认知语言学领域，关于语法的研究呈现出多种路径并存的现状，比如construction grammar（Lakoff 1987；Goldberg 1995，2006）、radical construction grammar（Croft 2001）和cognitive grammar（Langacker 1987，1991）。不过关于语法的本质、语法的习得和功能等，各方达成了一些共识，Holme将这些共识总结为如下几点：

1）语法由一个个的符号综合体（symbolic complex）或构式（construction）构成。

2）语法能够表达意义，图式结构（schematicity）原则和承继（inheritance）原则对语法意义起着至关重要的作用。

3）语法意义像词汇意义一样是经过概念化处理的范畴，它记录的是用一种特定的方式来认知某个情景。

4）语法在实际运用中习得。因为不同的语言使用者运用语言的方式各不相同，所以他们头脑中储存的关于同一种语言形式的心理再现方式也可能各不相同。

本章的主要篇幅用于讨论上述认识对二语教学的启示。Holme首先参照Goldberg（2006），将构式定义为"与其他的意义相结合，产生从各个组成部分无法推测出的新意义的意义"（a meaning that combines others to create one that cannot be predicted from the combined parts, p. 178），比如，由介词+冠词+名词构成的介词短语就是英语中的一个构式，在语言的实际运用中，这一构式可以不同的面貌出现，比如，to the house，in the room，on the floor等等，这些介词短语都产生了它们各自的组成部分（to/in/on，the，house/room/floor）单独无法表达的意义。Holme认为，在二语教学中，教师首先应该帮助学生识别哪些词串构成构式，哪些词串不构成构式。比如，在"They have to work very hard just to buy a bowl of rice"中，"hard just to"和"buy a bowl of"就不是构式，而"they have to work very hard"，"a bowl of rice"以及"just to"都是构式表达，分别体现的是"sb. have to do sth."，"a CONTAINER of SUBSTANCE"和"do sth. just to do sth. else"的构式。

从教学的角度出发，Holme将构式分为三类，分别是：

1）filled constructions，即单词或词素均明确出现的构式；

2）partially filled constructions，即部分单词或词素明确出现的构式；

3）unfilled constructions，即单词或词素均未注明的构式。

filled constructions以俗语和惯用法为主，比如，"to be tarred with the same brush"，意思是"to have or display the same faults, bad habits, or unpleasant characteristics"；partially filled constructions则包括各种名词词组、动词词组、介词词组等，比如，the + n.，to give sb. sth.，in front of sth.；unfilled constructions则包括英语的不及物动词用法、及物动词用法、双宾语动词用法、系表结构等。

与前面各章一样，Holme在本章也设计了一些示范练习，说明教师可以通过帮助学生识别构式、在实践中总结构式的结构、在语境中尝试构式的具体形式等方法来促成学生的二语习得。

# 第九章 认知语言学指导下的教学大纲

这一章既是对全书的总结，也是对在认知语言学的理论框架下设计二语教学大纲的前景的展望。传统的二语教学大纲可被分为重视过程的分析型（analytic）和重视结果的综合型（synthetic）两类，前者强调学习者必须识别应该掌握的语言元素，并据此设计教学活动；后者强调对语言元素的提炼和对与之相关的语言技能的操练。在认知语言学的框架下，人类的物理和社会经验影响着人类对世界的认知，人类对世界的认知又影响着人类语言的发展；语言的形式（包括词汇、语法）是人类蕴于身体的心智活动（embodied mind）的反映。因此，二语教学应该突出语言形式背后的embodied mind，具体做法可参照下述原则：

1）通过设计适当的教学活动，追溯语言形式及其所表达的意义的空间意象和动作起源；

2）有意识地让学习者分析语言的形式和意义之间的关系，帮助他们识别语言中大量存在的构式；

3）通过在具体语境中的交流活动，帮助学习者在实际运用中习得不同级别的构式。

Holme最后总结了教师在教学中应该注意的几点。首先，对语言形式的习得应该在不断反复中巩固；其次，在纠正学习者的语言错误时，教师宜着眼于学习者想表达的意义进行拓展；第三，配合学习活动的对学习者身体动作的调度宜贯穿始终，因为身体动作能帮助学习者接受和内化新的语言形式；第四，鼓励学习者将每一次与目标语的接触都视为探索和掌握目标语中的构式的机会而善加把握；第五，教师和学习者都应该认识到语言既不是不断变化的动态体系，也不是一成不变的条条框框。语言既有内在的灵活性，同时也不缺乏稳定性。二语学习的目的是帮助学习者从容应对未来各种需要对目标语进行创造性运用的场合。

## 3. 结语

　　近些年有不少学者尝试将认知语言学的一些理念运用于二语教学实践，并且发表了相关文章，不过对认知语言学与语言教学的结合进行系统阐述的专著还不多见，Holme的这本著作应该说是这方面的一个大胆且有益的尝试。本书的最大亮点是作者并没有空泛地倡导用认知语言学的理论指导二语课堂教学，而是有针对性地设计了不少练习和活动，其中既有词汇学习方面的，也有语法学习方面的。

　　当然，作为一部探索性的著作，本书不免存在一些问题。比如，作者的定位不够明确，摇摆于对认知语言学的理论进行阐释和对语言教学的课堂操作进行指导之间，这使得一方面作者关于认知语言学的介绍显得比较零散，另一方面关于语言教学的探讨也显得比较混乱。再有，作者在每一章都只采用了一级标题，这使得章节内部的结构不够清晰，增添了读者阅读的难度。这一点在后面几章表现得更为明显。总体而言，本书适合于对认知语言学有相当程度的了解、对语言教学也有较深体会和认识的读者；如果这两方面的知识缺一，那么从本书所能得到的收益恐怕就会打点折扣。

# Contents

*List of Activities*   xxiii

*List of Figures and Tables*   xxv

**1 Introduction**   1
  The linguistics applied approach: generative linguistics and second language learning   2
  The applied linguistics of second language learning   4
  Language as a social semiotic   5
  The emergence of cognitive linguistics   6
  Ending the LA–AL divide   10
  The purpose of the book   12

## Part I  Embodied Experience

**2 The Problem of Linguistic Meaning**   17
  Introduction   17
  The problem of meaning   17
  Language learning as category learning   21
  Conclusions   27

**3 Conceptualisation, Embodiment and the Origins of Meaning**   29
  Introduction   29
  Proprioception: how the body remains aware of its own position in space   31
  Not seeing but conceptualising   32
  Cognitive development and infant movement   33
  Aplasic phantoms   34
  Mirror neurons   35
  The nature of language: image schemas and embodied cognition   36
  Education and embodiment   39
  Language teaching and embodiment: language as rhythm and movement   41

Language teaching and embodiment: mime, enactment
and movement .................................................. 44
Language teaching and embodiment: rethinking TPR ...... 48
Conclusions .................................................. 52

## 4 Gesture — 54
Introduction .................................................. 54
The importance of gesture in communication ............ 54
Gesture in education ........................................ 56
Gesture and teaching prepositions ........................ 58
Gesture and English articles ............................... 60
Conclusions .................................................. 62

# Part II Conceptualisation

## 5 Language, Culture and Linguistic Relativity — 65
Introduction .................................................. 65
The Sapir-Whorf hypothesis ................................ 67
Meaning and conceptualisation ........................... 69
Linguistic relativity: how different is different? ......... 75
Experimental evidence for linguistic relativity .......... 77
To learn new meanings, do we have to conceptualise the
world differently? ........................................ 80
Second language errors and linguistic relativity ......... 81
Errors that use first language forms and meanings
within the second language ............................. 84
Errors that over-generalise some acquired formal or
semantic feature of the second language ............. 86
False friends .................................................. 88
The problem of separating meaning from conceptualisation ... 89
Can one change a conceptualisation? ..................... 90
Language, culture and conceptualisation in the classroom ... 92
Language, culture and learning ........................... 95
Different meanings for different languages .............. 100
Conclusions .................................................. 108

## 6 Conceptualisation and Construal — 111
Introduction .................................................. 111
Construal operations ....................................... 112
Attention and salience ...................................... 113
Attention, salience and enactive SLA ..................... 113
Metonymy: attention and salience ........................ 117

| | |
|---|---|
| Scope of attention | 120 |
| Scalar adjustment | 123 |
| Dynamic attention | 125 |
| Judgment and comparison | 129 |
| Category formation | 129 |
| Category formation and language teaching | 130 |
| Metaphor | 134 |
| Metaphor and language teaching | 134 |
| Metaphor analysis | 135 |
| Metaphor and target language differentiation | 136 |
| The explanatory power of metaphor and analogy | 136 |
| Using metaphor to learn second language lexis and grammar | 138 |
| Figure–ground conceptual operations, force dynamics and action chains | 142 |
| Perspectives and situatedness | 147 |
| Deixis | 150 |
| Constitution/gestalt | 152 |
| Geometry | 155 |
| Conclusions | 157 |

## Part III  Meaning and Usage

**7  Teaching Encyclopaedic Meaning** — **161**

| | |
|---|---|
| Introduction | 161 |
| Word networks: hyponymy and schematicity | 163 |
| Word networks: meronymy | 165 |
| Crossing category borders | 167 |
| Knowledge types and encyclopaedic meaning | 168 |
| Finding the frame | 169 |
| Phonological sense relations | 171 |
| Conclusions | 174 |

**8  Usage and Grammatical Meaning** — **177**

| | |
|---|---|
| Introduction | 177 |
| Constructions | 178 |
| Type and token | 179 |
| Usage | 181 |
| Language learning as construction learning | 183 |
| Recognising constructions | 183 |
| Teaching constructions | 184 |
| Teaching filled constructions: idioms | 185 |

Teaching partially filled constructions: lexis, meaning and
  conceptualisation ... 186
Teaching partially filled constructions: bound morphemes,
  inflections and lexis ... 187
Teaching partially filled constructions: bound morphemes ... 188
Teaching partially filled constructions: lexis and
  morphemes ... 192
Teaching partially filled constructions: lexis ... 197
Teaching unfilled constructions ... 201
Routines for more advanced students: lexis, meaning and
  conceptualisation ... 205
Encountering constructions ... 205
Finding useful forms ... 206
Conclusions ... 212

## Part IV  Conclusions

### 9  Towards a Cognitive Linguistics Syllabus ... 217
Introduction ... 217
Product and process ... 217
Language teaching implications ... 218
Re-embedding linguistic form in the imagery and
  movement from which it emerged ... 219
Engage the learners in the explicit analysis of form and
  meaning ... 220
A forum for usage ... 226
Sequencing ... 227

*Bibliography* ... 231

*Index* ... 244

# List of Activities

| | | |
|---|---|---|
| 1 | Stand your ground! | 23 |
| 2 | What I can't stand | 23 |
| 3 | Standing | 24 |
| 4 | On thin ice and in a situation | 26 |
| 5 | Feeling the stress | 41 |
| 6 | Chanting | 42 |
| 7 | Moving through language | 47 |
| 8 | Blindfold | 49 |
| 9 | What am I doing? | 49 |
| 10 | What am I? | 49 |
| 11 | Natural cycles | 50 |
| 12 | Move and talk: silent movies | 50 |
| 13 | Determined gesture | 61 |
| 14 | Surveillance | 61 |
| 15 | Culture game | 96 |
| 16 | Tracing it back | 97 |
| 17 | What we do with it | 97 |
| 18 | Collecting a culture as language | 98 |
| 19 | Cross-cultural meanings | 100 |
| 20 | Exacting movements | 102 |
| 21 | Furtive movement | 104 |
| 22 | Motion paths | 107 |
| 23 | Teaching the plural morpheme | 114 |
| 24 | Word building | 116 |
| 25 | The room | 119 |
| 26 | My what? | 120 |
| 27 | Through and over | 124 |
| 28 | The open road | 127 |
| 29 | Category building | 131 |
| 30 | Seeing time | 132 |
| 31 | Keeping it together | 140 |
| 32 | Switched histories | 146 |
| 33 | Construal | 148 |
| 34 | Someone else was there | 151 |
| 35 | Container or surface | 156 |
| 36 | Passed down? | 164 |

*List of Activities*

| 37 | What it really is | 169 |
| 38 | The basis of comparison | 193 |
| 39 | Pride and prejudice | 194 |
| 40 | Making constructions productive | 196 |
| 41 | Testing constructions to destruction | 200 |
| 42 | Identifying and exploring constructions | 210 |

# List of Figures and Tables

## Figures

| | | |
|---|---|---|
| 1 | The category relations for some of the meanings of 'stand' | 25 |
| 2 | 'On' versus 'in': an activity diagram | 26 |
| 3 | How cognitive blends work: counterfactuals, becoming another person | 73 |
| 4 | Complex and deictic time contrasted: using diagrams to help avoid schematic errors with tense | 85 |
| 5 | Why we do not use a determiner with abstract nouns that have a sole reference to what they describe | 87 |
| 6 | 'Up to' and 'up on': furtive and prominent motion paths | 105 |
| 7 | Scope of attention in discourse: using diagrams to master discourse structure | 122 |
| 8 | Scalar adjustment: different construals with 'through' and 'over' | 125 |
| 9 | The building: using hyponym charts to explore categories | 131 |
| 10 | Visual analogues of the language content of English: continuous aspect | 139 |
| 11 | Three action chains (Langacker 1987) | 144 |
| 12 | Who is Moll Flanders? Epistemic deixis and the creation of different character perspectives | 151 |
| 13 | Rubin's face diagram | 153 |
| 14 | Using meronymy for information transfer tasks | 167 |
| 15 | Illustrating phonaesthemes set in a poetic metre | 174 |
| 16 | How a construction's productivity can increase in proportion to its schematicity | 179 |
| 17 | Representing the English past tense as a category meaning | 192 |
| 18 | Using hyponym charts to explore construction meanings | 196 |
| 19 | The present perfect: extending the time of speech | 198 |
| 20 | Construction conceptualisation: between one thing and another | 209 |
| 21 | Using a prototype chart to explore constructions | 211 |

## Tables

| | | |
|---|---|---|
| 1 | Using frame semantics tables to extend learners' lexico-grammatical control: 'sell' | 170 |

*List of Figures and Tables*

2  Using frame semantics tables: 'go' 170
3  Using a substitution table to explore a transitive construction 207
4  Using a substitution table to explore a partially filled construction 209

# 1
# Introduction

Behaviourist and structuralist linguistics gave second language teachers a concept of form where the grammatical and lexical units through which a language was presented were held to be the same as those through which it was processed. This provided a unity of approach that was once an assumption of applied linguistics:

> There is no conflict between application and theory: *the methods most useful in application are to be found among those that are most valid and powerful in theory*
> (Halliday, McIntosh and Stevens 1964: 166–7; cited in Widdowson 1973; author's italics)

Unfortunately, this unity between the psycholinguistic and pedagogic approaches to language was achieved at the cost of a considerable simplification, both of grammar, and of the language learning process.

One problem derived from structuralism's analysis of form itself. A language structure is defined according to its properties of formal differentiation (Bloomfield 1914; Thorndike 1932; Skinner 1957). For the language learner this resulted in an over-emphasis upon the formal properties of language and their disassociation from the creation of useful meanings. Drilled through substitutions or transformations, the learner was forever producing versions of a structure that represented meanings they might never use. Moreover, the view of language as correct habits acquired through repetitive manipulation led to a stress upon providing students with the correct model of the target language, and hence a disproportionate emphasis on native-speaker teachers and teacher-centred classrooms.

The demise of behaviourism has left applied linguistics in no less a quandary, however. Fundamentally, we were left with a divided treatment where mainstream approaches to the description of form offered next to nothing to the teacher who was looking for ways to present second language content to learners. The language teacher fell prey to what Widdowson (1979) defined as a dichotomy between a linguistics applied (LA) approach and an applied linguistics (AL) approach. In the LA model, one accepted the dominant linguistic theory and examined its implications for second language learning. In an AL model one evolved modes of analysis that treated second language issues on their own terms, analysing the language that was used by learners and native speakers. This divide meant that teachers adopted one of two equally unsatisfactory approaches to teaching forms. On the one hand they searched for ways to apply descriptive procedures whose abstractness and complexity made them unusable as part of a language teaching approach. On the other hand they had to fall back upon rules of language use that were formulated for their transparency and not for their identification of the forms from which language was processed and produced. The first approach can be identified with studies that sought to apply generative linguistic theory to such processes as second language acquisition (SLA). The second is associated with the more social and discourse-oriented approaches to linguistic analysis typified by the systemic functional school.

## The linguistics applied approach: generative linguistics and second language learning

The inapplicability of generative theory is unsurprising, since it achieved theoretical consistency by recreating language as a stable entity within what was called an 'ideal speaker–hearer relationship'. Chomsky rationalised this process of abstraction inside another metaphor, the nature of water as it is studied:

> Why do chemists study $H_2O$ and not the stuff you get out of the Charles River? You assume that anything as complicated as what is in the Charles River will only be understandable, if at all, on the basis of discovery of the fundamental principles that determine the nature of all matter, and those you have to learn about by studying pure cases.
> (Chomsky *ca* 1985, cited by Cook 2005, personal communication).

The argument was that like water, language could not be understood in all its variable states. We had to reduce language to its essential common elements, otherwise we would be dealing with an entity whose almost infinite variation would make it impossible to study.

Not only did language have to be isolated from its social context to reveal its essential nature, it also had to be isolated from the mind's larger array of cognitive functions and their engagement with the plethora of scenarios that our reality presents. Language was therefore perceived of as cognitively modularised, or largely processed in a part of the brain that was isolated from others and structured for the purpose. Just as when we open our eyes we have no choice over whether we do or do not see the world before us, so when we hear a language that we know, we cannot fail to recognise its meaningfulness (Fodor 1985). Language was therefore described as occupying a specialised module in the brain. This module had an innate grammar that was the same at birth for every human. The parameters of this universal grammar (UG) were reset by the input of the particular language to which it was exposed from birth.

Some second language acquisition (SLA) specialists were attracted to the generative treatment of language because it allowed acquisition to be closed off as a process that was immune to social variation. In a generative model SLA was an interaction between a model in the mind of the idealised speaker–hearer and a language that could be construed as a logical system. But these scholars faced the quandary of how one could acquire another language when one had already set the parameters of a universal grammar within a first language, then modularised this knowledge as a set of reflexive operations with which the rest of the mind could not interfere. Broadly, three models were proposed. In the full transfer, full-access model learners were thought to transfer the settings of the UG that result from the first language. This created the phenomenon of first language interference. In the next stage we obtained access to our universal grammar and acquisition would then start to accelerate (see for example, Schwarz 1986, 1987, 1993). The second model could be called partial transfer. In this model learners could not access their universal grammar directly but could only do so through the grammar of the first language. In the third model there was held to be no access to universal grammar and second language acquisition was held to occur through alternative versions of the language derived by broader learning strategies (see for example, Bley-Vroman 1990).

The lack of resolution in the debate about these models has revealed larger problems, however. For example, the proposal that languages were only acquired from naturalistic input was demonstrably untrue. Because some students did learn second languages, albeit to different degrees, it became necessary to postulate modules dedicated to second language learning. Since first and second languages interfered with each other, this created a cognitive architecture where one module had throughput to another, thus undermining the very principle that modularity had sought to defend. More generally, by searching for applications for a theory that made a virtue of its inapplicability, generative SLA theory undermined the very integrity of the construct it set out to sustain. In other words, the generative model had achieved consistency by failing to notice the messier processes of second language learning and when it was brought into contact with these processes, that consistency could no longer be sustained.

## The applied linguistics of second language learning

After the demise of structuralism an alternative consensus to generativism perceived that language was finally about communication, or the conveyance of meaning. Conveying meanings is a social process so a language was a system that evolved to reflect its social role. Hymes (1971) famously argued that Chomsky's concept of competence would produce utterances that were socially so inappropriate they could only belong to a lunatic. This focus on the limited, extra-social nature of the generative conception of language knowledge missed how it was precisely these limitations which were perceived as essential to the scientific exploration of language (see for example, Chomsky 1985). In Chomskyan terms, Hyme's notion of a communicative competence was nonsensical. A linguistic competence arose when the parameters of a learner's innate and universal grammar were set by the language with which they came into contact. This contact was with the language as a performance, or as a contextualised and inconsistent entity. The external, social language then evolved into a 'steady state' through the process of its acquisition and could thus be studied as a consistent entity, or competence. Essentially, it took on an internal, extra-social complexion. To treat that competence as social or communicative therefore entailed its self-reaction as a type of performance. However, in their eagerness to grasp language as a social phenomenon, applied linguists ignored the evident contradictions of Hymes' conception by formulating it as a pedagogical goal (see for example, Brumfit and Johnson 1979; Savignon 1983). The objective of giving second language learners a communicative competence implied a strong link between linguistic form and the social objectives and meanings the form realised. Therefore support was sought in theories which saw language as structured by its social nature, or which perceived it as a social semiotic (see for example, Halliday 1993).

## Language as a social semiotic

This social conception of Systemic Functional Linguistics (SFL) appealed to language teachers because of the way grammar was linked to principles of use. However, SFL also raised a series of difficult problems. First, Halliday described language as an external entity, and so located it in exactly the realm of social confusion from which the generative linguistic wanted to remove it. The linguist therefore addressed a construct which was located outside a stabilising concept of mind. To provide stability in a social arena, scholars had to reify language as an extraneous object. It was now 'an outlying system for meaning exchange', which built cognition rather than being built by it (Holme 2007), for in Halliday's view, cognition was just 'a way of talking about language' (Halliday and Matthiessen 1999). The difficult implication was that language had to pre-exist the cognition it created, or was at least mutually constitutive of the same.

Linguistic form, or the lexico-grammar, then, was delivered to the classroom teacher as an entity that was simply a response to a social need. A difficulty was that there was no convincing explanation for the cognitive processes through which the development of those forms and their meanings had been mediated. An advantage of the structuralist concept of form had lain in how it came ready-packaged with a learning theory. The problem with a communicative notion of form was not that this package was unbundled, but rather, that learning arose purely from a social imperative. Reductively, the imprint of cognition upon language was effectively nullified because the mind was postulated as a kind of microcosmic society, building language as an unmediated response to social need. Teachers had been furnished with a concept of mind as simply reflecting social experiences then ciphering those reflections back into society. They lacked an understanding of how cognition had first to categorise and interpret experience before construing it as a usable set of meanings. In pedagogy, an even more reductive consequence of the reification of language as a social entity was to de-emphasise its grammar entirely. Language was perceived less as a rule system designed to match utterances to social objectives, and more as a set of pairings between fixed expressions and their functional meanings.

The need to treat language as an extraneous object found a supportive metaphor in the language corpus. Although research tools of great promise, language corpora postulated a metaphor of a language as something captured as a totality, or as an extraneous and complete product. Corpus studies themselves gave unwitting support to this metaphorical interpretation when they emphasised the repetitive and ritualised nature of much communication (see for example, Eeg-Olofsson and Altenberg 1994; Moon 1998). The argument that teaching should take greater account of these fixed expressions (Nattinger and DeCarrico 1992) helped develop a new lexical emphasis in the language teaching syllabus (Lewis 1993) that stimulated interest in the neglected area of vocabulary teaching, but which raised no concomitant theory of meaning, grammar and linguistic creativity. Students doubtless benefited from an enhanced repertoire of lexical phrases, but over-encouraged to seek the safety of the fixed forms, they still lost control of their larger meaning and found themselves stranded on phrasal islands of incongruous correctness by the error-infested nature of their larger sentence.

## The emergence of cognitive linguistics

Cognitive linguistics (CL) emerged largely from dissatisfactions with the limitations of formal linguistics and generative linguistics in particular. These dissatisfactions did not, of course, relate to the second language problem of applicability, for this was never an interest within the discipline. The issue was with the assumptions of the generative enterprise itself.

Generative linguistics had set itself the task of deducing the principles and parameters that are common to all languages from the data that these languages provide. Yet these principles have proved remarkably elusive and have hitherto amounted to little more than a few highly limited statements about the nature of language (Lakoff and Johnson 1999).

A second problem for generative linguistics lay in how it took syntax as the prime object of study. In Chomsky's minimalist model, language study was divided between syntax and the lexicon (Chomsky 1995). Words and their meanings were specific to a language, rather than to language itself, and therefore did not have structures that could be generalised across languages and established as a set of scientifically credible parameters. The generative interest was therefore in syntax. But it had always been acknowledged that the way syntax treated lexis was partly a consequence of the nature of that lexis, or of its grammatical marking.

For example, the lexicon would have to store verbs as either transitive or intransitive so that intransitive verbs would not be made available to a transitive sentence structure, or vice versa. However, students of syntax became increasingly aware that many idiomatic patterns violated the principles of such marking, making intransitive verbs transitive, or creating passive sentences from intransitive ones. The resultant expressions could be taken out of the syntactic system and set up as a rival system of semi-fixed expressions called constructions (see for example, Culicover and Jackendoff 2005). Constructions could then be seen as being learnt much in the way that lexis and idioms were, but their frequency seemed to make a language with two systems, one governed by syntax and one not.

A third problematic area concerned the relationship between the model of the mind postulated by the generative model and the picture of cognition that was starting to emerge. Central to generative linguistics was how the structures perceived in the language were thought to have been generated out of simpler common structures by a series of transformations. Finally a language could be broken down into the universal grammar which underpinned all languages. A model where basically more was made from less could therefore claim the virtue of cognitive efficiency, or the maximisation of what was thought to be limited cognitive space. It allowed us to produce an almost infinite number of sentences with limited grammatical means. But the transformations needed to achieve this were found to be incredibly complex. It therefore became increasingly difficult to postulate this as a cognitively efficient method of producing language. Further, new models of the brain questioned the requirement that models of language should be based upon limited processing capacity. Cognitive development was seen less as the exploitation of specific structures to overcome capacity constraints and more as an exercise in capacity reduction in order to focus on such tasks as language acquisition (see for example, Ramachandran 2005). Finally, UG was seen as a series of innate mental structures that were vested in a language module, but our increasing knowledge of the brain has failed to find any area that is structurally different in the way such a model requires (Edelman 1992).

A fourth problem related more to the formal approaches to linguistics themselves and to the question of how meanings were actually gathered from the world. As Saussure (1974) had recognised, language could not simply represent objects or states in the world. The word 'tree' did not represent a single object and 'happy' did not represent a one-off condition. The first term represented the thousands of trees we had seen and the putative trees that we had not. The formal response to our need to deal in meaning as a concept rather an exactly equivalent object was to suggest that a category such as 'tree' arose from its possession of an objectively identifiable set of features. Thus a tree had to have a trunk, sap, branches and leaves, or whatever. So finally 'a tree' was a tree when, and only when, it could be feature-matched with that concept. If the features were present, the item conformed to the category and if absent it had to be something else. However, as Wittgenstein had already understood, some of the entities that composed a category did not have features in common with all the other entities (1957). The category then seemed to have no binding set of features. Thus, in Wittgenstein's famous example, many of the activities that are called games had almost nothing in common with each other. For example, chess had little in common with a game of football and almost nothing to do with the meaning implied by the question, 'what's your game (job)?' Another problem lay in how abstract categories such as 'happiness' were derived from our experience of that state and had no objective set of features to which we could match anything.

The re-evaluation of how we derived meanings was further stimulated by Lakoff and Johnson's exploration of the nature of metaphor (1980). Lakoff and Johnson built on work in philosophy which had already reopened a longstanding enquiry into metaphor and the questions that it raised about the relationship of language and meaning (Richards 1936; Black 1962; Ricoeur 1975; Derrida 1978). Metaphors asked severe questions of truth-condition semantics, or of a view where the meaningfulness of a proposition rested in how well it corresponded to the facts of the world. When we used a metaphor, 'Juliet is the sun', for example, this was technically meaningless, because we knew that Juliet could never be a solar object. Yet in the world of rhetoric such metaphors were intensely meaningful.

Lakoff and Johnson's first contribution was to consolidate the understanding that metaphorical language was not confined to the literary domain. They thus developed Michael Reddy's (1993) insight into how a metaphor could structure our everyday discourse and fashion our perception of a given topic. Reddy had perceived that the abstract idea of 'communication' was structured by what he called 'the conduit' metaphor. For example, we talked about 'getting through to' somebody or perceived the act of communication as a 'channel' through which we could 'pass' our message or 'get it across' (*ibid.*). Lakoff and Johnson (1980) saw in this insight a larger process where much of our everyday discourse was structured by metaphors. For example, we perceived happiness as being 'up' and sadness as being 'down'. Equally, consciousness was 'up' and 'unconsciousness' was 'down', 'buried', or 'under' as when we slept *deeply* then woke *up*. Other examples were our conceptualisation of people as 'plants' that must be 'nurtured', and emotions as temperatures, as when feelings were 'cold' (indifferent to hostile) or 'hot' (angry or passionate).

Lakoff and Johnson's enquiry did not just confine itself to metaphor. Metonymy was also analysed as fundamental to how we grasped our experience of the world (see for example Lakoff 1987; Gibbs 1994). The exact nature of a metonymy was a topic of some debate, but at root it represented a relationship where a part stood for a whole as in a 'sail' for a ship, or 'smoke' for fire. Thus, in British English, we identified one of the government's most senior standing committees after the type of room where it was sequestered away, thus calling it a 'cabinet'. In this way a physical space or room in which a council met was used to conceptualise and name the council itself.

The enquiry into metaphor and metonymy furnished three key points to the larger cognitive linguistic enterprise that has developed since. First, meaning-making could no longer be treated as the straightforward symbolisation of the facts of our world. The understanding that we used metaphor and metonymy to capture such common meanings as 'happiness' or 'time' refocused attention on how a meaning had to be a product of some form of conceptual process. The second point was that our conceptualisations were derived from experience. The third was the often improperly accredited adoption of Merleau-Ponty's idea that experience was shaped by our physical interactions with the world (Merleau-Ponty 1945, 1962). In other words, cognition was not a straightforward repository of perceived reality but was itself embodied, or shaped by our bodily existence and the nature of the anatomy on which it depended.

Lakoff and Johnson's interest in how the conceptualisation of experience underpinned our meanings has been further extended by our larger perception of meaning and category formation. Since all meaning is basically categorisation, all linguistic meaning is abstracted to some extent and so requires an act of conceptualisation. The study of how categories are conceptualised has been extended into a larger examination of the ways in which language reflects our cognitive grasp of the world.

To see grammar as derived from experience was also to understand that it was not simply some organisational principle from which we interpreted meanings. Grammar, in Langacker's (1999) view was itself 'conceptualisation'. Grammar was therefore meanings that had been conceptualised out of the wellspring of experience.

The CL interest in metaphor and metonymy was only part of a broader concern for linguistic meaning, for how it was derived and how the process of its derivation structured language. Language's central feature was therefore the more traditional one of meaning representation or symbolisation. Key to the symbol was the fact that it was a conventionalised entity. Thus we did not interpret a symbol because it was like its meaning or in some way physically associated with it. A symbol's meaning arose from a social consensus. In this cognitive model, language's social nature was thus restored to it but as a function of our need for a society and culture in which to conventionalise signs as symbols.

## Ending the LA–AL divide

The LA–AL divide was unsatisfactory because it amounted to an admission that both of the enterprises it characterised would end in failure. On the one hand we were saying that to construct an adequate linguistic theory we had to idealise language. Having done this, we would then be unable to apply the idealised model to the language we found in the world or in the classroom without the model coming apart. If, on the other hand, we tried to develop an applied approach to the complexity of those circumstances we risked obtaining no more than a series of fragmentary observations that would never coalesce into an idea of over-arching explanatory power. CL provides a path out of this dilemma because it proposes a concept of form that is at once cognitive and socio-cultural.

In CL, form is cognitive because it is derived from the way the reality we inhabit is a product of cognition. For example, when we look at a scene, one object in it will capture our attention whilst the others will be de-emphasised. Cognitive psychologists called the object of attention a 'figure' and the rest of the scene 'the ground'. Sentence structures reflect this. They pay attention to one entity as a subject and process it against the 'ground' or an object (Talmy 1978). This is fundamental to how language structures its representations as a reflection of experience.

In CL, linguistic form is also social. First, form is honed by the social function of passing experience from one person to another then it is collected as the repository of meanings that constitutes a culture. Second, linguistic form is social because the cognition whose operations it encodes is also social. This can be exemplified most clearly if we think about the symbolic nature of language.

It is self-evident that words are meaningful, or are symbols. Less self-evident is how we bind words together into *constructions* that are also meaningful. For example, a transitive sentence, 'Nancy loves John' proposes 'John' as a love object and Nancy as the agent of the action. English uses a construction of Agent (Nancy) +Process (loves) +Object (John) to express this state of affairs. This is a symbolic complex or construction. Japanese, on the other hand, might use 'Agent+Object+Process', or particles that mark grammatical functions to express that meaning. Thus each language expresses the same meaning with a different construction. Like words, these forms mean what they do as a result of a social convention. Symbols need society, and a society needs a culture to preserve and develop the conventions that determine what symbols mean.

Language, then, cannot exist in an autonomous and extra-social modularity. Language expresses how a given society conventionalises its grasp of experience over time. Language is in this sense cognitive, and cognition is experiential and social. 'Languages are viewed as nothing other than sets of social conventions by means of which human beings communicate with one another about their experience' (Tomasello 1998: 486). Language's response to social need is 'composed of the same basic elements as many other cognitive skills, event cognition, categorisation, joint attention and cultural learning' (ibid.).

This is not to suggest that CL is conceived with the applied linguist in mind. It is not an enquiry that is limited by some concept of how useful it might be. But, for the applied linguist, CL offers a less fractured starting point because it treats language as cognitive and assumes cognition to be social. In this book, language can be seen less as a 'mirror of mind' and more as an evolving response to how we conceptualise the world through mind and body. According to such an understanding, the human infant does not *acquire* a language because they have an innate grammar whose parameters are reset by that language's input. By the same token, the human adult does not fail to achieve a native-like knowledge of a second language, because their maturity denies them access to that innate grammar. Second languages are difficult to acquire for the same reason that first languages are easy to acquire (Larsen-Freeman and Cameron 2007). Languages have evolved in ways that make them friendly to infant cognition. If they had not they would have died out. When we obtain maturity we also need to retain a language and its meanings. We therefore resist the new, or need to operate its new forms with our previously acquired meanings, creating the types of distortion that are characteristic of second language use.

A first language also gives second language learners the capacity to interfere positively and negatively in their need to *proceduralise* or gain an automatic control over the forms they encounter. Different individuals will learn differently, with some setting out to consciously analyse a form, and others trying simply to acquire it through practice. In successful learning, conscious analysis, however, can promote greater uptake through usage, or by keeping a form and its manner of use in focus. Thus we no longer need to see language teaching as being an activity that either promotes the conscious isolation and presentation of form, or encourages an intuitive uptake through usage. In the model that will be proposed, the first activity will support the second.

We do not have to de-emphasise 'form' by stressing that language should be arranged around 'topics' or that usage should be promoted through tasks. The analysis of a form must be a preliminary to the promotion of its use, and usage the precursor of a form's isolation and analysis. Further, to see the uptake of a language feature as usage-driven also means the learner must disengage it from the context or situation through which it is first practised. For example, if a conditional construction is presented through a scenario of advice-giving, as in 'if I were you I would...', the form should then become a vehicle through which its larger meaning can be explored in other analogous contexts. Thus, for the conditional, advice can be developed into a negative appraisal, as in 'if we took that road we could get help up here', and the student's grasp of the form's meaning will be extended. Finally, it is more important to explore a form's meaning across contexts than to express a context through an array of different forms. If this principle is adopted, we can grasp the difference between the classroom and the language-using world outside as one of the degree to which we exploit our linguistically constructed ability to focus language upon itself, and the learner upon the processes of learning.

## The purpose of the book

In this study, our objective is to begin looking at how the classroom teacher can make use of some of the key principles of CL, and hence develop a pedagogy that will start to bridge the AL–LA divide. To achieve this aim, each chapter will set out a central tenet of cognitive linguistic theory then show how it might re-orient our approach to classroom language teaching. CL is quite a new enterprise, so it contains some quite strong areas of disagreement. In a book of this length I am unable to focus on the detail of these disagreements. Instead, my strategy will be to adopt the perspective that is most consistent with the production of a new model of second language teaching.

The book is divided into four parts. Each part summarises a central tenet in CL then looks at possible classroom applications. Within each chapter I will exemplify my broader discussion of classroom relevance by setting out teaching activities. The larger summary of these methods can then be construed as a first step in the formulation of a CL approach.

Neither the activities nor the book as a whole make any claim to methodological novelty, however. The language teaching literature already abounds with prescriptions for how to teach a certain item of lexis or grammar, or how to foster second language use in class. The activities detailed here do not try to open new methodological ground so much as to exemplify the types of approach that CL emphasises.

The activities have been set out in an instructional format that addresses the teacher directly. They have also been the subject of some classroom experimentation and adaptation. In the main, however, the experimental process is not recounted, since the larger aim was to typify an approach with a repertoire of usable teaching ideas. My objective was not to show how those ideas were derived.

The activities are written for people who are familiar with teaching. The need for clarity means that they are written as instructions. However, finally they are ideas for adaptation that let the teacher decide whether they will fit the level, age and interests of their class. Some may find them under-specified – for example I do not indicate the age or level for which they are suitable. This is because they are not provided as a resource for instant access but as a way of exemplifying an idea that the teacher can adapt to the circumstances in which they work.

Part 1 of the book considers how CL sought answers to some traditional or classical problems concerning the nature of meaning. It then sets out some of the broad tenets of CL regarding experience and embodied cognition. Theories of embodied cognition are found to have particular relevance, not just for how we teach language but for education generally. This relevance is explored in more detail when I look at some research on gesture.

Part 2 looks at meaning as a product of conceptualisation. This topic provides us with two broad themes. The first considers how conceptualisation entails that different cultures and their languages operate with different meanings. This extends the language teaching task into the domain of meaning exploration and comparison, then argues that teachers should look more closely at the cultures from which their target language meanings have evolved. The second theme will be to examine the difference between conceptualisation and construal, then to consider how construal operations shape language and language teaching activities.

Part 3 takes language's symbolism as its theme and explains a usage-based approach to meaning. It looks first at the CL notion of encyclopaedic meaning and discusses its significance for second language learners. It then looks at the concept of a construction, or at a meaning that combines others to create forms beyond the word.

Part 4 draws conclusions and isolates some principles that the designers of second language syllabi should take into account.

# Part I
# Embodied Experience

# 2
# The Problem of Linguistic Meaning

## Introduction

Straightforwardly, language learning would seem to be about matching new forms to old meanings. Learners therefore take the meanings they have already acquired and try to match them to these forms. This learning assumption rests in how all speakers of the world's languages look out on the same reality with the same mind and will thus break it down into roughly the same meanings.

In this part of the book, I question the assumption that linguistic meaning is a straightforward representation of what we see in the world. I pose this question by exploring how words link multiple meanings together in ways that cannot be matched to the world we see. I then consider how meanings are better considered not as parts of our reality but as categories, or as ways of pulling together and pegging down different fragments of experience. Languages use category meanings and these are fashioned from the common imagery established by experience over time. In recounting this view I will consider some of its pedagogical implications.

## The problem of meaning

Even a straightforward concrete term such as 'house' or 'tree' is used to refer to quite variable phenomena in the world. Thus one can imagine occasional disagreement as to whether a given structure is really a house or not. When we start to consider a phenomenon such as colour the disagreements are likely to become more frequent and more intense. The paradox of meaning is that it is fixed enough for us to be able to understand each other but fluid enough for us to be able to apply it across contexts. The problem is to know how this is possible.

One way that formal philosophy tried to resolve the problem of meaning was to see the language we used as directly reflecting some state or condition in the world. Thus, in Tarski's truth-conditional semantics, one could say 'snow' was 'white' only if this was demonstrably true when we looked at the snow lying outside our window (Tarski 1935). Thus words were made meaningful by the fact that they corresponded to some verifiable state of affairs in the world. Meaning, in other words, was obtained by different people observing the same phenomena with the same means of perception.

But there are several difficulties with the above position. Consider statement (1):

(1)  He is my brother

By a truth-conditional argument, the statement would be true only if the subject shared a parent with the speaker. But Chinese people will sometimes talk of having a brother when this person is actually a close friend who feels bound to look out for them. If the speaker were a woman, the statement might also be a way of saying that she was close to this man but did not have any type of physical relationship with him. If the statement were made in a Western monastic community, its significance could change again. 'Brother' could mean somebody who is simply a member of the same order, or even more loosely a 'monk'. In the West, there was also the expression 'brothers in arms' where people felt that they were bonded together by a common enterprise or common dangers. Sentence (1) could be an affirmation of such a relationship.

When we think about the way we use almost every kinship term across cultures and languages we start to produce problems of the same kind. Consider, for example, the threat of the late President of Iraq, Saddam Hussein, when he warned that those who tried to force his troops out of Kuwait would face 'the mother of all battles'. The phrase was meaningful both in its original Arabic and in English, despite having little directly to do with the biological relationship normally expressed by the term 'mother'.

Evidently, Saddam's use of the term could be classed as a metaphorical extension. Thus it was using metaphor to stretch the meaning of the word 'mother' in a new direction. Metaphor is ubiquitous in language and did not escape the interest of those who sought to see meaning as logically derived from some state of affairs in the world. Arguably, therefore, Saddam was not saying that the battle was a mother in any normal sense but rather that it was in some way comparable to a mother. The metaphor need not of itself invalidate the argument that meaning is created out of a match with some state of affairs that exists in the world. It could simply be that the state to which the term was being matched was not the conventional one. One proposal for 'mother' in this metaphor might have been that the word's meaning depended on its possession of certain core features. Thus to be a 'mother', in a literal sense, a creature had to be animate and to have given birth. In the metaphor, some of these core features would have had to be cancelled out by the term to which it was compared. Thus some formalist students of metaphor argued that when we heard 'the mother of all battles' we would have cancelled out the animal features of 'mother' because these could not be found in 'battle'. A remaining meaning would have been that of a progenitor. Thus the battle would have been progenitor of other battles but not human in any sense. This gave the metaphor meaning.

However, it is often difficult to explain the totality of a metaphorical meaning in this way. In 'the mother of all battles' it is clear that some other meaning concerning size has crept in, and, although this may be derived from the first meaning of a progenitor, it is not really contained by it. We must therefore recognise a fundamental feature of metaphor that was first identified by Aristotle (Cooper 1986), then mentioned more recently by Ricoeur (1975). This was that a metaphor could create new meanings. Unfortunately, this made it difficult to see how that meaning was built up from more basic constituent states which could be found in the world. Another problem for a truth-conditional view of meaning was perhaps more fundamental. Although we could allow that metaphors created new sets of references to states in the world, making 'mother' mean 'cataclysmic', for example, we could no longer use the world as an inviolate reference point to validate these claims. If 'mother' could mean both 'cataclysmic' and 'a biological parent' we could say that any word meant almost anything. In short, words would have no stable meanings which we could validate by looking for an equivalent state in the world.

The problem of meaning becomes more difficult when we consider, further, how it operates across languages and cultures. I have already alluded to possible confusion when some Chinese people talk about their brother. When such a speaker may actually possess a biological brother, I sometimes have trouble knowing who they are referring to, particularly when one is not used to hearing them use the term in this way. This confusion points up something which second language learners must come to recognise very early in their studies. This is that different languages operate with different meanings. Evidently, if this quite basic fact is accepted, it becomes still more difficult to think of meanings as simply lying out there in the world until gathered up by language.

Broadly, we can now garner three important issues about meaning. Each of these issues bears upon how we set about the language learning task:

meanings are complex and extensible;
meanings differ among languages;
meanings are not stable entities that can be taken back to some set of shared, common perceptions.

In CL, meanings are generally referred to as categories. This word captures their complexity and potential extensibility. A category implies a grouping of related items rather than the denotation of a single phenomenon. A straightforward term such as a 'tree' groups many different phenomena and can be extended to refer to types of diagram or family relationship. And apparently straightforward concepts as 'love' or 'hatred' will group many different conditions and states. For example, sentences (2), (3) and (4) typify some quite different types of emotional condition:

(2) I am desperately in love with you
(3) Chocolate is a particular love of mine
(4) I have a love–hate relationship with Venice

The differences in these sentences do not just relate to different love-objects. They are about different categories of emotion that originate in different forms of experience.

The fact that meanings are categories ensures that they will vary somewhat between languages. For example, many learners of French come to recognise early that the French language does not distinguish between the categories of 'like' and 'love' in the same way as English, though it does possess the capability of grading this type of emotion:

(5) Je t'aime
(6) Je t'aime bien

Clearly the meaning of 'aimer' (to love/like) is binding together some core meanings in a way that is different from English.

Clearly then, different languages are not all mining the same semantic resource then putting this into different words. The meaning which a language attaches to a word is often fluid and complicated, and not fully captured by definition or by a condition that exists in the world. Word meanings are therefore better construed as categories. Therefore language learning means setting out to master new categories, or new networks of category–form pairings, and this is perhaps its most fundamental problem.

## Language learning as category learning

Consider Gibbs' (2005: 174) analysis of the many meanings of the English word 'stand'. One can gather these meanings into three distinct types, or sub-categories. The first type is the literal sense of achieving or occupying a vertical physical posture. The second is the meaning of retaining a vertical posture or, by a metonymic extension, a position, whilst under pressure to let it go. For the third, the meaning derives from how 'standing' makes one more visible or prominent. Finally the word is more a network of related categories than a single one. For the language learner, acquiring such a complicated category network is hugely problematic. In fact non-native speakers will only develop control of such a category over an extensive language-learning life.

Sub-category 1:   Achieving a vertical posture

(7) My leg hurts, I can't stand/stand up

Sub-category 2:   Retaining a vertical posture

(8) We must stand our ground
(9) Stand up to adversity!
(10) I cannot stand that kind of music
(11) I'll stand you lunch

Sub-category 3:   Becoming prominent through a vertical posture

(12) They were stood down at nine o'clock
(13) She's standing in for Sally today
(14) She really stands out in a crowd

(15) I stand for freedom and justice
(16) He/She was just a one-night stand
(17) She/He's a person of considerable standing

Another concern is how these meanings are built from the core physical meaning, given in the first category. This is the meaning that will be learnt by beginners in English everywhere and which lends itself to a basic 'command–response' procedure where the teacher asks students to stand or sit and demonstrates how they should respond. Even here, learners face a meaning difference, however. This difference lies in the contrast of 'stand' and 'stand up'. 'Stand up' tends to mean the achievement of the expressed posture or its retention when this is becoming difficult, but 'stand' is simply maintaining the position:

(18) He's standing by that desk
(19) He's standing up now

The word is one example of how many metaphorical and abstract meanings can be developed from a word's core physical sense. All of these meanings link back to our experience of standing and obtaining the necessary 'balance' to do so. They also originate in how we feel this posture to be the one in which physical 'resistance' to contrary forces is most easily accomplished. Gibbs has conducted a series of experiments which show how people 'make sense of these uses of stand' because they have built mental patterns or *image schemas* around this experience of obtaining balance and the associated physical action (Gibbs et al. 1994). Image schemas are the patterns of experience that we build up from infancy. For example, the meaning of 'stand' was built out of various central and culturally constructed experiences related to obtaining a vertical posture. Thus the infant experience of standing upright develops into one of balance. Through balance we experience how being upright is advantageous when we have to resist forces. The image schema of balance allows us to grasp the relatedness of such meanings as 'don't stand for such treatment' and 'stand against the odds' (Gibbs 1994, 2005). It is also the case that teaching, of whatever subject matter, should try to tap into our image schemas, if only because they are productive of the larger meanings that education will always aim to develop.

Since meanings develop from concrete bodily experience towards the abstract, it makes sense if pedagogical sequences do also. Therefore, teachers who can cope with the health and safety implications of

Activity 1 might want to use 'stand our ground' as a bridge between concrete and abstract meanings in the way shown.

Activity 1    Stand your ground!
1 Tell the class to stand up then to sit down.
2 Two students of approximately equal size and weight 'stand' and come to the front of the class.
3 The students to face each other, press their flattened palms together and lean forward, supporting each others' weight. Tell them on no account to 'give ground', saying 'stand your ground' many times. Encourage the rest of the class to chorus 'stand your ground!'
4 In pairs, students rehearse a point of argument. For example, Student A likes a particular film and student B doesn't. Ask one pair to unfold a discussion in front of the class, point by counter-point. After each point/counter-point, the class encourages their opponent by saying 'stand your ground!'

The meaning, 'stand your ground', relates to 'I can't stand that book', but the connection is not so obvious. Thus teaching 'standing one's ground in an argument' not only teaches a fixed expression and extends the 'stand' category, but it also provides a bridge between the word's evident physical meanings and the other more abstract ones. This can also be made evident by a straightforward activity that links the metaphor of 'stand' as holding up an object, to that of 'like', then more commonly to letting it fall as being unable to stand it:

Activity 2    What I can't stand
1 Bring another student up and ask them to think of something they dislike.
2 Give them a heavy book and tell them to raise it as high as they can safely on the flat of one hand. Tell them that this book is the thing they dislike.
3 Tell them they 'can't stand it' and get them and the class to repeat this with venom. Tell them to drop the book. Look at the fallen object and say they 'couldn't stand it'.

These activities may seem an over-elaborate way of accessing a few meanings, but they illustrate the larger principle of how abstract meanings can be developed from those that express physical posture and of how teachers can tap into the image schemas involved. More advanced students might also try developing a conscious knowledge of the larger category through the following text-based activity:

Activity 3    Standing
1 Give students the following text and ask them to read it:

### 'Stand'

'Stand' has many meanings in English. But all of these meanings are connected to the basic sense where we occupy or achieve a vertical position, as in 'stand' and 'stand up'. When we stand we can apply pressure more easily and are also more prominent or visible. The other meanings of stand develop from these core senses. The meaning of resisting pressure is associated with the more literal sense of holding a position in a fight, as in 'stand our ground'. We also use this meaning to express that we will not concede a point in argument, as in 'stand our ground'. This gives us a general abstract meaning of standing as resisting pressure or misfortune, whether intellectual, physical, or both. From such a notion we obtain a contrary *refusal* to stand one's ground or resist, then by extension it becomes a refusal to support or resist pressure and hence to put up with something adverse or distasteful as when we say 'I can't stand that film'. We also use the idea of standing as supporting when we say 'we will stand them a meal', meaning we will pay for their meal.

Standing expresses a profile that is prominent, as opposed to crouching or hidden. People who are wealthy or important are therefore thought to have 'standing' in their community, whilst 'high visibility' means simply 'standing out'. We also stand up to make our opinion clear and so stand for an idea, and hence come to represent it. Closely associated is the concept of standing for parliament, and its earlier association with standing on a platform to ask to be elected. Therefore, when we attach ourselves to a cause 'we stand up to be counted'. We may obtain the sexual meaning 'one-night stand' from this idea of prominence: performers play music on a 'stand' to show themselves to the audience. A one-night stand was a performance for one night. The expression then developed to mean not a one-night musical show but a one-night sexual relationship. Closer to the idea of prominence is how we signal our presence by 'standing' and so 'stand in for' another, and conclude by 'standing down' from a position.

2 Give students the category diagram shown in figure 1 but delete all the expressions apart from those shown in the double-outlined ellipses.
3 In groups, the students use the text and the following expressions to fill out the category diagram, showing how some expressions relate more closely to one meaning of 'stand' than another.

   *Expressions*: I stand for freedom and justice. I'll stand you a lunch. He was just a one-night stand. She stood them down at nine. She's standing in for Sally today. Stand up straight. I can't stand that film! Stand up to adversity.
4 Discuss the result by showing the students figure 1. Make clear that there is not always a right way and a wrong way to do this. For example, there does seem to be a close relationship between 'stand in for somebody' and 'stand them down', but either of these meanings could relate more or less closely to 'stand out from the crowd'.

In a process called *conceptual projection* (Lakoff 1987) we can explore the imagistic potential of image schemas by creating related sets of

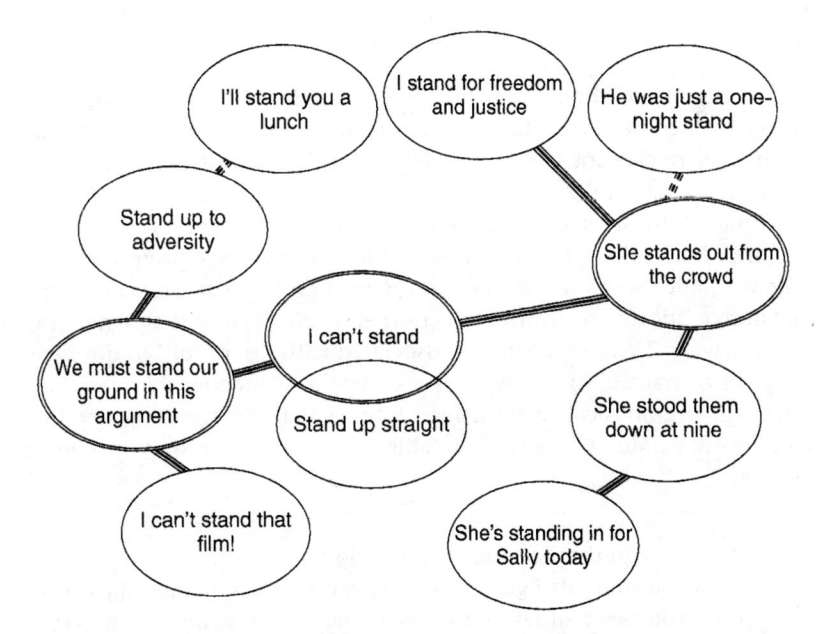

*Figure 1* The category relations for some of the meanings of 'stand'

26  *Cognitive Linguistics and Language Teaching*

The water's in the tank    The man's in the water

He's in deep (The situation is hard to get out of)
He's in a crisis

The man is on the horse.    The horse is on the road

He's on the edge of disaster

---

We are in/on
trouble, the shit, a road to no-where, target, a situation, it up to our necks, thin ice, weak ground, poverty, the way (blocking progress), the way (going towards our goal), a mess, the brink, the dark, a new path, a roll (winning and winning), a bad way, schedule, the right direction

*Figure 2* 'On' versus 'in': an activity diagram

metaphors from them. Consider, for example, how we can use the concept of containment to understand why certain sets of abstract relationships involve the use of the preposition 'in', whilst others use 'on'. The preposition 'in' generally evokes a container schema, derived from a primal physical sensation of being a living organism that is physically distinct from others, or contained within a form. When projected onto the world, it also proposes an enduring relationship, since it is more difficult to extricate one thing from another when it is in it than when it is on it. Figure 2 relates meanings associated with 'in' or 'on' to different degrees of tractability or tenuousness. The first anchors the meanings through the physical relationships from which the meanings evolve, and so illustrates the more tractable types of relationship expressed by 'on'.

Activity 4    On thin ice and in a situation
 1 Show the students figure 2 and explain how the images show that 'on' expresses a situation as easy to get out of, whilst 'in' makes it seem more difficult.

2 Reinforce by getting students to perform associated actions and say what they are doing (standing on a chair, for example, or putting a paper in a drawer, and a book on a shelf).
3 Remind them how 'in' relationships are more secure than 'on' ones. Illustrate by showing one object slipping over another then by taking a different object and rattling it inside a container.
4 In pairs, the students decide which of the idioms at the bottom of figure 2 is completed with 'in' and which with 'on'. They match each complete idiom to a situation from the following list:

- What we're doing has no future
- Our project is keeping to time
- Our argument is very weak
- We're winning and winning
- We have difficulties
- We have big difficulties and will be blamed
- Our activities are illegal and we can't escape that
- Our situation is very confused and chaotic
- We are poor
- We are not far from disaster
- We are stopping somebody from doing what they want to do or from going where they want to go
- We don't know what's happening
- We've found a new way to do something
- We're going where we want to go

5 In pairs, student A uses an expression from the above list to sum up their circumstances and student B agrees with an idiom. For example:

Student A: *What we're doing has no future*
Student B: Yes, we're on a road to nowhere

The above activity also reminds learners of the image schemas that lie behind how English prepositions express meaning and so helps them to operate these meanings as part of a broader category with a common conceptualisation.

## Conclusions

In this chapter I have broached how CL arose from the difficulties that linguists had with producing a formal theory of meaning. I illustrated this by discussing the multiple meanings of some terms, then looked at the types of pedagogical issue which these gave rise to. I described how CL sees meaning as rooted in embodied, physical experience and the image schemas that such experience produces. Last, I gave some thought as to how teachers can use image schemas in language learning. They can do this by asking learners to mimic the bodily experiences in which a schema originates. Alternatively, they can ask learners to trace the metaphorical or metonymic relations that bind categories together.

It is also important to point out that both the activities discussed here make 'language' into a topic of classroom focus, and can be used to develop discussions about meanings. Exploring the cultural and historical origins of meanings and their associated imagery will help the retention and understanding of pairings between form and meaning (see for example, Boers 2001; Holme 2004). Further, I emphasise the much older principle of deductive or cognitive code-learning and its insistence that when we have to work for understanding we will retain knowledge more successfully. In the CL-based model, I carry cognitive code-learning away from the deduction of grammatical rules and towards an exploration of the connections between meanings by asking students to discuss the significance of how forms are arranged in the charts. Finally, it is not new to propose that we can advance the retention of meanings if we re-associate them with the physical activities from which they were derived (Lindstromberg and Boers 2005). This proposal is rooted in a strong language teaching tradition of what can be called E&M (enactment and movement routines). CL furnishes a stronger rationale for an E&M approach whilst also stimulating a somewhat different take on how, when, and why they are implemented.

# 3
# Conceptualisation, Embodiment and the Origins of Meaning

## Introduction

Recalling a problem voiced by Socrates, philosophy has given the name 'Meno's problem' to the question of how we come to translate reality into thought. Socrates wondered how an ignorant shepherd boy could manipulate objects as if he were aware of their geometric properties. The larger question was how we come to know anything when we do not already know it. The problem rests in the perception that there is a subjective 'I', or person, looking out on the world, and an objective 'it' which is being looked at. Because the world and its observer are effectively separate, it is impossible for the subjective, thinking being ever to know the objective world without making it part of their thoughts. As soon as the world does become part of our thoughts, however, the objective form is made subjective. Therefore we can never really get to know what is out in the world, because all meanings are products of the subjective mind. We might conclude then that it was meaningless to talk of an objective reality because we could never cognitively manipulate it. But this view leads to a logical nonsense where, because reality would be constructed by the subjective mind, it would always be fashioned by the whims of the thinker – and we could never be contradicted by circumstance.

The model of mind and body that was long dominant in Western thought was often called Cartesian, because it could be traced back to the seventeenth-century French philosopher, Descartes. The Cartesian model treated the body as a vehicle for the mind, and the mind as a kind of command and control mechanism for the body. The body's function was to relay back sense impressions of reality to the mind. In an objectivist view, the mind processed these perceptions as meanings and represented them as language. The mind's capacity to shape abstract meanings was a flight from its physical circumstances. When the mind dealt with abstraction it entered a realm whose truths were transcendental. Reason was seen as God-given and forged from our capacity for abstract thought into an instrument of bodily control. This dualism risked making rational thought insubstantial, because it manipulated ideas which it had constructed from itself.

The philosopher, Merleau-Ponty (1945–58) formulated one of the more recent responses to Meno's dilemma. For Merleau-Ponty there was a third element in the subjective-mind (internal)–objective-world (external) relationship, which was the human body. We experience our bodies as extensions of our subjective thought processes and we experience reality as an interaction between the body and the world amidst which the body moves. The body, therefore, was neither a subjective mental condition nor an objective physical one. The body was a third term that mediated between subjectivity and objectivity. The body enfolded the world and so shaped reality as an extension of its own identity. The mind was not some separate perceptual instrument but an extension of the body and suffused with bodily imagery.

A larger conclusion was that experience was a product of both body and mind. Cognition was not the passive receptacle of sense experiences relayed to it by the body. Cognition was *enactive* and reality was experienced as a function of cognitive and bodily activity. The body, 'through its motor abilities, its actual movements and its posture', informed and shaped 'cognition' (Gallagher 2005).

What began as a philosopher's attempt to solve an ancient problem has become a much larger enquiry into the relation of mind, body and reality. This enquiry has embraced the disciplines of psychology, biology, neurology and linguistics whilst also bringing them together into the domain now known as cognitive science.

Evidence for this concept of an embodied mind has been found in many areas, but most notably in:

- the broader concept of *proprioception*, or of how the body remains aware of its own position in space;
- studies of object perception and the way we do not just 'see' the phenomena we encounter but may conceptualise them in terms of our embodied nature;
- the correlation between cognitive development and infant movement;

phantom limb syndrome, where those who have lost or been born without limbs may still feel they have them;

the discovery of 'mirror neurons' as evidence for how the brain simulates movement without the body's actual engagement in it;

the study of how language uses schemas of bodily form and function to conceptualise meaning;

studies of body language, gesture and their relationship to learning and speech.

I will now elaborate briefly upon these sources of evidence but will leave the last, which looks at gesture, to the next chapter. I will then explore how these ideas should affect our approach to language education.

## Proprioception: how the body remains aware of its own position in space

Socrates exemplified Meno's paradox with a discussion of geometry. The crux of Socrates' puzzle was how a shepherd boy could be capable of precise movement without knowledge of the geometry that would allow him to calculate where to put each limb. Plato was posing a broader philosophical dilemma, but he was prescient to use spatial movement to express the problem. In the twentieth century, Merleau-Ponty would again take the perception of space as an example of his theory of embodiment. Instead of seeing space as an objective entity in which the body moved, he saw it as produced out of bodily movement:

> Far from my body being no more than a fragment of space, there would be no space at all for me if I had no body.
> (Merleau-Ponty 1945/1962: 102; cited in Gallagher 2005: 59)

*Proprioception* describes how we maintain an awareness of where our various limbs are positioned in space. Such an awareness is essential to almost any physical activity. If you reach for an object in the dark, you will not know exactly where that thing is placed, but as you reach towards it, you will know where your hand is in relation to yourself. All our motor actions and skills depend on proprioception even though it is generally registered unconsciously.

Studies of proprioception have done much to re-work our view of the mind–body relationship in a way that has made Merleau-Ponty's solution to Meno's paradox seem more plausible. Over a century ago, Munk

(1890) and Wernicke (1900) described the mind as carrying within it a homunculus (small man), or map of itself, on which it could register its own movements. The homunculus metaphor allows one to imagine a still image of a man and a moving one. The mind tracks the movements of the body by relating a moving diagram to a static one. Whilst no such imagery is realistically postulated, it does point up how the mind must possess a set of stored images of the body, using these to maintain spatial orientation by mirroring the body's movements in a continuous process of imagistic adjustment.

More recently, proprioception has been understood as a function of both mind and body. Thus we depend upon *proprioceptors* which, though part of the central nervous system, are distributed throughout the body and relay information about posture and position back to the brain (Gallagher 2005: 6). Proprioceptors relay information back to the brain as attributes of the central nervous system but also extend the brain into the body. They propose that movement is not a response to some mental command and control centre but is cognitive activity extended out into the body. By the same token, thinking is partially constructed out of the imagery of bodily movement.

One of the strongest challenges to traditional perceptions about mind–body relationships has come from studies of imitation among newborn infants, or neonates. Traditionally, thinkers such as Piaget (1962) thought that neonates were incapable of imitative behaviour because of the complexity of what was involved. When a caregiver moves their tongue, for example, an infant must observe the action, map the caregiver's part of the body onto their own equivalent one, and must have observed themselves to recognise the equivalence, then finally must have developed an awareness of where this body part is in relation to themselves, and of themselves in relation to it. However, recent studies have found imitative behaviour in infants of 2–3 weeks, making such a complex procedure unlikely (Meltzoff and Moore 1977). A more recent analysis is that the neonate is born with an innate sense of itself as an embodied entity, or with a body image which can recognise the body of another as both separate from and similar to itself (Gallagher 2005). Finally, a neonate's imitative behaviour originates in the unconscious recognition of its own humanity and the common physical heritage that this entails (*ibid.*).

## Not seeing but conceptualising

When we reach for an object it would seem that we are moving our hands towards something which is out there in space with measurable dimensions. However, there is substantial evidence to show that we do not assess the object only straightforwardly according to its size, colour and shape. We also assess the object according to how easily we will be able to manipulate it, or by whether we can pick it up or not (Jeannerod 1994; cited in Gallagher 2005: 8). Further, the straightforward perception of an object may actually involve the activation of some of the neurons that are implicated in picking it up (Gallese 2000; Murata et al. 1997; Rizzolatti et al. 2000; cited in Gallagher 2005). In other words, we do not just perceive the object as an objective form in space but also conceptualise it in terms of how it may affect us. By the same token, our visual perception may actually stabilise an object when it is in motion (Martinez-Conde et al. 2000; cited in Gallagher 2005: 8). We therefore conceptualise forms in ways that will allow us to make a better assessment of them and not according to some idealised construct of how they actually are.

Studies of animal perception have also suggested that the 'perception of objects in space is based on a person's anticipation of the sensory consequences of actions that could be performed in a given situation' (Gibbs 2005: 69). For example, blindness can result simply by severing the areas of the brain responsible for movement from those responsible for visual perception (Nakamura and Mishkin 1980). In other words, movement may be the necessary correlate to how we see. It is also significant that those blind from birth may be capable of spatial perception. For example, by running their hands over the raised surfaces, or tactile pictures, they can obtain pictorially correct representations of their immediate environment which they can then map back onto that environment and use to negotiate a way through its obstacles (Kennedy et al. 1991; cited in Gibbs 2005: 50–1). In other words, their proprioception is helping them to construct the world out of their movements through it.

## Cognitive development and infant movement

If space is internalised as an attribute of bodily movement, cognitive development and language acquisition may not begin in processes of seeing and starting to grasp the names of what is seen. Rather, greater infant crawling and mobility correlates with enhanced cognitive development and by the same token a 'retardation' in development has been associated with a lack of early crawling experience (Gallagher 2005: 145). Crawling and general locomotor experiences in infancy can change how the infant will evaluate a height (Bertenthal and Campos 1990; cited in Gallagher 2005: 145). Crawling facilitates the infant's development of proprioception and enhances their spatial perception. In other words, the way that the infant perceives space becomes inextricable from their growing awareness of their own bodily movements within it (*ibid.*).

## Aplasic phantoms

The phenomenon of *aplasic phantoms* refers to how amputees may continue to experience a limb as if they still had it despite being consciously aware that they do not. The phenomenon is far from universal among amputees but has been the subject of some quite intensive study because of how it indicates that the brain's body image is constructed more around the mental image of it that we have and less around the form that it has physically assumed. Poeck (1964: 272), for example, noted how a woman who had lost her thumb would constantly attempt to handle objects as if the thumb were still there (Gallagher 2005: 90). The vividness of the phantom limb experience has been associated with how we can forget about posture and the position of body parts, relying instead upon the schema that we have of these. Incredibly, phantom limbs are not unknown among people whose defect is congenital, pointing to how the schema from which they are generated may be innate.

Human movement unfolds with varying degrees of consciousness. For example, when walking we can choose to deliberately put one foot before another or step between the lines on paved ground, but may then walk without any awareness of what we are doing. The varying extent to which we consciously intervene in our physical actions furnishes a clear parallel for language, making far-fetched the insistence that we depend upon some cognitively isolated module whose operations are always reflexive, but pointing to different degrees of interference from other cognitive functions in how we transform meaning into words. In relation to bodily function, Gallagher (2005) has related this shift between unconscious and conscious modes of operation to a movement between the use of what he calls the body-schema and the body-image. The schema unconsciously locates our body in space and furnishes us with a mental image strong enough to make aplasics think they are physically complete. Unlike the schema, body-image is more the awareness of our physical selves that we construct from birth. Evidently, it will also be shaped out of the way in which the culture into which we are born also perceives the body and its physical functions. In the same way, we can also understand how language *automaticity* is on a continuum, as if between reflexive schemas and constructed images (Kahnemann and Triesman 1984). Even when it is proceduralised knowledge, language does afford us choice over such aspects as word selection. The extent to which we make use of these choices is open to conscious control. Exerting such control is similar to making decisions about where we put our feet when learning dance steps. Language and movement centres in the brain are closely associated. Centres for language may have borrowed from how those for movement permit different degrees of control. This function is both applicable to use, as when we re-word a difficult point, and to learning, as when we try to assemble words into an unfamiliar pattern.

## Mirror neurons

One of the most far-reaching aspects of work on embodied cognition concerns the discovery of what are called mirror neurons. This discovery gives further evidence for the close relationship of proprioception, locomotion and how we grasp the world (see for example, Gallese and Goldman 1998). Experiments with macaques found that activity in the brain's ventral pre-motor cortex was triggered not just by actions themselves but by the observation of them in others. In monkeys and humans the ventral pre-motor cortex is associated with movement, and this part of the brain registered similar neuronal activity when a monkey observed another reaching for a stick as when it actually performed the action itself. A direct study of this type of brain activity in people has been ethically impossible, but the use of indirect brain-imaging measures, or EEG scans, suggests that humans also show this type of 'mirror' activity in the part of the brain responsible for movement (Fadiga et al. 1995).

Intriguingly, the site of activity for mirror neurons in humans is Broca's area, a part of the brain previously associated with language, and at one point with syntactic functions (Gallese and Goldman 1998). Mirror neurons in humans may therefore be associated not just with a passive response to others' activity but with the ability to imitate others' actions that is essential to all language learning. By cognitively enacting what others do as if we had done it ourselves, they propose that others' actions can be mapped back onto our own body image. This allows us to imitate each other with relative ease, an attribute that is essential to the acquisition of language and gesture.

Tomasello (2003) perceives the grasp of another's intentions as an essential prerequisite to first language learning, as the infant, on hearing a given expression must deduce what is intended by it. Understanding another's intentions also depends on our capacity to model them without their having occurred. In essence, mirror neurons can afford us this capacity by relaying others' actions to ourselves as if they were our own. They could thus be fundamental to our ability to empathise, to read others' intentions, and hence acquire language.

The condition of autism is characterised by an inability to empathise or emotionally connect to others. It is also associated with delayed first language acquisition, an excessively literal speech and an inability to use or process metaphor. Researchers have found anomalous or partly suppressed activity in the motor neurons of subjects with higher-functioning autism (Oberman *et al.* 2005) indicating that this condition might be related to defects in mirror neuronal functioning. Two of the characteristics of autism, the inability to empathise, and the problem of language delay, can both relate to a failure to read another's intentions.

Finally, those with autism can find the use of imagination and non-literal language difficult. Seminal to imagination may be a capacity to run the types of simulations of others' actions that mirror neurons afford. Failures in the simulation of movement may also relate to a failure in imagistic grasp of others and of their world. For example, we may be unable to see things as having the potential to move, or not. The object world is thus left anchored in a perceptual here and now and deprived of the potential for movement and change that our imagistic grasp of it affords.

## The nature of language: image schemas and embodied cognition

Cognition and our cognitive processes are in part shaped around the image of the body that they manipulate. In its turn, the reality experienced by the mind reflects the nature of the body that moves through it. The world is no longer some independent and objective information source, but is re-worked by the physical form of the information gatherer, and by the cognitive processes that are also structured by that form's image. Experience is structured by the forms that our bodies have and the movements that they make. Cognition is therefore embodied, first, because it's finally an aggregation of the experiences that are thus structured by the body, and second, because it cannot be disaggregated from the body map that makes those experiences what they are, and the mind what it is.

Cartesian philosophy saw logical and mathematical thought processes as transcending our physical and emotional nature. Cognitive linguists have shown much logical and mathematical meaning to be derived from bodily experience, however. For example, number systems are commonly based on ten. But twelve is more composite, or has more factors, and has been used to create theoretically effective *duodecimal* systems. However, the origins of number manipulation in finger counting may make ten conceptually easier. Mathematics then, which is traditionally construed as 'pure reason', is conceived out of the embodied form to which it was once thought antithetical (Lakoff and Nuñez 2001).

One of the many contributions made by Johnson (see, for example, 1987), Lakoff (see, for example, 1987) and Lakoff and Johnson (see, for example, 1980, 1999) was to understand how the embodied nature of thought influenced the structures of language. The influence could largely be seen in metaphor. Lakoff and Johnson developed Reddy's (1993) insight into how a metaphor could structure our everyday discourse and fashion our perception of a given topic. Lakoff and Johnson (1980) saw in this understanding a larger process where much of our everyday discourse was structured by metaphors. For example, we perceived happiness as being 'up' and sadness as being 'down', and consciousness as 'up' and 'unconsciousness' as 'down' or as being buried or 'under' (sleep 'deeply' versus wake 'up'). We also saw people as 'plants' who must be 'nurtured', and emotions as temperatures, as when feelings were 'cold' (indifferent to hostile) or hot (angry or passionate).

A new perception of metaphor as the result of a cognitive and not a linguistic process required a new terminology. In cognitive theory three terms are used to encapsulate how metaphor is the consequence of a conceptual process. Thus, in the metaphor 'the child is a tender plant', 'plant' is the *source domain*, because it is the concept through which the identified entity is conceptualised, and 'child' is the *target domain*. For the child to be given the attributes of the plant, we can say that the meaning of plant is *mapped* onto that of child (Fauconnier and Turner 1997) and our conceptualisation of the child is structured by some of the attributes of a plant.

Perhaps Lakoff and Johnson's most significant point, however, was that the figurative language summated the cognitive processes through which we derive meaning from experience (1980). This was a process that can be traced back to infancy. For example, an infant pulling themselves upright for the first time will often smile and experience a glow of pride and satisfaction. Falling a few seconds later they may experience some pain and humiliation. The state of being 'up' thus acquires positive associations, and that of being 'down', negative ones. These experiences developed mental patterns that helped us conceptualise our future experiences of joy and sadness (Johnson 1987, 1989; Grady 1997). The state of being 'up' thus shapes schemas of verticality and balance. These allow us to conceptualise various other conditions such as consciousness and happiness. Thus the coincidence of feeling happy about standing upright means we cognitively *map* our feeling of well-being onto this schema of uprightness, shaping what is called a *conceptual metaphor*. This could be expressed linguistically as 'up is conscious' or 'up is happiness', though the more schematic mapping would always be sub-linguistic.

Our analysis of 'stand' in the last chapter showed how these schemas may be used to extend one basic meaning of physical position to many more abstract ones such as 'resist' or 'put up with'. In reverting to the previous problems of meaning, we can see how our notion of happiness is not really a definable entity with a fixed set of features. Happiness is conceptualised through our experiences of well-being, among these those of balance and verticality will feature strongly, as will also the satisfaction of hunger. The meaning of happiness is also 'embodied' because it is conceptualised through a coincidence between the positive physical experiences of obtaining 'balance', being upright, or appetite satisfaction and the positive sensation that results from these states. Of equal consequence was the view that these meanings were not being conceptualised out of the world itself but from our experience of it. The source of meaning was therefore experiential, and created image schemas which were in turn used to fashion the conceptual metaphors out of which much abstract meaning was shaped.

As discussed, for human beings perhaps the primary physical experience of the world is as space unfolded from movement. Grammar is itself structured by our discovery of the relationships between our bodies, entities in space and the impacts that these have upon each other. A process of grammaticalisation was thus postulated and studied, where the meanings that originated in the orientation of the body to its environment became grammatical (see for example, Traugott and Heine 1991; Heine 1997). An almost self-evident example concerns how in many languages some prepositions begin as body parts, as in the English 'be-*hind*' (Heine 1997). Thus, we use our body's orientation to objects to map the relations that they have to us, then, by projection, between themselves, creating an abstract, grammatical word out of one that made a lexical reference to one of our physical features.

## Education and embodiment

The more specialised influence of a theory of embodied cognition in language education can best be grasped by first considering some precepts from education generally. An implicit metaphor of education as movement or exploration has been prevalent among some thinkers for a considerable time. In fact the metaphorical origins of the terms associated with education suggest this. 'Educate' comes from a Latin term meaning to 'lead out', for example, whilst a 'course' supposes a route or path. A more conscious connection between education and movement was made by the eighteenth-century philosopher Rousseau when he advocated that infants should not be kept swaddled but need to stretch their limbs and explore their environment (1911, first published 1762). Rousseau further put forward a model of education where the role of an idealised tutor was more to manipulate the environment of their pupils so that they might learn from it and less to inculcate them with knowledge. Knowledge was gleaned from movement in a world that was experientially arranged and enriched. More than a century later, the American educational philosopher, John Dewey (1896) gave such ideas a more precise and practical form in his development of an early model of discovery learning. Dewey noted, for example, how the stimuli that we perceive did not simply vary in themselves as external agents, but according to the 'physical value' that we placed upon them. Thus we could not simply objectify external stimuli but needed to consider them as inextricably bound up with our mode of processing them:

> We do not have first a sound and then activity of attention, unless sound is taken as mere neuron shock or physical event, not as conscious value. The conscious sensation of sound depends upon the motor response having already taken place.
> (Dewey 1896, cited in Gibbs 2005)

Concomitantly, education was in part about the development of these subjective modes of experience through immersion in what he called 'the consciousness of the race'. This immersion was a process, where, for example, 'the response which is made to the child's instinctive babblings' makes 'the child' aware of what 'those babblings mean', so transforming them into 'articulate language' and introducing 'the child' into the 'wealth of ideas and emotions which are now summed up in language' (Dewey 1897). Cognition, in this model of learning, is enactive, with the child using adult input to construct their own sounds as meaning, not simply making meaningful sounds in imitation of adult speech.

More tellingly, Dewey understood that the relationship between the psychological and social sides of education needed to be 'organic', without either aspect being treated as dominant. Treating education as enforced socialisation subverted individual freedom and intellectual autonomy. As for Rousseau, education therefore had to mean remaking the child's environment in ways that afforded an inventory of experience that would be more concentrated and better focused than outside the schoolroom. Accordingly, physical activity would not be subordinated to the rest of the curriculum, as was traditional, but should become the medium through which more abstract forms of learning such as mathematics were expressed.

More recently, mathematics educators have given form to Dewey's ideas by helping children develop concepts of number from their manipulation of concrete objects. Studies now show how calculation and learning to calculate can be made easier when students learn by handling concrete objects. In one study (Kirsh 1995) participants were shown two sets of 30 coins, then asked to calculate the amount in dollars and cents. People got a faster and more accurate results when they were allowed to touch the coins than when they were not allowed to use their hands (Gibbs 2005: 193).

Embodied education does not simply mean object manipulation or teaching through realistic contexts, as when one learns how to calculate areas by measuring the classroom. Rather it should be an appeal to 'what human ideas are', to 'the conceptual systems in which they are organised', and to the way these are grounded in reality (Nuñez *et al.* 1999: 51). Metaphor becomes the essential vehicle of that appeal, taking ideas back to modes of conceptualisation from which they evolved. Accordingly, the 'continuous function' in mathematics is derived from a metaphor of 'a traveller' tracing a line. Thus the essential conceptualisation is to see a static line as continuous and hence as unfolding before us in a state of fictive motion. The perception of the static as moving is dependent on the conceptual metaphor of 'fictive motion'. This conceptual metaphor is manifest in such everyday expressions as 'just before Highway 24 *reaches* Walnut Creek, it *goes through* the Caldecott Tunnel'. This conceptual operation originates in our sense of self as a body whose motion unfolds the space by which it is surrounded. Accordingly, children can be encouraged to transfer the imagery built out of their own movement into that which underpins logical and mathematical concepts.

The ideas of another pioneer, the Swiss music educationist Jaques-Dalcroze, were also closely aligned with the concept of embodied knowledge because they perceived the target concept, music, as an entity that would not simply be grasped as a facet of the mobility afforded to the child's body, but as internalised by the forms this body assumed in dance and mime, or through a process he termed eurythmics (Jaques-Dalcroze 1988). Although focused on music, Dalcroze did not see his educational ideas as restricted to that subject. He criticised the educational practice of his time for not allowing people to learn from experience until released from formal education into the world, considering that we therefore missed aligning the physical and mental development of our children at a time when it was most achievable. We needed to encourage 'active experience' right at the start of a child's studies 'when body and brain' were 'developing in parallel' and were 'constantly communicating their impressions and feelings' to one another. Dalcroze wanted children to learn music through movement, experiencing the physical nature of rhythm, and regarding the body itself as a kind of musical instrument.

## Language teaching and embodiment: language as rhythm and movement

Dalcroze's interest in internalising music through movement can also stimulate thought about a language's rhythmic nature. Learners whose first language is tonal may find particular difficulties with a stress-timed language such as English, and the opposite can also hold true. A very simple procedure, that can be inserted into almost any other activity that introduces new lexis or form, is to have learners stamp out the stress pattern of a word as they say it by inserting it into a line governed by iambic metre.

Activity 5　　Feeling the stress
1　Introduce a new item of lexis by inserting it into an iambic line. Any line that scans with stress/unstress will do, for example: 'cupboard':
　　Thĕre ĩs ă cūpbŏard ĩn mў hōuse
2　Walk and say the line at the same time. Try to say it by taking a small quiet step when the syllable is unstressed, then stamping when is stressed.
3　Bring one learner up and ask them to walk and speak exactly as you do.
4　Ask the class to tap out the stress with their hands on the table.

Learners of a tonal language can try a similar activity where they conduct the tone with their hands or fingers whilst they say it. Such a procedure can also be used to practise intonation patterns.

Clearly such activities will be less resisted by younger learners, as will any approach involving linking language to movement. However, some types of material have the potential to interest learners of all age groups. Jazz chants have evoked interest in ELT because of how they can fix language with rhythm (Graham 2001). In its turn, the rhythm can be linked to movement.

Carol Graham has adapted stories into jazz chant rhythms, and these can be combined with dance and mime, where one or several performers illustrate the actions that the chanted story unfolds (1988). Dramatisation with choral chants was central to Ancient Greek theatre with the chorus sometimes pursuing the principal actors as an incanted embodiment of their impending fate. Teachers can revive this type of choral chant to link target forms to rhythmic movement.

Activity 6    Chanting
1  Take a Jazz chant that can be easily divided into parts of a dialogue, for example:

> Do you know Mary?
> Mary, who?
> Mary Macdonald
> Course I do.
>
> Do you know her little brother?
> Yes of course I do
> I know her little brother
> her mother
> and her father too.
> (Graham, 2001: 3)

2  Stand the class and group them in a horseshoe round one member who should face them.
3  Tell the class to ask the first question as a chorus (this present simple question is the target form).
4  Have them practise moving in time to the stress, a step forward on the stressed syllable as they speak, then back to receive the answer, for example:

Do yóu (step)
knów (step)
Már (step) -y

5 Ask the lone student to respond in the same manner, gesturing affirmatively and moving into the space that the chorus vacates when they step back.
6 Encourage improvisation of the surrounding patterns and associated movement.

The extent to which students respond to rhythm and movement is of course subject to huge cultural variation, but dance, unless temporarily suppressed by a fundamentalist creed, is universal. In a schoolroom in East Africa I once observed an entire lesson sequence conducted in rhythm, maintaining a ritualised question and answer routine between students and teacher, with the student rising to respond, and the class offering rhythmic applause for each correct answer. Some might argue that if such an approach completely takes over the class it will ritualise linguistic production to a point where children fail to develop an expressive capability, but in an elementary phase it may help a class attain the rote mastery of stock phrases upon which a more creative and generalised use will later be based. Such techniques have also entered into phonics-based reading lessons with children assembling phones into words to a rhythm tapped out by a teacher's baton.

Boers and Lindstromberg (2005) also found that alliteration made language more memorable. Daunted by the insistence of the lexical approach upon the need to help students acquire a vast repertoire of fixed phrases, they thought the task might be facilitated by emphasising the alliterative properties of some forms. They based this assumption on an experiment with learning alliterative idioms such as 'bite the bullet', 'get short shrift' or 'beat about the bush' which showed that even when the students' attention had not at all been explicitly directed at sound patterns, 'alliterating phrases were more likely to be remembered than the non-alliterating ones'.

Poets in oral traditions were well aware of how alliteration could help them remember long texts. Alliteration is important in oral poems that were subsequently written down, such as the Homeric epics or the Anglo-Saxon *Beowulf*, often consolidating the poem's larger structure around repeated imagistic chunks. Alliteration gives language a tangible contour, making a single portable object from its otherwise disparate elements. Clearly, it can form a base from which to help students build the repertoire of the fixed forms that may in some cases be used for more creative generalisation.

## Language teaching and embodiment: mime, enactment and movement

Activities that link movement, stress and rhythm also link language, as a remembered entity, to the use of the body as semiotic device. One has only to enter a Khoranic school to see how closely physical and rhythmic movement can be associated with the memorisation of a foreign language text. In discussing language evolution, Donald suggests a stage where mimetic skill served as a precondition for language (1997). A capacity to use the body for meaning-making coincided with the cognitive ability to control the retrieval of items from memory. He also points out how the imitation of each others' physical actions remains essential in many types of training, whether for sports, dance, or workplace skills. Theories of mirror neurons emphasise how bodily movement can be associated with the origin of voluntary memory retrieval, elementary meaning-making, and the rehearsal routines that underpin language learning.

Working in both L1 and L2 contexts, researchers have found that 'vocabulary learning can be helped by the physical enactment of vocabulary' (Craik and Lockhart 1972; Duffelmeyer 1980; Boers and Lindstromberg 2005). Further, as Donald claims, many of us will recollect how when memorising we move and walk. Also, when we want to solve problems or unfold complex thought, we move as if tracing the path of our ideas.

Rehearsal routines, where people speak in response to movement, and move to express their own uttered meanings, may thus be central to both language *phylogeny* (its evolutionary development in the human species) and its *ontogeny* (its development within a single individual). In the second language case this may be captured by Saville-Troike's observation of a Japanese ESL child who moved around the classroom repeating 'walking, walking' (1988; cited in Lantolf 2002). The child's actions are also helping it to place a verb that specifies a manner of movement, 'walk', within an image schema of 'motion', as this is built up from the action. For Lantolf the event also represents an important assumption of agency, in that the private speech of a child talking to itself is translated into an action. The action begins as the speech act's meaning but then becomes its implemented consequence. The repetition does not simply signify agency in relation to the action, it also signifies the child's decision to use this speech–action relationship to promote their learning.

The imagistic thought that completes a meaning may evolve from physical movement. Words such as 'ball' or 'wheel', whilst connoting fixed object categories, derive much of our sense of what that category actually is from a potential for movement. One can thus argue that when learning meanings our movements may help to re-access that motor imagery, or even to re-fashion the same, thus embedding second language vocabulary within its appropriate imagery. Using this assumption, Boers and Lindstromberg taught such English manner of movement verbs as 'trudge', 'saunter', or 'shrug' by having students enact the actions themselves in an experimental group whilst a control class was learning the same verbs though explanation (2005). Boers and Lindstromberg found that 'enacting or miming a verb resulted in better retention than explaining it'. When the students said they had learnt a verb by practising its expressed action they expressed a correct response to it in 89.47% of such cases, compared with 72.34% under the control condition, with chi-square tests showing this difference to be significant. Perhaps an even more interesting conclusion was reinforced in another study described in the same article which showed that 'merely watching someone enact or mime a MM verb' could 'have a positive effect on learning'. Here, the conclusion was that 'physically enacting or miming the literal sense of a MM verb, or watching someone else do so' could promote recognition of the rich imagery behind its use in a substantially unfamiliar, latently metaphorical context.

Enactment and movement (E&M) based pedagogy can also be built into lessons that do not have motion as their explicit focus. Some teachers worry that changing the configuration of their classroom from the serried and teacher-centred form, to making group-based islands, then back, is too great a waste of time, and they may therefore sabotage their own impulse to do group work by trying to conduct it with students leaning back or talking across each other. However, I have also observed classrooms where changing the configuration of the classroom is part of the lesson drill for students during the first lessons of the year. When conducted in the target language, such drills can reduce changes in the class configuration to less than a minute, whilst also becoming pedagogically powerful E&M routines that stretch beyond the straightforward, row-to-island change and include semi-circles, desks against the wall, or the movement of children forward into a story, or presentation space. Thus, some pedagogical thought about the physics of language can embed language into the physical routines needed to make a creative use of classroom space. The set-up time for a task or activity can then be used as profitably as that of the activity itself. Teachers who think that such movements are linked to a very limited repertoire of language should reflect on the variety of lexico-grammatical forms that can be used to detail these complex movements of people and objects in space.

My earlier emphasis upon the poetic or dramatic aspects of language should also remind teachers of the usefulness of drama and drama techniques generally. A dramatic production, whether for film or stage, will involve direction and movement in the dialogue between director and cast. Drama links movement to meaning, both as gesture and as changes of position and posture. To promote usage, a key function for the teacher is not to simply direct, but to work with student directors, if only at first as ciphers for their more expert input. Another strategy is to frame drama within a role play, making a stage production into the central outcome of the task but impeding or facilitating the process by asking class members to take on such roles as those of the egocentric director, the actor who is something of a prima donna, or the ever-compliant props director.

Holme and Chik (in submission) completed a project in a Chinese Hong Kong secondary school where children were taught by teacher trainees to direct their own films. A director from among the school children was appointed to each group. One of the objectives was to script movement, then to give the script spoken form through the director's instructions. The first phase worked well, but the second was less satisfactory since the director's instructions were invariably given in the children's native Cantonese. The project received a positive response from the teacher trainees, however, who saw considerable potential for language practice in the procedure.

Procedures that use mime and drama are a recognised part of the canon of ELT Activities (see for example, Maley and Duff 1982; Heathfield 2005). Teachers can, for example, tell learners a story then ask them to mime it back, after demonstrating how to do so with an example, to help them overcome any feeling of self-consciousness. In the same vein, teachers can give different stories to different groups of learners then ask them to mime the action whilst getting the class to say what is going on. Those who want a more exact lexical focus can try using games such as charades where one group of students will mime different syllables of a word and the others have to guess what the syllables are and then assemble the word from them.

Mundane events are a ready, but sometimes neglected, source of material with a learner being asked to act out some event of the day whilst the class try to produce a commentary upon what occurred. For example, students can mime walking to school and stopping at a shop on the way, waiting for public transport then boarding, or going home and eating. A more elaborate linkage can be made to ethnographic projects where learners are asked to observe the customs of whatever projects they are in. For example, I have had students study the behaviour and conversations of the British in bus queues. These can be dramatised through mime and a contrastive version from another culture also produced for comment. Another activity divides a story into discoursal moves then asks different groups to mime each move.

Activity 7    Moving through language
1 Give the class a short story of appropriate level that can be easily divided into the sequence of Abstract, Orientation, Complicating Action, Evaluation, Resolution, Coda (Labov and Waletsky 1967).
2 Ask the class to divide the text into appropriate discoursal moves, for example:

- I had rather a strange journey home yesterday (abstract)
- And, as you know, I only live a few streets away from school (orientation)
- When waiting at the lights, I saw a man lift a wallet from a lady's shopping bag (complicating action)
- He didn't look threatening (evaluation)
- So I decided to follow him without saying anything (complicating action)
- Then something totally unexpected happened (evaluation)
- Suddenly he seemed to notice me, turned and held out the wallet and said, 'here', giving me the wallet before running into the crowd (complicating action)
- I handed the wallet into a police station but of course there was no money in it (resolution)
- And I'm still amazed at the nerve of the man (coda)

3 Check that each group produces an acceptable analysis.
4 A pair of students leaves the class. Call them the narrators, take their texts from them and give them the moves only. Ask them to recall the text and write it down, filling in each move.
5 Assign one or more moves to each group at random until each move has been given out.
6 In groups, the students rehearse their move as a mime.
7 The narrator comes back into class.
8 Each group performs their mime out of order.

9  The narrator assigns each group a number according to where the group's mime occurs in the story sequence. They can ask a group to repeat their scene as often as needed.
10 The narrator moves among the class pointing to each group to ask them to mime their part of the story. The narrator then says what has been shown and the class corrects.

In the above, 'the narrator' reconstitutes discourse as a sequence of movements in space.

## Language teaching and embodiment: rethinking TPR

The above technique begins with an imagistic use of memory then makes a physical and linear instantiation of this, building a bridge between movement, imagination and recollection. More straightforward E&M routines were found in the language teaching technique of TPR (Total Physical Response; see Asher 1979). This was originally associated with the principle of input-based second language acquisition (Krashen and Terrell 1983) but merits revival in an age that is focused on an embodied cognition. TPR was based on Krashen's assumption of a 'Silent Period' and an input-based model of second language acquisition (1981). In the Silent Period, learners supposedly processed the language input they received with what Chomsky (1965), when describing first language acquisition, had then termed an LAD (language acquisition device). The objective of TPR was therefore to get students to physically respond to language without any obligation to actually say anything. They would therefore be given instructions in the target language that they would have to move physically to carry out. After a phase of this type of exposure and response to input, the idea was that the Silent Period would bring itself to a conclusion when the learners started an unprompted use of the second language with each other.

If founded on this theoretical base, TPR runs counter to the view of an enactive cognition put forward here. However, the insistence of TPR upon an early physical response to meaning, and hence the tacit recognition of its embodied nature, may account for why it continues to enjoy some success. One way to integrate the method more firmly into a CL framework might be to encourage private (or public) speech related to the movements that are being performed. There are many types of activity that can make this connection between movement and language. For example, blindfold activities are an excellent way for students to incorporate directions as a physical response:

Activity 8    Blindfold
1 Blindfold a student and hide an object somewhere in the class.
2 Remove the blindfold from the student and tell the class to give them step-by-step instructions on how to find the object without ever mentioning its location.

Unlike in straightforward TPR, instigating an action can be the responsibility of the student:

Activity 9    What am I doing?
1 Ask the class to think of some simple (and sensible) action that they want another student to perform, such as cleaning the board or opening a window.
2 Ask one student to instruct another how to perform it without saying what it is, whilst the other carries it out movement by movement and never doing more than instructed.

Teachers need to think beyond instruction and response routines when considering the linguistic forms that can be embodied as action. The form does not have to be instructional, for example, but can address quite complicated issues such as the 'water' or crop 'cycles'.

Activity 10    What am I?
1 Give students a card telling them they are some functional artefact (e.g. a washing machine).
2 Tell them to think how they would imitate and express the object's function, taking it through its functional cycle (e.g. wash, rinse, dry), then how they would ask another student to mime that cycle.
3 In pairs and by turn, student A tells student B how to mime the cycle without saying what the cycle is. The class guess what the mime is about by saying what is happening at any given moment.

Activities such as 9 and 10 can also practise tense and aspect. When a student is performing an action, another can provide a commentary in the continuous present whilst just after the action a third student can say what 'they have done', as soon as they have moved. In another permutation, the teacher can turn their back to the action, call out each instruction and wait until the class relay the information that the student 'has moved'.

Activity 11    Natural cycles
1 Tell students about a straightforward natural cycle. For example, the growth of trees and the water cycle.
2 In groups of four to six, give each student the role of an item in the cycle. For example, tell one that they are a tree and another that they are the sun, the sea, clouds, rain, or water in the soil. Ask them to think how they would mime that cycle.
3 One member of the group offers a commentary on the cycle whilst the others put his words into mime.
4 In turns, the groups mime the cycle whilst another group offers a commentary on what is happening.

A more ritualised variation on the above instruction-movement-commentate routine involves mimed dramatic sketches where the actors speak their thoughts:

Activity 12    Move and talk: silent movies
1 Divide the class into groups of between four and six students.
2 Ask each group to write a short narrative that they will have to mime. This should not last more than three minutes. You can provide themes:
   (i) A husband tries to take his wife's money so that he can go gambling. The wife tries to stop him.
   (ii) A teenage child tries to sneak out of the house when their parents have told them they must stay home. The parents try to stop them.
   (iii) Two children are in a shop when one sees something they want. They ask the other to distract the shop keeper whilst they take it.
   (iv) Two people get on a train and recognise each other but don't want to show recognition because last time they met they had a big argument.
3 Explain that whilst the students mime they will have to tell the audience what they are doing and what they are thinking. They must express their thoughts and actions in movement and gesture whilst speaking to them at the same time. But the scene itself is a mime. For example:

*The character introduces himself*: I am Paul Chang. Last night I lost all my money gambling. (gesture of despair, and turning pockets inside out) But tonight I know I will win it back. (grasps the air and brings his clenched fists towards him) So I will take it from my wife (points at wife, sitting quietly, then nods a greeting towards her).
*Wife is sitting*: I know Paul lost his money last night. I must hide my savings so he will not take them (puts her bag behind her back).
4  Work with one group to get a model of what you want. Demonstrate your sketch then give the other groups time to rewrite their own.
5  Ask the groups to perform sketches and commentaries.

Teachers with the skill and inclination can also think about the opportunities of using sport and sports coaching as a subject when taking a content-based approach to language teaching (see for example, Stryker and Leaver 1997; Brinton *et al.* 2003; Hall and Austin 2004). Learning sports routines, whether in relation to individual skills, team-work, or implementing more elaborate strategies with the requisite debriefing, can all serve to embody not just instructional language but also the language of analysis (in the 'what did I do wrong?') mode of instruction.

Elaborate linkages between instruction, movement, and announcing the completion of an action have also been obtained by using kit-building activities with Lego, or other construction sets. These were popular in ESP teaching because of their focus on instructional and semi-technical language (see for example, Holme 1996). Teachers who want to force linkages between a more elaborate language use and illustrative movement can work with divided groups or pairs sitting opposite but at a distance from each other. One side of the group will have the plan of a model. The other will have the pieces of the kit. The group with the plan relay their instructions across the classroom, the group with the kit decipher the instructions into actions and call back what they are doing. Some teachers have tried this back-to-back or with screens between the groups to increase the need to communicate effectively, but it may be more effective to let the students with the plan to talk and gesture at the same time, thus helping to embed the language in gesture, and the schematic meanings that gesture expresses. A less forced routine involves making the kit-building a group or pair activity where the learners sort out who does what and discuss how to build it. However, target language use will be reduced unless the students either have high self-discipline or the class is multilingual.

Blind-box activities also help students to build meanings out of their interactions with objects. In one permutation a blindfolded learner reaches through a hole in an upturned box to feel out the form of an object placed inside it. The student then describes the shape and texture of the object while the rest of class try to guess what it is. Fruit can challenge linguistic resources in the area of texture; toys, such as model cars or animals, can stimulate a more elaborate enquiry about the relationship of form and function, with the teacher asking what it could be used for, and even trying to force the student to justify quite fine distinctions, as between a toy van and a car, or a plastic donkey and a horse.

An intriguing and less appreciated feature of blind-box activities may lie in how a withdrawal of the stimulus may do more to foster language use than its presence. Working in mathematics education, Cary and Carlson (1999) found that subjects found calculation easier when physically manipulating dice-like markers, and also supported the activity less with private speech. Since language teachers are more focussed on language use than an ability to perform calculations they might want to think about puzzle tasks that move from object manipulation to a conceptual version of the same. They can therefore help students make a shift into abstraction and the use of the appropriate language in a way that may help them conceptualise what they are trying to do. For example, when teaching numbers, it may help if one starts by asking students to count objects. In a second phase one can give them simple oral addition tasks. Equally, if working with descriptions, one can begin by taking learners to look at a scene, then to make a prolonged mental sketch before returning and describing it. After the outing one can ask them to recall that scene to the class, then finally to re-imagine it after some catastrophic changes, such as a forest fire, and describe it again.

## Conclusions

Teaching an embodied, enactive cognition posits education as the design and provision of a knowledge-rich environment that the mind can be stimulated to explore. It further supposes the design of activities that develop that exploratory need. In language education the supposition is that because linguistic meaning and its modes of symbolisation have together evolved from embodied experience, then these symbolic structures will be made more memorable if they are reinvested in the movements, gestures and imagery from which they were conceptualised. The body can be rethought as the expressive instrument of the language that must be learnt. This posits the following types of activity:

command and physical response (teachers and students speak, students and teachers make an appropriate bodily response);
mimetic activity and language response (teachers or students move and describe their movements);
move to speak and learn (students can be encouraged to learn and speak 'on the hoof', using movement to unfold thought);
imagined movements in recollected worlds and the appropriate descriptive response (students envision movement and describe the same).

Nor should we forget that writing is itself a type of embodied linguistic activity. It reintroduces language to the type of controlled bodily activity from which it may once have emerged. This may explain how educators have always intuited that writing is a powerful bodily mnemonic, something well-understood by more traditional approaches to education.

Finally, there is some evidence from animal experimentation that learning may be improved through physical exercise. For example, when mice were given an exercise routine followed by problem-solving tasks in mazes, the results indicated that physical activity impacted positively on 'synaptic plasticity' and hence on learning (Gómez-Pinilla et al. 1998). The benefits of warm-up and physical relaxation routines have long been recognised by both drama teachers (see for example, Tourelle 1997; Hodges Nelson and Finneran 2006; Johnson 2007) and by language instructors with an interest in affective methods (see for example, Moskowitz 1978). They also have the benefit of being a command and response routine themselves, but one that has the added benefit of making the student more receptive to knowledge generally.

# 4
# Gesture

## Introduction

Any observer of human communication understands that language is not used in a vacuous physical space but is accompanied and supported by movement or gesture. Those who doubt the significance of this might observe somebody on the phone. Gesture has therefore become an area of increasing research interest, and has come to be treated not just as central to the development and use of language but to its evolution also. For example, Ramachandran (2005) has theorised that the connection between language, mirror neurons, simulated movement, and gesture provide a basis for understanding how language may have evolved from a gestural communication system. Recent studies of gesture create a considerable body of supporting evidence for language's close relationship to bodily movement and the mimetic representation of meaning (McNeill 1992; Goldin-Meadow 2003).

## The importance of gesture in communication

Traditionally, gesture was seen as ancillary to speech. For example, Argyle (1975) thought that gesture 'could express emotion, convey interpersonal attitudes, present one's personal attitudes, and help manage feedback, and attention', but 'gave it no role in conveying the message itself' (Goldin-Meadow 2003: 12). However, studies of first language development suggest that infant acquirers tend to gesture when they are limited in what they can say (see for example, Bates 1976). Most typical is the deictic or pointing gesture where a child wants a desired object but cannot name it (McNeill 1992). In a second phase, the infant will use a word or garbled version of the same in combination with a gesture, and will thus integrate language and speech (Goldin-Meadow and Butcher 2003). In the third phase, we can find combinations in which gesture and speech may convey different information. The fact that this phase occurs after the second suggests strongly that 'gestures and speech are products of a unified system in which the two modalities work together' (*ibid*: 93).

Streeck (1996) and Kita (2000) proposed that gestures were virtual actions. In other words, 'pointing' to an object could be interpreted as an analogue of actually taking hold of it and moving it around. However, Gallagher found this interpretation also to be insufficient (2005). Like Goldin-Meadow (2003) he saw gestures not simply as analogous motor-actions but as in fact fashioned by meaning itself. In respect of story-telling he noted that gesture was not some method of dramatisation or message reinforcement which operated within the space that the verbal narrative had itself created. Gesture helped 'create the narrative space' (2005: 117). Gesture was not action conscripted from the motor system to support that of linguistic communication, but originated from our broader ability to communicate. Evidence for this came from a much studied subject, Ian Waterman, who after damage from illness had no proprioception, and no sense of touch below the neck. When deprived of visual feedback and performing motor-tasks such as object manipulation, he did not know where his hands were at any one time but could still gesture meaningfully when talking (*ibid*: 108–9). In other words the use of the body as a visual semiotic endured when other movements became difficult, suggesting its close association with meaning-making.

For cognitive linguists a central property of gesture lies in the clues it gives to the conceptualisations that lie behind the language with which it is concurrent. Arguably such uses of sign have a central role in shaping image schemas, creating a space into which a more exact meaning may be inserted by the onset of language. This role also means that as gestures endure into adulthood, they can also become clues to the types of conceptualisation that have been formed and to how strongly they may endure or be carried from a first to a second language (Kellerman and van Hoof 2003). Gesture can be seen as 'a window' into the 'mental processes' that hark back to the earliest conceptualisations from which meanings develop (McNeilll and Duncan 2000). As this window on cognition, gesture affords some interesting opportunities for those interested in second language acquisition (SLA) research whilst also proposing various techniques for those interested in an embodied approach to language learning. Because the issues for SLA researchers fall under the more general interest in conceptualisation I will look at the SLA questions more closely in the next chapter. In what follows I will consider how gesture can be exploited in the classroom.

## Gesture in education

The link between the use of gesture and cognitive development has been most researched in the domain of maths education. Metaphor shows us how reason is conceptualised from bodily action and movement in space, a feature implicit in much of the language of logical deduction (see for example, Lakoff and Johnson 1980, 1999). For example, a result *leads to* a conclusion, an argument *is founded on* a premise, one idea is implicitly contained in another before being *de-duce-d* from it, or literally in Latin, 'led' from it. However, the embodied nature of the number system, and our broader cognitive capacity to reason, bear as much upon the development of individual understanding as upon the social development of the concepts themselves. For example, it has been found that children who are exposed to gesture and who gesture themselves might better represent the relations between objects in the world. In this way a use of gesture may help children achieve a better representation of the relationships between numbers and symbols in maths problems, whilst also facilitating the construction of underpinning mental models and concepts (Roth and Lawless 2002; Roth and Welzel 2001). Relatedly, children who are allowed to gesture can count more accurately than those who are not permitted to do so (Valenzeno *et al.* 2003).

Gesture can both help and hinder how children grasp mathematical concepts. Valenzeno *et al.* (2003) presented elementary-school children with a taped lesson on symmetry. However, only one lesson included gesture. After the administration of a post-test it was found that the children who saw the lesson with words and gestures scored higher than those who had just listened to an explanation (cited in Goldin-Meadow 2003). More pertinently, a similar study was conducted on two groups, one of native speakers and one of Hispanic children who were learning English as a second language. Although the native speakers performed better on both pre- and post-tests, both groups were helped by speakers with gestures in equal measure (Church *et al.* 2004). In another study it was also found that misplaced gestures can do much to hinder conceptual understanding. When asking students to solve the simple equation: '7+6+5 = \_\_\_\_\_ +5', the teacher was unaware of how she was pointing across the whole expression and so encouraging the child to produce an incorrect answer or '23' (Goldin-Meadow 2003).

In language teaching, one of the most extensive uses of what could be called explicit, emblematic gesture was to be found in the method called 'the *Silent Way*' (see for example, Gattegno 1971). The gesture was explicit because it was consciously used, and emblematic because it was constructed to represent quite specific meanings.

The Silent Way was postulated as a broader process of subordinating teaching to learning and enjoyed some popularity in the 1970s and 1980s. The method was also used in maths education. The premise of the Silent Way was to minimise the teacher's presence by maximising student output and their 'push' to discovering knowledge when assisted by the teacher's use of gesture, pantomime, pointing to pictures and manipulation of objects or Cuisenaire Rods (coloured wooden blocks that can be used to symbolise words, their meanings or the relationships between them). The teacher was thus silent and used gesture and phonetic charts to help students converge upon the correct form and, more challengingly, a correct pronunciation of it.

Like many methods that aspire to be total instead of supplementary, the Silent Way took a sound pedagogical premise and exaggerated it to a point of absurdity, suppressing language's aural nature in favour of imagistic visual input from the teacher. It also ignored the imitative and usage-based aspect of language learning in favour of the need to perceive it as an exercise in hypothesis formation and deduction. The interest of the Silent Way probably lies now in how it has passed to language teachers generally a repertoire of gestures which can help students work back through errors to find correct solutions. It also enforces the general principle that teachers sometimes need to talk less to persuade learners to talk more.

The use of gesture can transfer from the teacher to the student to help them internalise the correct forms such gestures are designed to elicit. For example, in the Silent Way, finger correction asks the student to say the problem phrase or clause back whilst the teacher counts off each word until the poorly formed or omitted item is reached. This visual cue is intended to get the student to self-correct the appropriate part of the phrase. Teachers familiar with this technique might also want to try getting the student to count off the words of the correctly formed phrase to help them internalise it as a complete sequence. This can also work for single words where a morpheme has been omitted or mispronounced.

Other emblematic gestures are sometimes used to correct tense. Thus assuming the schema of the past as behind the speaker and the future as in front, teachers will gesture back over their shoulder with the thumb to persuade the student to correct to a past tense, or point forward to elicit a modal for the future. A present perfect can be elicited with an emphatic down-beat of the hands, pointing to the event's occupation of the same space as the speaker, as in 'I've done it!' A technique that merits more research would be getting students to self-correct whilst the students themselves use these gestures, thus helping them to map a form's representation of time onto their own sense of themselves as located in space.

Other work in the use of explicit gesture to advance language teaching has been in the Canadian Accelerated Integrated Method (AIM). AIM uses a corpus-based approach to teach French, by targeting a vocabulary of 700 of the most frequently used words. Gestures are used to teach this vocabulary, with children associating actions with the requisite gesture, shading the eyes with a hand when they say 'voir' (see), for example. Great stress is put on verbs which tend to be under-taught in methods that relate language to social function. This interest in verbs gives linguistic form to the method's focus upon enactment and movement. It is also worth noting that both CL and traditional grammars stress the verb as central to how a clause unfolds, determining the meanings that are possible in the rest of the clause. Knowing verbs and obtaining a full grasp of their meanings can therefore help learners to control a larger construction. Gesture-based, choral learning also extends into drama, music and dance. The AIM syllabus is itself shaped by this dramatic focus, with creative writing activities being evolved from a focus on stories in preference to topics. The method, which has been focused on children of primary age, makes anecdotal claims to bring about huge increases in the students' motivation for learning French, with concomitant impacts on performance (Maxwell 2004).

## Gesture and teaching prepositions

Broadly, CL divides words into two kinds, those that express 'things' and those that express 'relations' (see for example, Radden and Dirven 2007: 42). Traditionally considered grammatical and closed class, prepositions are particularly crucial to how English expresses relations. Prepositions and, by association phrasal verbs, have therefore received a substantial degree of attention among applied cognitive linguists (see for example, Lindner 1981; Boers 1996; Dirven 2001; Kurtyka 2001; Queller 2001; Rudzka-Ostyn 2003; Holme 2004; Littlemore and Low 2006).

Expressions such as 'I went *over* the topic' or 'I took it *for* cleaning' show the difficulty prepositions pose for learners of English. They also reveal that their difficulty lies chiefly in how they are used to represent abstract relations between concepts through metaphors of spatial relations and associated movement. A key to a successful use of prepositional expressions may therefore be a well-grounded understanding of their spatial reference. Arguably this can be obtained through the early association of prepositional meaning and gesture by the learner. Gestures can thus help distinguish between the core physical meanings for 'up' and 'down' that were analysed by Lindner (1981):

- 'up' as an expression of movement or a path: raising the hand above the head;
- 'up' as a static location: hand held above the head;
- 'down' as an expression of movement or a path: index finger moving down below the waist in the direction of the ground; and
- 'down', as a static location: hand below the waist, palm flat towards the ground.

A more difficult area still is the difference between 'across', 'through' and 'over', in 'I walked across/over/through the field'. 'Across' assumes a birds-eye view of one's own completed action whilst 'over' summates an unfolding trajectory that places the 'field' beneath one's feet. 'Through', on the other hand constructs the field as a potential impediment to progress (Langacker 1991). These distinctions can also find gestural representation:

- 'Across' (hand flat and palm down sweeps over the floor);
- 'Over' (hand extends and arm arches up and over);
- 'Through' (hand pushes effortfully forward).

In this case, the intonation and the gesture can reinforce each other:

- 'Across' (flat, rapid and dismissive);
- 'Over' (rising intonation on the first syllable, fall on the second, extension of the first syllable o___ver);
- 'Through' (effortful, as if pushing against an obstacle).

Learners can also be encouraged to use gesture to invoke the imagery in which to embed new meanings:

- 'Across' (look down from a raised point and trace a trajectory across the floor);
- 'Over' (Stepping or leaping over an object or space);
- 'Through' (miming wading through thick muddy water).

Also problematic is making a schematic distinction between 'of' and 'for'. Langacker perceives 'of' as sometimes predicating a relationship between two entities where 'one is a subpart of another'. Again this can be usefully expressed through explicit imagery and associated gesture. Thus when the expressions below are repeated by the teacher or the students, they can be supported by clenched fists being pushed together in front of the body to indicate attachment:

- 'The leg of the chicken'
  'The wheel of the car' (clenched fists moving together)

'For' on the other hand has implicit motion or transfer of possession:

- 'I've got something for you' (hands cupped around an imagined object reach forward to the recipient).

All gesture and E&M classroom routines can be problematic with adults and adolescents, though much depends on the type of learning expectations that are engendered and the ability of the teacher to free learners from self-consciousness. However, teachers who persuade students to ground meanings in gesture may furnish an imagistic base that can be used later to help grasp the metaphorical relations between abstract concepts that prepositions also express. For example, the phrase 'something for you' and the appropriate gesture can provide a rationale for such stock phrases as '*for* example', or 'exchanging oil *for* food'.

## Gesture and English articles

Another difficult relational grammatical area in which gesture can help develop a student's grasp of meaning is the definite determiner, 'the'. The concepts of definiteness and indefiniteness, and of determination generally, can be highly problematic for learners whose languages do not have these parts of speech. Langacker (see for example, 1990) perceived determiners in general as exercising a grounding function or as clarifying which of a given class of entities was under discussion. He also perceived them as summating our larger sense of what we mean by a noun phrase. We can see this in the close relationship between English determiners and prepositions, with some being interchangeable:

(20) Give me that book
(21) Give me that...

The juxtaposition of examples (20) and (21) shows that the pronoun in clause (21) looks as if it is simply a determiner whose noun has been omitted. This impression extends into the role of 'that' as a subordinator:

(22) I said that it was true
(23) I said that...

The subordinate clause is itself behaving as a noun or noun phrase for which the determiner (or subordinator) has opened a schematic space. The determiner thus represents a type of indicative schema, or has the gestural meaning of pointing to something. The gesture of pointing has its meaning completed when our eye finds the indicated object and the same is true for the determiner when its phrase is completed by a noun. The general schematic meaning of the determiner is thus given precision by whatever meaning the noun or the rest of the noun phrase specifies.

We can understand this more clearly if we take the definite determiner 'the' and embed it in a clear indicative gesture.

Activity 13    Determined gesture
1 Show the class similar but distinguishable sets of objects such as books on a shelf or pictures on a wall.
2 Ask students to select objects by pointing to them and using the definite article ('I want the red book on the right').
3 After a few objects have been distributed, ask other students to ask each other for them using phrases of possession ('I want the red book that Jane has').

A follow-up, or more elaborate and less concrete, procedure involves a surveillance scenario:

Activity 14    Surveillance
1 Students imagine that they are police engaged in a surveillance operation radioing back the movements of various suspects.
2 The teacher tracks the movements of a suspect and talks as if radioing back the information. In pairs, student A repeats what the teacher says. Student B asks for clarification and more information. For example:

Teacher: The suspect has a red bag and is leaving a restaurant.
Student A repeats the teacher's sentence.

Student B: Which restaurant?
Student A: (improvises) The Macdonald's near the bus stand.
Teacher: The suspect's walking down the High Street and turning left. They're passing the bag to a man in his thirties.
Student A: Repeats the teacher's sentence.
Student B: Which man? Where?
Student A: The one running across the road, now.

3  Control how the story unfolds. When the students identify a person or object try get them to point as if at an imaginary person in the room.

Activity 14 also shows how we can move from gestures that single out actual objects and classroom movements to those that accompany imaginary things and actions. Finally we may produce the mental gestures that help conceptualise the determiner's schematic meaning.

## Conclusions

Few concepts illustrate the broader principle of this book as successfully as that of an embodied mind. The principle lies in the relatedness of language form and meaning to the processes from which they are conceptualised and the methods by which they may be best learnt. Put very simply, cognition is embodied, language as a cognitive entity is embodied, and learning as a cognitive process can also be embodied. This does not mean that learning should avoid an advance into abstraction, for clearly that movement is fundamental to how education is conceived. Rather, the implication is that this move towards abstract language and learning is better achieved when students use gesture to help them understand and learn how meanings have been conceptualised from the gestures they make and the way that they move.

# Part II
# Conceptualisation

# 5
# Language, Culture and Linguistic Relativity

## Introduction

In the CL view, experience is embodied and provides the image schemas through which we conceptualise meaning (Johnson 1987). If we accept this, we encounter the problem of how the different experiences that people have can be gathered into common conceptualisations that build common meanings. The solution lies in how human (and to some extent, animal) societies develop cultures. A culture is finally the collectivisation of experience, allowing some approaches to conceptualising, explaining, and manipulating to take preference over others. Essentially, a culture gathers common modes of conceptualisation, making some dominant and others less so. Yet, using the existence of culture to explain how we develop common conceptualisations and meanings will itself create another problem. We might be able to hypothesise a situation where cultures develop differences in meaning that are radical enough to make intercultural communication a somewhat vain hope and second language learning an almost impossible challenge. The defining attribute of cultures is that they differ from each other. However, these differences arise from how a common cognitive and anatomical architecture are interacting with environments that, though different in climate and featural detail, will share such basics as gravity, the contrast of light and dark, and pre-eminently, the various behaviours in which humans engage. Thus the myths that may take hold could have common themes but will express those themes in quite different ways. What is more difficult to assess is whether such evident variations simply put the same ways of seeing reality to different uses or whether they in fact evolve from fundamental differences in how we grasp and categorise the world. In other words, the question is whether we treat experience as broadly a common cognitive resource from which we shape different mental artifacts, or whether that resource is itself constructed differently by different peoples.

At one level, the CL hypothesis anticipates that different cultures will reveal fundamental differences in their modes of conceptualisation. A language should encode such differences and transmit them from generation to generation. A common cognition interacting with a different environment will produce different types of experience and these will build their own ways of looking at reality. But this argument produces several quite difficult questions. First we might ask what 'seeing the world in a different way' actually means. For example, it could be saying quite simply that a language uses different meanings. Thus when we walk through a rain forest with a tribe indigenous to it they might recognise trees as having an individual identity where we see only an oppressive forest canopy. Yet this scenario could postulate something more fundamental than an ability to distinguish and name individual trees. Thus the tribe's emphasis on the individual identity of certain phenomena might actually give the observed entities more visual prominence. Their world might then look different to them in a quite fundamental way. In extremis, the way their language divided up the categories of plants and wildlife might be so different that it would be almost impossible for us to translate meanings from one language to another.

Every aware language learner and every translator knows that languages do not operate with quite the same meanings. They also know that translation may sometimes be difficult but is rarely completely impossible. We do communicate across cultures, sometimes with difficulty and often with relative ease. If we have problems we can often find a vocabulary in which we can identify meaning differences. The question we need to answer then is not about whether we can sometimes bridge cultural and linguistic differences or about whether these exist. The answer is affirmative in both cases. The question is about the scope and nature of the difference that can lie between two languages and their cultures, and how this affects our approach to language learning. This topic is not at all new and is now generally called 'linguistic relativity'. It has been asked over time by various philosophers and the answer given has depended upon a fundamental difference of approach; in a modern context, we can call this difference 'perceptual versus conceptual'.

In a perceptual view, human cognition mirrors reality. What we see is what is there. This means that, with a few trivial differences, what we represent in one language will be broadly the same as in another. In the conceptual view, which is that of cognitive linguistics, reality is a function of the mind, or mind and body, that experiences it. This does not suggest there is no such thing as a world outside ourselves, but it does say that we can only experience that world as a function of the mind and the body that we have. From a perceptual view, therefore, the answer to the question must be that differences in the meanings of languages are trivial and that the major task of second language learning is not in operating new meanings but in matching old ones to new forms. In the CL, or conceptual view, the issue does not bear on whether significant differences exist, but on how deep they go.

For language teachers, the last question is important for the following reasons:

- If languages hand down different conceptual systems, then learning them will require some quite fundamental cognitive adjustment. How and what should teachers do to facilitate that adjustment?
- If conceptual differences are embedded into the language's culture, then does successful language use demand some process of acculturation?
- If some areas of second language use involve both acculturation and re-conceptualisation, could the problems of attaining this account for how we often fail to fully master target language forms to native-speaker level?

In this chapter I will explore these questions by first looking at the relativity hypothesis. This exploration will show how CL reshapes linguistic relativity by discussing the issue of language, meaning and conceptualisation. Next, I will turn to how differences in language may promote a different way of looking at reality. After that, I will propose how teaching can accommodate the need to see meanings as different. I will therefore argue for a pedagogical accommodation that treats the adoption of different modes of conceptualisation as a form of acculturation, and which also introduces a language's host culture into the classroom. This last issue raises the concern of what acculturation means when a language has become a vehicle for international communication.

## The Sapir-Whorf hypothesis

Pre-war American linguistics was partly motivated by a desire to collect and describe the languages of endangered Native American cultures. Any such anthropological motivation focuses on the larger cultural context in which a language operates, and in how such contexts differ. If culture is finally the collective formulation of an environment as it is explored and explained by a given social group, then a culturally focused enquiry must delve into meaning. Famously, Sapir and Whorf held that the grammatical forms of a language could actually influence the way we saw our world, becoming a factor in why one culture differed from another (Sapir 1949; Whorf 1956).

Sapir and Whorf worked from the structuralist assumption that the forms of language had a role in shaping our meanings. In their model, formal differences in language furnished the boundaries that separated one meaning from another. Formal differentiation thus provided the semantic boundaries that constituted a collective interpretation of reality. This interpretation was carried into the culture. Sapir-Whorf's conclusion, then, was that people from different cultures would see their respective realities somewhat differently. They might impose structures upon time or the natural world that were not quite the same, for example. They would do this because they used languages whose structures had divided up reality in different ways. Language shaped culture and thus influenced thought. Whether this was true or not became known as the 'linguistic relativity' question.

The Sapir-Whorf hypothesis encountered considerable criticism. It challenged the central philosophical assumption that if we ignored one or two minor differences in how languages segmented reality into categories, we were all looking out on the same world and simply rendering it into different linguistic forms. Sloppy fieldwork did not help Whorf's larger claim. Notoriously, he claimed that the Native American Language, Hopi, had no concept of time, when some further acquaintance with the language showed that it did. He also said that the Inuit of Alaska and Northern Canada had a large number of words for 'snow', but subsequent research has shown that they had not (Pourcel 2005).

Interest in the Sapir-Whorf hypothesis dwindled when generative linguistics became a dominant approach. The generative interest was in treating different languages as products of a single universal framework. If language structures were fundamentally the same, then they could not partition meaning differently in ways that were anything other than trivial. One of generativism's more recent advocates, Steven Pinker, argued that thought delivers our perceptions of the world pre-formed to language. Accordingly, we do not even think in language but rather we have translated our already formed ideas into it, as if out of some other universal human tongue (Pinker 1994). According to this contention, the differences in meaning imposed by linguistic form could not be large enough to account for divergences in the world's cultures and belief systems. Differences in belief systems had to be analysed as different ways of using the same semantic material.

The CL view of meaning is therefore almost the opposite of the one just ascribed to Pinker. CL sees meaning as derived from physical experience and conceptualised through the nature of our bodily response to the same. CL therefore affords cognitive space for different methods of partitioning reality as meanings, not just between groups of individuals and their cultures, but idiosyncratically as well. However CL is not advancing a Sapir-Whorf view of relativism either. Whorf, we should remember, worked with a structuralist assumption both about the nature of language and of culture. For him, human beings sought to make sense of the world by imposing structures upon it very much as the anthropologist Claude Lévi-Strauss famously proposed that we derive central ways of organising reality from such formal constrasts as 'raw and cooked' or 'moistened and burned' (1969). For Whorf, a language was operated as a set of such formal contrasts or structures, both at the level of its meanings and its grammatical organisation. He therefore suggested that the way a language's grammar did or did not structure such meanings as time or the attributes of space would affect how the language's culture treated these concepts, thus influencing that culture's larger grasp of reality. CL is suggesting that when a common cognitive architecture interacts with variable types of environment then different types of experience will be conceptualised. Further, as in any evolutionary or adaptive process, there will be a randomness of response to circumstance, particularly within processes of symbol creation where the conventionalisation of new meanings becomes a response to how the old have evolved. Within the framework of a culture, these meanings may then hand down the modes of conceptualisation from which they have evolved. If such a process has some descriptive validity, the consequences for language learners will be profound, so before looking at these, we need to look more closely at the evidence for this relativity claim. To understand this better, I first need to discuss how meaning and conceptualisation do and do not inter-relate in the CL model.

## Meaning and conceptualisation

Meaning and conceptualisation are not easily separated. Their inseparability is made evident by some thought about how the selection of one meaning as opposed to another may be a consequence of how we conceptualise a scene. However, a meaning implies a greater stability in the relationship between a sign and its signification than could be produced if we were constantly reconceptualising the world when we put it into language. We can see this in the emergence of meaning from conceptualisation over time (see for example, Heine 1997). For example, in English, a noun representing a body part, 'head', has evolved to represent various relational meanings. Because our eyes are set in the head and look forward not sideways we conceptualise our heads as pointing in our direction of travel. We therefore conceptualise a direction through a body part. The head is generally the front or top as in the expression 'at the head of the column'. In Old English 'a' could mean 'on', so that when it became attached to a noun, for example, 'head', we conceptualised a direction as 'on' the forward-facing 'head' or as 'a-head'. This direction is now a meaning which is stabilised by the symbol out of which it was conceptualised. A convention arises where 'ahead' no longer refers to a body part but to a forward direction. 'Ahead' is now a symbol. However, this convention is still bound up with the metaphor from which the word emerged. For example, we cannot say 'go ahead the house', because the word's meaning is still conceptualised as bodily direction rather than as a more metaphorical relationship between one entity and another. In short, the word is perceived as a description of a direction rather than of a relationship. This is why 'ahead' remains an adverb, which posits an alternative type of conceptualisation to a fully relational expression such as a preposition.

Meaning emerges from conceptualisation. However, it is important to understand that this process is neither top–down nor bottom–up. Conceptualisation does not begin in an objective world that constructs cognition from experience. If it did, it would be called perception. According to an enactive view of cognition, the world cannot be known as an objective entity that exists independently of the body that explores it. Equally, our cognition is not some disembodied entity that is informed by bodily experience. Experience is produced out of the embodied nature of cognition, and cognition is developed by the nature of experience.

To be part of linguistic meaning and shared across cultures, conceptualisations must be *symbolised*. Again, this does not assume a bottom–up process where we have a meaning that is looking for a *symbol* or a symbol for a meaning. Early last century, the defining attribute of a symbol was held to be its conventional nature (Peirce 1931–1958). We do not understand a symbol because it is similar to what it represents. If this were the case it would be an *icon*. Further, we do not grasp a symbol's meaning because it and the sign adjoin spatially, as fire does smoke. In that case the sign would be *indexical* (Deacon 1993). We understand symbols because our culture has agreed to give them a certain meaning. In other words, it is conventions that give them meaning. If we do not know the conventions, we do not know the meaning.

One effect of how symbols achieve meaning through convention is that it is impossible to disengage them from what they signify. Icons and indexical signs, on the other hand, can have an independent semantic identity. 'Smoke' is 'smoke' and only sometimes comes to mean 'fire'. In the iconic metaphor, the ship 'ploughed' through the sea, where 'ploughed' can refer to a ship crushing through the waves, but it develops this meaning by retaining its original reference to furrowing the soil. A symbol can only be itself, on the other hand. When the conventions are known, we have no choice but to understand a symbol's meaning, and will even decode meanings we would rather not know. So a symbol and its meaning should not be described as if they were two separate layers of the same object, with one being detachable from the other. The symbol is better seen as a peg that holds down a network of meanings. Lift the peg and those meanings will merge into others, losing their separate identity.

Because symbols are created by conventionalisation they are instantly recognisable. Further, once we are aware of a symbol's conventions, we do not need to cognitively track back along the conceptual history of a word such as 'ahead' in order to understand its meaning. Such conceptual imagery is not disassociated from the symbol it has helped create, however. We can see this in gesture, as when for example we talk about a 'far-off time' and gesture as if to a point over the horizon. We do not need to delve into some conceptualisation of 'time as distance between two points' to interpret the adjectival phrase 'far-off'. If, however, somebody then describes a time as 'hidden-away', the less conventional nature of the expression might cause the activation of the imagery out of which it has been created. Thinking from a perspective of language production, this is also how we extend meanings with considerable facility, moving away from the conventional to the conceptual then back. Significantly, tapping into a meaning's conceptual imagery does not seem to be particularly effortful or to take an unusual amount of processing time (Gibbs 1994). Further, the processes of symbol interpretation and conceptualisation relate closely, with one evoking the other when necessity requires. As already discussed, we evolve meanings from image schema that are in turn shaped by experience. Although symbols are conventionalised entities, they are embedded in the richer and more flexible imagery from which their meanings have been conceptualised.

The cognitive processes essential to conceptualisation are implicit in everyday meaning-making and comprehension. How this happens can best be explained by the theory of mental spaces (Fauconnier and Turner 1998, 2002). Mental spaces hold 'packets of knowledge' about a given concept whilst we are engaged in constructing a meaning (Evans and Green 2006: 279). They are therefore essential to our use of a given item within discourse, as well as to how we can keep one meaning in mind whilst stretching it towards something else, as in a metaphor.

For example, consider sentence (24):

(24) If I were John I would be devastated

'If I were John' is an expression that is counterfactual, or expresses the impossible. To express this impossible situation we have to build a space where the impossible can hold and 'I' can be someone else. To do this, we need first to construct a space where we hold a meaning of ourselves, as we are. For sentence (24), this self-conception probably includes an assessment of our self as a sensitive person who reacts badly to some kinds of adverse circumstances. This is input space 1 in figure 3.

'John' must also be placed in a conceptual space where he is the person we know and recognise. In this case, John's circumstances are clearly adverse, and we need that information to fully construct his identity. This information is also held in input space 2. When 'I', the speaker suggest that 'I' might be 'John', my identity is mapped onto John's. In other words, information from input space 1 is mapped onto input space 2. But 'John' and 'I' are both individual people, and our individuality obstructs that blend because it makes us incapable of assuming each other's identity in any literal sense. This common feature passes to the generic space. With the obstructive individuality of each of us taken away, we can now be blended as a single sensitive individual facing adverse circumstances. This occurs in the 'blend space' (see Fauconnier and Turner 2002). This space permits the conceptualisation of one person as having the temporary identity of another.

Cognitive blends are conceptual operations that underpin much figurative language and are essential to many grammatical operations such as the use of the second conditional to represent a counterfactual in a sentence such as 'If I were you I would be happy'. For now, they show clearly how grammatical and lexical meaning must be derived through conceptual operations. Words such as 'if' can even be characterised

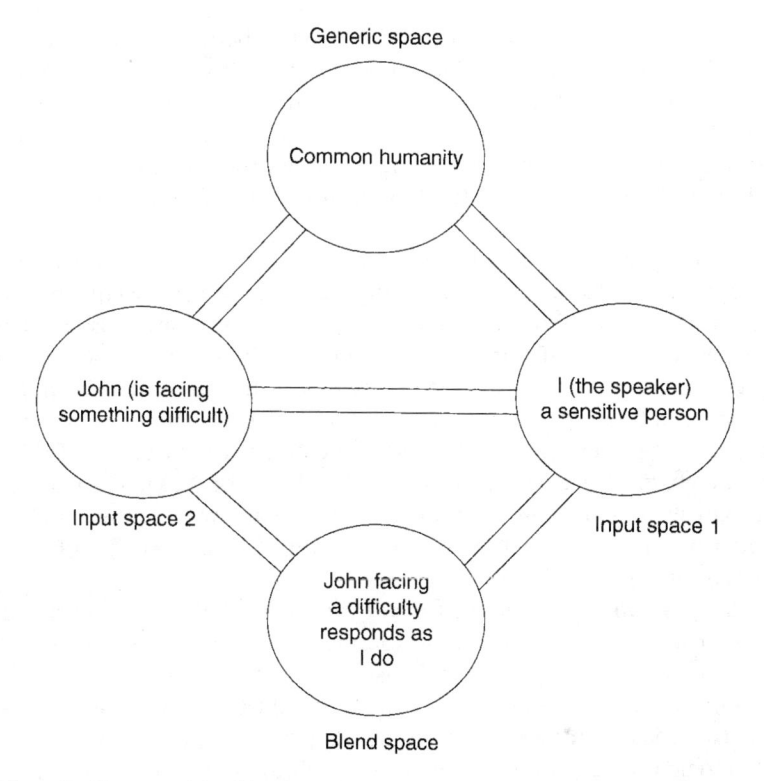

```
                    Generic space
                         ___
                        /   \
                       |Common|
                       |humanity|
                        \___/
                       /     \
                      /       \
                 ___/          \___
                /   \           /   \
          John (is    \       /  I (the speaker)
          facing       |-----|   a sensitive person
          something    |     |
          difficult)   /     \
                \___/         \___/
          Input space 2        Input space 1
                  \             /
                   \    ___    /
                    \  /   \  /
                     |John facing|
                     |a difficulty|
                     |responds as |
                     |   I do    |
                      \___/
                    Blend space
```

*Figure 3* How cognitive blends work: counterfactuals, becoming another person

as 'space-builders' because of how their meaning initiates conceptual operations (Radden and Dirven 2007). 'Grammar', as Langacker said, 'is conceptualisation' (1987).

Another example of how a meaning and its conceptual imagery interrelate closely can be found in studies of language and gesture. As physical movement, a gesture is closer than a word to the imagery of movement from which much meaning derives. One study that illustrates this quite graphically looked at the use of the Turkish determiners, 'şu' and 'bu'. Ostensibly, these words would seem to operate a contrast familiar from demonstratives such as 'this' and 'that' where the reference is either to objects that are close or distant. However, by studying the use of these items in relationship to eye-movement, Özyürek and Kita (2000) found a much subtler distinction. Using naturalistic data they found that that the distinction did not encode the distance of an entity from the people who were talking about it. Eye movements showed how the use of a determiner related to whether or not a speaker's visual attention had been placed upon it. Thus if a speaker's gaze was not on the object being referred to then they were more likely to use 'şu' than 'bu'. Such studies make the larger point that conceptual operations are part of on-line processing, helping to situate meaning as part of the wider conceptual scaffolding furnished by the body's movement in space.

Arguably also, a first language may stress one type of conceptual imagery over another. Thus many languages hand down a set of schemas that categorise phenomena according to whether they are substances or shapes. It is not difficult to imagine how an infant will experience a plastic brick in their grasp as very different to the seeming unbounded expanse of flooring that they crawl across. However, a function of a culture may be to exaggerate the image schema derived from one of these types of experience and to downplay the other. For example, some languages such as Japanese treat objects as shape first whilst others such as English may conceptualise objects according to a quality identified as *boundedness* (Langacker 1987).

Entities conceptualised as *bounded* can be individuated or outlined. They can thus be counted and grounded by the use of the indefinite determiner which signifies 'one'. Just as they can be counted as a single item, they can also be seen as many and pluralised. Unbounded entities are treated as continuous or un-individuated. Like liquids, powders and materials they cannot be counted so much as apportioned. Therefore, when something is seen as unbounded it cannot be counted or pluralised, and cannot take numerical or indefinite determiners. Arguably, infants acquiring shape classifiers or article systems based on boundedness will find that the language biases their way of seeing in favour of form over substance.

Various studies have claimed to find evidence that shows language will favour one mode of conceptualisation over another in a way that affects how people see their world. For example, the expression of spatial relations has been categorised as either absolutist or relativistic. Relativistic languages such as English express spatial relations from the perspective of where the speaker is situated. Thus 'up' generally indicates motion to a point above the speaker. In an absolute system such as that of the central American language, Tzeltal, space is conceptualised from reference points external to the speaker. It is as if instead of saying go 'left' we said go 'west'. This means that speakers need to make a geometric calculation to say where something is located.

Putting forward his famous staged model of ontogenetic development, Piaget claimed that children could not deal in basic geometric concepts until they were eight or nine (Piaget *et al.* 1960). Tzeltal children, however, are able to do this at an age that is much younger than Piaget would predict. A possible implication is that linguistic meanings appear to be enhancing cognitive development if only because they require an ability to deal in a given conceptual system (Brown 2001).

A larger conclusion is that a meaning and a conceptualisation are the products of two distinct but closely related processes. Conceptualisations produce meanings but meanings will affect the types of conceptualisations that occur. In the CL model, languages do not just divide the world into slightly different semantic packages. Different linguistic meanings will sometimes demand acts of re-conceptualisation from their learners. Grammatical meanings may pose particular problems because they instantiate a more fundamental and more imagistic type of meaning. This makes grammatical meanings harder to grasp and explain to learners whose first languages have not developed the same conceptual framework. Significantly also, Whorf's original relativity hypothesis was largely focused on grammar.

Arguably, the conceptual preferences that languages show can also affect how we assess and analyse the world, encouraging us to prefer one type of meaning, or even facilitating types of cognitive operation. The key question for learners, therefore, concerns the magnitude of the conceptual adjustment that has to be made to the second language, and whether there is a realistic chance of making it.

## Linguistic relativity: how different is different?

Our discussion of Tzeltal should show that language itself provides one of the most readily available sources of evidence for how languages may hand their users different ways of grasping reality. One of the most salient of such sources lies in the metaphors out of which meanings are conceptualised. Some conceptual metaphors should be fairly constant from culture to culture because the source domains and the image schemas from which these are derived are fundamental to human experience. For example, 'sexual desire is heat', or 'time is an object moving in space' concepualise common bodily feeling and observations. However, Kövecses (2005) has pointed out that even the most consistent experiences can be treated differently in different cultures in respect of such features as their intentionality. Thus English conceptualises 'desire' itself as 'heat' and makes fewer projections of that state onto a person who feels that sensation, with the expression, 'she is hot', being more the exception than the rule. Chagga, a language of Tanzania, on the other hand, projects 'heat' onto the condition of the female party in a sexual relationship with such expressions as 'néóka' (she roasts), or 'nékeha' (she burns). In this way, a common experience and its resultant image schema can conceptualise a different target, as between arousal itself, and an aroused woman. Consistent experiences and image schemas do not always produce universal conceptualisations, therefore.

For Kövecses (2005), it is not just the target domain which may change from language to language. For example, it is unsurprising that 'play' as a common infantile experience should be used to conceptualise many states and conditions. Arguably a cultural variant is found in the common 'sports' metaphors of British and American English, or Chinese. But these will vary according to the dominant games in each society. British cricketing metaphors, such as 'a straight bat' will baffle speakers of American English which prefers baseball and American football metaphors, whilst Chinese prefers images of volleyball, ping-pong and soccer (Yu 1998: 120).

Another potential area of variation is in the entailments of a metaphor and how these are developed within a particular culture. An entailment is our exploration of the inferences of a given comparison. For example, natural forces such as storms, waves, and earthquakes furnish image schemas across languages and provide the metaphors through which we conceptualise anger in both English and the South African language, Zulu. Yet, in Zulu the entailments are worked far more extensively. Thus one can say of an angry person that ' "the sky became dark with thunder" or, "the sky", a metonym for lightning, "almost singed us" ' (Taylor and Mbense 1998; cited in Kövecses 2005: 128).

Kövecses (2005: 14) sees our social constructions of meaning as given a 'bodily basis' whilst 'bodily motivation is given social-cultural substance'. Thus, while anchored in human physiology, our conceptualisations of emotions may vary along several dimensions. For example, a Zulu speaker who is learning English does not just need to ask if both languages conceptualise 'anger as heat'. They also need to understand how the entailments of English will be relatively under-worked. Equally, French native speakers learning English will find that words like 'stand' make a fuller use of the schema of verticality than they will have developed from their own language.

However, the fact that our study of the metaphorical structure of languages reveals evidence for different types of conceptualisation or different ways of using the same imagery is not of itself enough to say that these different forms actually change how we perceive the phenomena in question. Here there is need for some experimental evidence that different language speakers really do see reality somewhat differently.

## Experimental evidence for linguistic relativity

Colour is essential to how we distinguish one object from another and hence to our larger perception of reality. Even the 'colour-blind' are differentiating one form from another in shades of grey. We also know that our categorisation of one object as being one colour rather than another is an area likely to evoke strong areas of disagreement even among users of the same language. The linguistic difficulty becomes greater across languages. One language, spoken by the Dani in New Guinea, has a spectrum of two colours. For the proponents of linguistic relativism, therefore, colour seemed a perfect area in which to study how those who spoke languages that conceptualised reality differently might also process reality differently.

Some of the first studies in the area of colour gave little support to proponents of linguistic relativity. Eleanor Heider Rosch found that we still operate with what are called 'focal' colours even when these are not defined by a language (Heider Rosch 1972a, 1972b; Heider Rosch and Olivier 1972). Thus whether or not a language could name 'red' or 'blue' was found to be irrelevant in relation to a subject's propensity to single out objects that were so coloured, ignoring the less salient, such as purple or grey. However, Heider Rosch's views have not gone unchallenged. Lucy and Shweder, (1979), for example, raised questions about the validity of her procedure. The work of Kay and Kempton (1984) gave a more mixed result, however, showing that the way we classify the colours we see may sometimes be influenced by the colour spectrum that our languages affords us, whilst at other times no such effect is evident.

The methodology used in the Kay and Kempton study was also criticised (see for example, Saunders and Van Brakel 1997) and the failure to derive any secure strong evidence for a conceptual effect from a language's colour spectrum has made many cognitive linguists more hesitant about advancing a strong view of linguistic relativism.

There is more evidence for the enactive view of cognition that would underpin modern theories of linguistic relativity, however. Thus we cognitively compensate for variations in how things appear, and overcome such variations as are created by light or movement to create such entities as colour or shape as stable entities anchored around best examples, or 'focal' types (Thompson *et al.* 1997).

To argue that we inhabit a reality conceptualised from a common cognitive architecture may actually be to argue against a strong version of linguistic relativity, since it postulates that the same mind is reducing a variable reality to a common form. Accordingly, Lakoff (1987: 335) predicts that conceptual variation between languages is less likely to occur in observable entities such as colour. Abstract concepts such as 'nature' are a more likely area for relativistic thinking. This yields what has been called the weak Sapir-Whorf hypothesis, namely that the more cognitive work we have to do to obtain a concept, the more likely it is that the concept will vary between one language and another (Pourcel 2005). Evidently, therefore, a grammar remains a prime topic of interest because it is quintessentially about the conceptualisation of the abstract, dealing as it does not in concrete phenomena but in the relations that hold between them. Some evidence to support this perspective has come from studying whether the different ways in which grammars divide meaning affect our wider conceptual process.

Yucatec, a language of the Maya of Central America, is a classifier language, and in this respect is not dissimilar to Chinese or Japanese (Lucy and Gaskins 2001). In Yucatec the classifiers can be essential to the discrimination or separation of an entity from the substance of which it is composed. Thus the word for candle, 'un-tz'íit kib', is literally built of a classifier, 'one-long-thin' ('un-tz'íit'), and a substance, 'wax', 'kib' (*ibid.*). The classifier thus bounds the unbounded substance, then grounds it with a quantifier, 'un' (one). English and other Indo-European languages do not need such classifiers because their lexis distinguishes between mass and substance, as between 'candle' and 'wax'. For Lucy, a consequence of this linguistic difference is that 'Yucatec speakers should attend relatively more to the material composition of objects and less to their shape' than English speakers, and English speakers will do the reverse (*ibid.*: 262). They will do this because a user of English is operating a conceptual system where objects are predetermined on the basis of their shape. In other words in English and in many other languages, objects are bounded, so that they can be named, or bounded by the act of their being named, whereas in Yucatec they are first and foremost a substance which is individuated by a need for grounding.

To find evidence for this contention, Lucy and Gaskins showed sets of three objects to a sample of Mayan children then asked them to choose whether to classify them on the basis of shape or substance.

The experiment was then repeated with English speakers. Thus the children were shown a nail then asked to pair it with either a pencil or a piece of metal. The results showed that the English speakers would tend to pair the nail with the pencil, or classify according to shape, whilst the Yucatec speakers tended to match it to the metal, or classify according to substance, thus arguing that the manner in which we conceptualise objects is heavily influenced by whether the language identifies them as primarily substance or shape.

The validity of Lucy and Gaskin's study was questioned, however, because shape identification could be a property requiring more abstract knowledge and hence favour the larger amount of schooling received by the English-speaking sample. When Imai and Gentner (1997) conducted this type of experiment with Japanese and English speakers, they were therefore careful to match the samples in age, and hence, schooling. They also used a different procedure, where the subjects were asked to decide whether objects should share the same label on the basis of common shape or common substance. The results were not as strong as with Lucy's sample but they did show 'a bias' in the mode of classification 'built up by language-specific grammatical categories' (Imai 2000: 159). Malt (1995) has also pointed out that we do not conceptualise phenomena of whatever nature in easily divisible categories (cited in Imai 2000). A given entity may bias our perception of it towards shape or substance because of what we use it for. For example, because a nail's form is defined by its function we might move our categorisation of it more towards shape.

Generally, studies on linguistic relativity provide some evidence for a weak linguistic relativity hypothesis, but little for a strong one. The area of greatest conceptual shift for language learners is therefore likely to be found in that of the schematic and imagistic meanings which are encoded in a grammar. The difficulties implicit in reconceptualising the imagery that underpins a new grammatical system may therefore epitomise the learner problem of operating second language forms with first language meanings (Slobin 1985, 1996). It may also mean that teachers need to re-evaluate the second language learning process as entailing a conceptual shift, at least in the domain of abstract, schematic meaning. Such a re-evaluation of the language learning task raises two further questions:

> Where TL meanings differ as a result of different modes of conceptualisation, can one acquire them simply as different meanings or must one change one's mode of conceptualisation also?

If one must change one's mode of conceptualisation, how well can one actually achieve this, or does our failure to do this account for why we never learn a second language as well as a first?

I will answer the first question by looking at the types of errors students make when using a second language. The second question requires a look at some interesting research into gesture, cognition and second language use.

## To learn new meanings, do we have to conceptualise the world differently?

Broadly we should grasp that although some errors may be conceptual in origin, they can be the direct result of failing to operate the target language with the appropriate meaning. In other words, second language learners will generally be operating with the meanings of their first language. For example, let us say that a native speaker of English learning Spanish says 'mia manzana esta verde' and wants to say 'my apple is green'. The proposed sentence is wrong because 'estar' generally expresses a condition not a quality. So they have in fact said that the apple is green in the sense of unripe. We can guess that the error has been made because the student is operating with a first language that does not treat stative relations as expressing either qualities or conditions. Traditional approaches to these problems meant doing one or more of four things:

1 reminding the student of a rule of thumb that makes the distinction clear, for example: (estar = be-temporary-condition; and ser = be-enduring-quality);
2 encouraging the student to deduce the rule from a series of examples;
3 promoting acquisition by providing further exposure to the correct form;
4 adopting a lexical phrase-based approach and telling the learner they simply have to learn an inventory of the adjectival and participial expressions that occur with 'estar', and the nominal or adjectival expressions that occur with 'ser'.

Each strategy is problematic because it does not take the second language student closer to how a Spanish native speaker operates these meanings. In the first case we are giving the student a rule of thumb. The rule is an attempt to define a distinction between two types of meaning that Spanish makes and that some other languages do not. Effectively, the learner is using the rule to help construct a type of meaning that their own language does not conceptualise. This is a somewhat cumbersome and cognitively burdensome process where they have to consult the rule, use the rule to help them select a meaning, then translate that meaning into the correct form.

The second procedure of encouraging the deduction of a rule has the advantage of affording better exposure to how the form is used. Such exposure helps the student to build the conceptual difference between conditions and qualities, then encode this in the different relational meanings of 'ser' and 'estar'. However, another step is added to the procedure which may in fact increase the possibility of the learner acquring the wrong rule. This possibility may be increased because the rule is never explicity taught and there is no certainty that they will derive the correct one from even a long list of examples.

In the third case, the alleged process of unconscious acquisition may simply never happen, and in its place the student will fossilise the use of the wrong form, or make their error permanent.

The fourth case treats grammatical structures as having to be learnt as fixed forms. The risk is that it will encourage an identifiable preference among learners for fixed chunks of lexis that will inhibit the development of the more creative control of language needed to respond to novel situations.

A fifth strategy would be to encourage the student to attempt what Spanish speakers may actually do. This would be conceptualising meanings according to whether they are conditions or qualities. Such basic types of categorisation lie at the heart of many semantic systems. One other such is the distinction between countable shapes and uncountable substances, or between bounded and unbounded. The first step to helping learners acquire novel modes of conceptualisation can mean getting them to grasp how it is inappropriate to conceptualise the second language category in a way determined by their first language.

## Second language errors and linguistic relativity

Interestingly, it is plausible that the mechanisms that allow accurate language acquisition are also those that encourage us to make errors. The two cognitive processes identified by Michael Tomasello (2003) as crucial to first language acquisition were *reading intentions* and *pattern-finding*. 'Reading intentions' is more relevant to a case where linguistic meanings have not already been set down. In second language learning, pattern-finding is the more interesting process. Pattern-finding is a form-based operation where one group of words is perceived as having similar properties to another without being identical to it in all respects. A form is then perceived as a pattern rather than as a grouping of individually distinct items. Pattern recognition, which is finally a basic type of form-based categorisation, has been identified in infants confronted with visual stimuli (Haith and Benson 1997) but has also been found as a response to auditory stimuli (Safran *et al.* 1996). A central subcategory of pattern-finding is the ability to 'create analogies across two or more complex wholes'.

Gentner and Markman found evidence to show how people perceive analogies as stronger if there is similarity not so much between features as between how they relate to one another (1997). We can grasp this through a Galilean analogy. It was once argued that if the earth were moving, a cannon ball dropped from a tower would not fall directly to the ground beneath but would be displaced by earth's movement. Gallileo wrote that by analogy a ball dropped from a ship's mast would be affected by that boat's movement when you knew that it was not. If this analogy were based on a featural rather than a relational similarity, we would say that the ship was like the earth and the mast was like the tower. But this would say little. Stronger is to treat the relationship of a moving ship and mast to the trajectory of one dropped ball as the same as that of the tower and ground to another such projectile. On the ship we know we are moving when we look at the sea. The ship's movement does not affect the trajectory of the ball. So there is no reason to suggest that the ball's fall from the tower would change if the earth were moving. Effectively we have set up a counterfactual hypothesis similar to an 'if I were you' statement (Fauconnier and Turner 2002). We are saying: 'if the ship were the world then what is true for it is also true for the world because the relationships that pertain in each are the same'. Analogies are thus strong examples of cognitive blends, and as such are fundamental to how we make hypotheses about the world.

Using Gentner and Markman's concept of strong analogy, Tomasello demonstrates how infant acquirers construct language from an intuitive process of analogy formation (2003: 163). For example, a hypothetical acquirer hears sentences (25) and (26), below:

(25) Daddy is eating the chicken all up.
(26) The cat is fighting the dog.

The infant does not just perceive this as a pattern of 'A is B-ing C' but a pattern where the relationships of A, B, and C to whatever situation prevails in the world and hence to each other are similar. This means that B (for example, 'eating' or 'fighting') is schematised as a *process*. A, (for example, 'Daddy' or 'The cat') is schematised as the *agent* that is capable of initiating the process, and C as grounding the initiated process in an *object*. Creating a pattern out of featural relations where objects furnish the ground for agentive processes will allow one perceived pattern to become a vehicle for the construction of sentences that the child has not heard. Thus the perception of 'the cat' and 'Daddy' as sharing an agentive role in relation to the verb would help the infant schematise the notion of an agent, thus laying down the central features of this semantic role and helping to establish productive schemas of 'Agent+process (verb)+patient'.

The processes of pattern-finding and analogy formation are central to all learning. In the second language case they may operate at both an intuitive and at a conscious level. A conscious command of processes such as pattern-finding is a result of having already learnt one language. Conscious control means that second language learners can make decisions about whether they explore patterns or let them pass unnoticed. It permits the development of of both conscious and reflexive thought experiments with grammatical forms that are not dissimilar to what happens in the Galilean example just cited. When this experimentation goes wrong, the learner creates what is commonly called an over-generalisation error. We can categorise such errors as occurring in three basic ways:

1 a use of first language forms and meanings within the second language; (a first and second language form or meaning are mistakenly perceived as analogous, and the thought experiment produces a false inference)
2 the over-generalisation of some acquired formal or semantic feature of the second language; (a meaning or form is perceived as being part of a pattern when it is not – this is the equivalent of making a false analogy)
3 an inappropriate use of borrowings and cognates (the formal properties of the two languages are mistakenly perceived as analogous where they are not).

Effectively, each of these categories of error could also be a function of the under-generalisation of the correct form or meaning, where these are known. When discussing the teaching of grammatical forms in Part 4, I will give more thought to how we can help students to generalise constructions more effectively, and what this might actually mean in a CL analysis of grammar or lexis. I will therefore leave the issue of 'under-generalisation' for now and instead discuss how each of the above three categories is derived from analogy formation and pattern-seeking, whilst also showing how it relates to some form of conceptual process, or could be corrected through reference to the same.

## Errors that use first language forms and meanings within the second language

One example of this error type is when a French user of English says:

(27) The teacher is going to precise the schedule [author's data]

The student knows that English and French share the cognate adjective 'precise' (précis). They thus assume that like the French, 'préciser', English can also make a verb from the adjective. Their assumption may also be over-generalising a conceptual difference between the languages by treating a given state (being precise) as the process through which it is achieved (making something precise). They thus operate English by analogy to their native French and create an English verb 'to precise' where none exists. This is surely the main source of the error. However, there may also be some influences from the student's perception of the TL. English allows the creation of verbs from adjectives as in expressions such as 'calm down', 'blank the screen', or 'white out the error'. It also often disrespects part-of-speech boundaries. So there may also be some influence from the TL's different conceptualisation of the experiential boundaries that parts of speech reflect.
Another example is given in sentence (28)

(28) Yes, I have done the work at 10, yesterday [author's data]

Here the speaker imports a semantic pattern from spoken French. The speaker's mother tongue does not distinguish between a completed past action and one that is perfective.
Using perfective time requires the grasp of a complex schema that students often fail to master. I illustrate an aspect of this in figure 4. Here,

*Language, Culture and Linguistic Relativity* 85

I show how one can divide the English perception of time into complex and deictic (Radden and Dirven 2007: 204). In spoken language, deictic times relate straightforwardly to the moment of speaking. They are located simultaneously to the speech moment (the present); are behind it (the past), or in front of it (the present). In a simple past expression such as example (29) below, the speaker remains in the present time, and is, as it were, looking back on an action whose *reference point* is in the past, or at 10.00 o'clock. In using deictic time expressions, the speaker's *view point* is therefore rooted in the present time. In complex times, the speaker can move their view point. This may be simpler to grasp in a past perfect expression such as 'I had never thought about it before,' where the speaker, although still talking in their present, positions themselves in a past before which they had never thought about the issue they are discussing.

For Radden and Dirven (2007), a speaker using the English perfect will perceive the completed action from the perspective of the past and from

Deictic time

I live in an apartment now.
Once I lived in an old house.

The past

The speaker keeps their point of view in the present (speaking) time. When they talk of the past it is as if they are looking back in a way that allows them to see the event as a whole.

Complex time

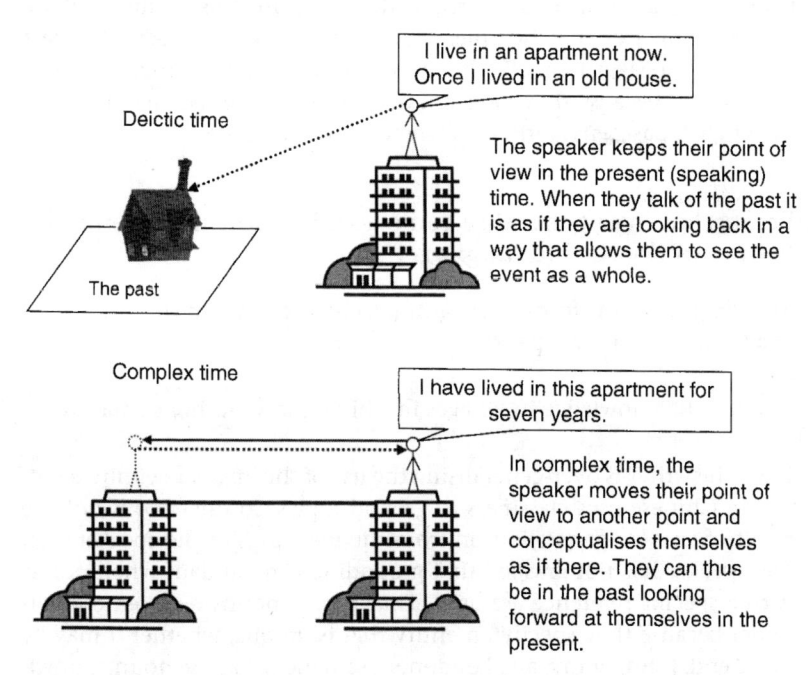

I have lived in this apartment for seven years.

In complex time, the speaker moves their point of view to another point and conceptualises themselves as if there. They can thus be in the past looking forward at themselves in the present.

*Figure 4* Complex and deictic time contrasted: using diagrams to help avoid schematic errors with tense

that of the present. The action's reference point is like a reflective surface in which the speaker can see themselves looking back. They therefore connect the event time to their present time, or watch the event as if it were coming up towards them. This act of shifting the reference point is fundamental to the English present perfect. In the error in example (28) the speaker has expressed deictic time in an expression reserved for complex time. They have done this because spoken French reserves complex time for expressions such as the past perfect ('je l'avais fait') or the future perfect ('je l'aurais fait').

(29) I've just done it
I've been away for a long time
I did it at 10.00

This type of error, therefore, may originate from two sources. First, French and English both have a perfect tense constructed with the possessive verb ('have'/'avoir') as an auxiliary and a past participle of the main verb. Second, spoken French does not use this to differentiate complex time from deictic time. Basically, the present perfect is the past tense. The speaker treats English as if it did the same thing. However, they do this because they have not developed an alternative schema for the English past tense, and its reference to deictic time.

## Errors that over-generalise some acquired formal or semantic feature of the second language

An example of this form of error in (30) has been taken from the work of a Cantonese native speaker:

(30) The knowledge in villages in China is low [author's data].

Here, the writer is over-generalising the use of the English definite determiner. Chinese uses classifiers to ground topics, so the error is not the result of an over-generalisation from the meanings of the speaker's L1. The speaker has not grasped that grounding is redundant when nouns with a specific reference are used. Thus proper nouns require no determiner because they specify an entity that is unique, whether it may be my friend, John, or my city, London. In sentence (30), the noun, 'knowledge' also treats its reference as unique: 'Knowledge is knowledge just as John is my friend John (Radden and Driven 2007: 101–2). Interestingly,

Language, Culture and Linguistic Relativity 87

if the student had written sentence (31), their use of the determiner would have been correct:

(31) The knowledge of children (about the outside world) in villages in China is low.

Example (31) shows how an English speaker sometimes conceptualises knowledge as a larger substance from which they can isolate a portion. They must then ground that they are talking about one portion of knowledge rather than another. For all we know, the writer might consider the knowledge of adults to be considerable. Figure 5 provides a graphic that helps students to conceptualise determinative meanings in this case.

Our understanding of embodied theory indicates how such graphics may help students more if they are given physical form, by, for example, cutting a circle of cardboard to represent a pie and labelling the pieces accordingly.

Knowledge is the basis of society.

Knowledge

The knowledge of geography

Knowledge in America is declining.

The knowledge of geography in America is declining, not the knowledge of religion.

*Figure 5* Why we do not use a determiner with abstract nouns that have a sole reference to what they describe

## False friends

Cognates and borrowings are most likely to be misused by speakers of *cognate languages*. These are languages whose speakers have been mixed up geographically or which have been themselves created as pidgins and creoles from such a process. Native English-speakers learning Romance languages will quickly understand how commonly they can simply take Latinate English forms and change them. They may also intuit, again through pattern, or through analogy, the types of word that are Latin in origin and will therefore transfer, establishing an equivalent between target and first language forms, or between the past participle ending '-ed' in English and '-i/-ado' in Spanish, for example. This may be a more intuitive search for analogues than we realise. The acquisition of an L3 by bilingual children requires more research, but I have observed that when very young bilingual children learn a third language, they tend to generalise in that language from the forms that most approximate to it. Thus, I observed a four-year-old Portuguese- and English-speaker learning French by turning to Portuguese lexis and grammar to help construct the TL. English teachers in Francophone Africa also used to assure me that pronunciation and grammar errors by young African, French and local-language bilinguals who were learning English could generally be traced to French rather than to first language interference. A probability is that children intuit the similarities between languages out of a more general pattern-finding capability, and that they do not, as some generative models would predict, suffer major interference from the parameter settings of their first language.

However, some cognates will have acquired different meanings in the language into which they have moved, furnishing the notorious 'faux ami' (false friend). For example, a Spanish-English faux-ami relished by teachers is 'embarrassed'/'embarazada' ('embarazada' means pregnant in Spanish). Although it is superficially a failure to pair the right meaning with a given form, this kind of error has a more interesting conceptual aspect. In origin the Latin root for 'embarrassed' meant 'blocked' or 'barred', and hence generally impeded. This original meaning is preserved in the English idiom, 'an embarrassment of riches', where 'wealth' bars one from the achievement of some goal. The earlier conceptualisation concept came to refer to an obstructive emotional condition in English and to an obstructive physical one in Spanish. For the learner, an error based on the use of the Spanish word with an English meaning is an issue of semantics not conceptualisation, but nonetheless the semantic trap is set by the way in which different cultures conceptualise the same condition differently.

## The problem of separating meaning from conceptualisation

Research into linguistic relativity does not support a strong Sapir-Whorf hypothesis, but research into such areas as classification and determination does give some support to a weaker version. We can therefore adopt the basic hypothesis that first language meanings will affect our conceptualisation of a given phenomenon. Further, the more abstract the meaning, the greater this effect will be. Such evidence gives some grounds for speculation that the successful acquisition of another language entails acquiring a somewhat different conceptual system, and that the difficulty of this task is very much dependent on the degree of similarity between the modes of conceptualisation implicit in the meanings of the languages concerned.

According to the CL view, meanings are not some fixed body of equivalences to forms, but rather encyclopaedic networks of knowledge about a given entity. Such *encyclopaedic meanings* are themselves extended by the imagery with which a meaning is imbued and from which it has been conceptualised. We cannot, for example, operate English determiners successfully without a conceptual grasp of the types of conceptualisation on which they depend. Thus, when using the indefinite article 'a', we need a broader grasp of the conceptual alternatives of bounded and unbounded, so that when we say 'a wine', for example, we need to know that we are treating this drink as temporily bounded, either because we are referring to one type of wine as distinct from others, as in 'a nice little Bordeaux', or because we are talking about a unit in a bottle or glass. Further, as our analysis of a few errors makes plain, the learner's generalisation of these semantic networks may stand a greater chance of success if it respects the imagery from which the form's meaning was derived. CL can offer the language teacher an enhanced understanding of this imagery, and thus of the reasons how and why a generalisation fails. What is less certain is how well the conceptualisations inherited from a first language can ever be significantly reworked to accommodate a second.

## Can one change a conceptualisation?

Because meaning and conceptualisation are so closely bound up with each other, it is difficult to find a way to show we are dealing with one and not the other. Yet, some thought about the embodied nature of experience, and hence of conceptualisation, has provided scholars with a way in. Our previous discussion of embodiment hypothesised how language originated in a gestural system. Gestures can also express the highly schematic meanings into which we embed the more precise concepts represented by many nouns and verbs. If gesture is closely linked to conceptualisation, the question of whether L2 users can change modes of conceptualisation inherited from the L1 can partly be studied through how much they change their gestures to fit adopted L2 meanings.

Clearly the expression of motion itself will be an area where meaning has a most straightforward relation to gesture. Gestures are themselves a form of movement and so are well suited to being an iconic vehicle for a broader expression of motion. Further, the conceptualisation of movement has attracted considerable interest in CL because of how it reveals the broader use of space to map grammatical relations.

Aske (1989) and Talmy (1991) described motion as conceptualised through four basic components:

a 'figure', or the moving object;
'the ground', or the space to which the movement is relative;
'the path', or the direction of the movement;
'the manner', or the way in which the movement is accomplished.

Aske (1989) and Talmy (1991) saw the path as the critical or defining element in the movement schema, since finally it plots the accomplished action. Talmy (1985) had further argued that language represented these components in one of two ways. Some languages such as French or Spanish (Romance) symbolise the manner of movement with words placed outside the verb. They are thus 'verb-framed' because the verb is dedicated primarily to showing 'path' and not manner. Others, such as English or German (Germanic), encode manner inside the verb but may indicate 'path' in an item outside the verb. For example, French tends to use the expression, 'on rentre à pied?', 'shall we return on foot?'. Manner, therefore, is outside the verb, and path is inside. English speakers are more likely to say 'Shall we walk back?'. Path is encoded outside the verb in 'back' and the manner 'on foot' has been placed inside the verb 'walk'. French may also use a gerund construction with 'il arrive en courant', carrying the path within the verb 'arriver' (arrive) and placing manner inside an added gerund, whereas English might often do the opposite, saying 'He ran here' (or to whatever landmark the speaker set down in the ground of the statement).

English is Germanic in origin but has borrowed French, then Latin, lexis, thus providing itself with some verb-framed expressions such as 'return', 'enter', 'ascend' or 'descend'. However, none of these are common when compared to their Germanic, satellite equivalents, 'go back', 'go into', 'go up' or, 'go down'. English also shows itself as fundamentally a satellite language in the vast and fascinating repertoire of verbs that encode the manner of movement, and which have to represent the path through adverbs, particles and prepositional phrases. A list of examples is given in the next section.

Various studies have tried to show how gestures illustrative of motion paths interact with speech that represents the same. For example, Özyürek and Kita (1999) recorded how subjects speaking a verb-framed language (such as Turkish or Japanese) tended to make no gestures expressing the motion itself, thus indicating that they conceptualised movement in a way where the manner was somehow secondary to the figure and path. Somewhat differently, other studies have shown that subjects speaking another verb-framed language, French, illustrate the path of movement with gestures that tend to fall on the verb itself, whereas speakers using a satellite-framed language, such as Dutch or English, will gesture concurrently with the adverbial phrase indicating direction. In other words, gesture indicates strongly that speakers conceptualise movement differently according to whether the language is verb- or satellite-framed (Kellerman and Van Hoof 2003).

More significantly, Kellerman and Van Hoof (2003) found that speakers often fail to change their gestures when they use a second language. One study investigated the gestures of native speakers of English, Dutch and Spanish by asking them to recount a narrative with a substantial need to express movement. When talking English, 65% of native speakers of Spanish still gestured in a way that showed they conceptualised movement as if it were verb-framed. They did this even if 'their verbalisations' were 'couched in nearly acceptable English' (*ibid.*). This finding has been supported in another study made by Negueruela and Lantolf (2004), but was not consistent with Kellerman and Van Hoof's other observation of Dutch speakers. Here they found that 55% of the Dutch speakers using English tended to gesture as if it were a verb-framed language. In other words, they conceptualised movement differently from their own language, treating English as if it were verb-framed. The English-speakers further confused the picture when speaking Dutch by gesturing on both the verb and the satellite. Thus Spanish-speakers tended to behave like Spanish-speakers whatever language they were using, whilst the Dutch-speakers treated English as if it were Spanish. However, this last result may be explained by the different ways in which Dutch and English express their satellitic conceptualisation. In Dutch the satellite, or prepositional phrase, is much more securely attached to the verb than in English. It is almost as if English grammar is developing in a verb-framed direction, a feature shown in the ubiquity of phrasal verbs and the tendency in some traditional grammars to treat the verb and preposition or particle as if they were a single constituent. Further, we have already alluded to how the large degree of transfer from French into English may make it less markedly satellitic than some other examples.

Perhaps most significant is how in Spanish, where the verb-framing is least equivocal and the culture perhaps more integral or less saturated by English media and its concomitant modes of thought, there is most resistance to conceptual reorientation. This is even the case among the Hispanic minority studied by Negueruela and Lantolf in the USA, where cross-cultural competencies have clearly been developed (2004). Evidently, some conceptualisations run deep and may not be wholly acquired from the language but from associated cultural perceptions that are encoded in gesture itself. Such a conclusion is supported by a much earlier finding that speakers gesture more when their knowledge of the second language is less (Marcos 1979). It is as if speakers whose words fail are falling back on dominant language conceptualisations to shape an elusive meaning, or even to give it visual form.

## Language, culture and conceptualisation in the classroom

For Sapir and Whorf, a language and a culture existed in a deterministic relationship where the language's segmentation of meaning shaped how the culture represented its reality. This is not the picture that emerges from our discussion above. True to its structuralist parentage, Whorf's model evolves culture from the human imposition of structure upon the world. Meaning begins in how a language compartmentalises its reality, or represents it as form. These meanings make the culture what it is, determining its compartmentalisation of such central features of human existence as nature or time. In CL, a meaning such as 'time' is conceptualised from experience, and human experience is conditioned by culture. Meaning and culture therefore fashion each other. The culture is both the pre-requisite and product of the conceptualisation as meaning.

Our conception of a culture has also evolved considerably since Sapir and Whorf proposed their hypothesis. Primarily, it can no longer be seen as a static and reified entity that imposes beliefs and behaviours upon its participants, whether through the mechanism of language or not. Such a model assumes that human societies are organised into closed tribal groups speaking different languages. Each such group is shaped in isolation from the other by whatever cultural practices hold. This social model summates a set of circumstances that probably never prevailed and which certainly has no application at a time when globalisation spreads belief systems across tribal and national frontiers. A culture is no longer 'a knowledge system inherited from the ancestors': it is rather 'a set of ideas, attributes, and expectations that is constantly changing as people react to' the different circumstances that cultures themselves create (Watson 2004: 145). Broadly, this model has evolved from the concept of a culture as shared social practices that was put forward by the French sociologist, Pierre Bourdieu (1977).

Social practices are the recurrent activities of a community. Thus a literacy practice could be 'blogging' and a given community of practice would be bloggers who were sharing the activity. In this sense practices are also linguistic and therefore fashion shared discourses, or discourse communities (see for example, Swales 1990). Communities of practice could also be shaped by professions, or the use of common skills.

Central to the conception of a social practice is its existence in time and space (Jenkins 1992). We can see how 'space' is critical when we consider how twenty-first century practices are fashioned by whether they unfold in a shared physical location or at an international distance but within shared cyber space. Their nature is then affected by the type of space, as when one can analyse a class from the perspective of how it arranges and uses the classroom, or appraise our own working practices through how they compartmentalise our desk space, or take us into the world outside. In each case the activity may unfold from real into virtual space and this will have a radical effect upon its nature. Even when it passes into virtual space, however, the practice may remain localised in both a metaphorical and literal sense. It is literally localised in that it can unfold in a computer user's room, positing lives of greater confinement than might have been tolerable in some older societies. It is metaphorically localised in that it might use a chat room that is reserved for a select community. But the same practice may be internationalised by how its participants are spread across the globe.

All human activity uses time, but any examination of this fact will quickly extend to an interest in the rhythm or non-rhythm with which the activity unfolds, and the frequency of our engagement in it. More profound, is how the way practices use time can be taken back to the fundamental cycles of season and reproduction. For example, computer gaming seems to exert a particular hold over male adolescents and thus posits practices that slot into a larger life cycle, perhaps substituting for other types of coming-of-age rituals. We can also see the role of time as crucial to how we engage in another type of practice that Bourdieu used to exemplify his concept, namely that related to sport.

Bourdieu's study of sport could be interpreted as carrying Merleau-Ponty's concept of the body into the laboratory of society. An enduring problem in linguistic relativism, and in sociology generally, relates to how far our actions are determined by the societies and cultures that shape our belief systems. For Bourdieu, the body was an encounter between the objective social structures that imprinted their culture upon it and the subjectivity of response allowed by its being an entity separate from others and suffused with an individual will. Sporting activity, such as a game of football, epitomised this image of the body as an encounter between subjective will and objective social structure, but one could just as easily refer to any collective human activity, such as a language class. Whether in sport or language learning, the body can be trained to make certain reflexive responses. For example, football training will try to condition players to look for a pass rather than risk losing the ball to an opponent. The consequence of this conditioning, however, is to allow to the individual player a series of choices or moves. In other words, the body ensures the mind's conformity with how the activity should unfold (looking for a pass) whilst also furnishing the material through which the individual can do something else (dribble the ball forward).

Language can also be conceptualised as a game. When using language, we construct a symbolic resource from the body and do so in conformity with an agglomeration of social conventions that are imposed upon it from outside, making those symbols what they are. However, we also operate these conventions with the accumulated imagery of individual experience, tailoring meaning to our individual expressive needs.

Language also proposes that the body is the zone of encounter where cultural conventions nurture individual choice. In learning a second language the student is therefore seeking out the meanings that regulate play, and the opportunities for individual choice that these come to afford. Gaining access to the meanings of a language proposes access to those of the culture in which they have evolved. It must take in also the practices for which the target language culture has had to develop specialist discourses. We can see this most clearly in scientific and academic practice, and can also understand how such cultural activities require new modes of conceptualisation from their participants.

When exploring the conceptualisation of meaning we may need to uncover the historical practices that have shaped a conceptualisation. In an age of international languages, however, the search for the conceptual origins of a meaning does not entail its treatment as some emblematic product of a national culture or even of its disintegrated empire. The search entails becoming alert to how international communities of practice take meanings developed in more localised contexts then evolve modes of symbolisation that are specific to them, whether these are focused on business, scientific or artistic activity.

Most relevantly, Byram (1989), Byram *et al.* (1991) and Byram and Fleming (1998) have proposed that 'learning a language should be completed by a sustained and ethnographically structured encounter with the practices of the language's culture' (Holme 2002). To fully support language learning one must therefore foster a cultural engagement, and one of the best ways to do this is to equip the student who is visiting a target language culture with the skills of an ethnographer who is going out to document unfamiliar cultural practices. Much of the work done in this area is focussed on study abroad, with students who were completing language studies in a given target language country being asked to conduct an ethnographic survey upon some aspect of its social practices. However, the approach can be linked to a wider ability to use a target language successfully in the communities of practice where it is required, and hence to understand the types of intercultural interaction and discourses that these require.

## Language, culture and learning

Broadly then, language students need to learn more about themselves, analysing their own subjectivity, belief systems and how these engage with the meanings of the target language. For example, they should probe each others' prejudices about the target language's host cultures and can also ask how certain cultural emphases should promote the study of different language topics in preference to others. This can be broad-brush, as when a cultural stress upon a religion, food, or other lifestyle interest will invite more study of the appropriate language.

Language students should also think more about sub-cultural practices and belief systems in their own culture. They can look at cults and lifestyle groupings such as Goths or Hells Angels, using a study of one of these to hone research skills and as a future base for cross-cultural study. For example, one might wonder how Japanese and English cultic adolescent groupings differ, and analyse whether these differences are evidence of some broader cultural effect.

Learners can develop their concept of culture and how to research and write about it by engaging in classroom 'culture games' of the type outlined in Activity 15:

Activity 15    Culture game
1  The class is divided into two or more groups with each group being sent to a different room.
2  Each group develops a culture, thinking carefully about its beliefs, rituals, and taboos. These practices should be easy to perform and demonstrate in class.
3  The groups swap 'anthropologists' who observe each others' practices then report back on the same. Each time they break a taboo they are immediately sent back to their group then replaced with another 'anthropologist'.
4  Anthropologists are sent back to their groups, which interrogate them about the other society, compiling a report on its beliefs and practices.

Learners can also be encouraged to think more deeply about which communities of practice will foster their use of the target language in a way that may be useful for them. They should also ask how they can be exploited. For example, business students can research the broader literature on contract negotiation, outlining this as a social practice with its rules of engagement and improvisational spaces. They then try to use this data in negotiation scenarios or role plays in class. In rehearsing these scenarios, learners should be asked to give more thought to a practice's accompanying gestures and the meanings these convey.

Learners should also examine the use or non-use of the target language within their own culture, and the way in which its meanings and expressions may be permeating their own language, or be being resisted by the same. They can then consider the relationship, or non-relationship, between some aspects of the language's idiom and their own cultural circumstance:

Activity 16    Tracing it back
1  Take an idiom or fixed expression.
2  Use library or on-line resources to trace its historical origins.
3  Present some facet of the historical background they reveal. For example, the place in English society of the horse, from horse metaphors: 'at the end of my tether', 'you can lead a horse to water but you can't make it drink', 'don't ride before you can walk', etc.
4  Ask students to translate similar expressions from their language, for example, 'you can lead a cow to water but you can't make it drink' (Cantonese) and discuss the cultural differences that these reveal.

Another interesting area concerns how cultures cross borders, allowing local interests and interpretations to break down trends and products that seem monolithic in nature. Globalisation is then far from being a straightforward process of one culture dominating another. For example, Watson (2004) remarked how the Hollywood epic *Titanic* enjoyed huge popularity among an older generation of Chinese men. This was because it became for them an expression of the lost dreams and opportunities of youth which they had suffered. The same author has also remarked upon how the globalising phenomenon of Macdonalds restaurants may be used in culturally different ways in different places. A *globalised* entity is thus *localised* as a cultural symbol with an entirely different meaning, and students can be invited to explore how this occurs.

Activity 17    What we do with it
1  In groups, select an international trend or product associated with a target language culture. For example a Hollywood film or international restaurant chain.
2  Out of class, the groups research local responses to the product, assessing how the same entity may be differently perceived.

Equally, an international language is indubitably a globalising phenomenon, but this may be localised by local expressions and metaphors. This is not simply a case of pidginisation, where the lexis or grammatical structures of the first language influence the way the second is used in a way that can be stabilised as an international variety (Kachru 1990).

For example, in Chinese Hong Kong, the word for a 'stamp' of the kind put into passports is a 'chop', thus using a metaphor derived from the sound and action of putting in the stamp.

In addition, both teachers and students can be furnished with stronger language awareness so that they may develop a greater understanding of language variation and its origins in how cultures foster the conceptualisation of certain meanings. Andrews (1998), McCarthy (see for example, 1991) and Mittins (1991) have all addressed the awareness of language variation in teacher training, whilst Adger *et al.* (1999) and Fillmore and Snow (2000) have argued that the development of such an awareness will both foster a greater understanding of their learners' cultural worlds and attune them better to the processes of language learning (Kelly Hall 2002). Less has been said about quite how this should be followed through into the language class, however. Providing teachers with a grasp of conceptual metaphor theory may be a good starting point from which to help students explore the acculturated nature of meanings and conceptualisation. The following activity shows how such knowledge can be used in what is intended as an extensive project about exploring meanings, or which could be one part of a larger examination of a culture.

Activity 18    Collecting a culture as language
1  Check that the students understand what we mean by a metaphor and collect as many examples as possible, asking each student to try to produce a different one. To encourage them you can write some common abstract nouns on the board, for example, 'life', 'love', 'time', 'hatred', 'hope', 'argument' etc. They will probably give a very literal interpretation of a metaphor, as 'NP is/are NP', or 'life is a difficult road', for example. Tell them to translate from their mother tongue if they have problems.
2  Extend their understanding of how metaphor may be carried in our use of verbs and adjectives by asking for entailments. For example, the teacher says 'Life twists and turns', then asks 'What is life?', to get 'life is a difficult road'. The teacher then asks students to follow a road in their minds to lead them towards, 'ups and downs', 'unexpected twist/turning' etc.
3  Group some of the produced metaphors according to an accessible conceptual metaphor. For example, 'life is a difficult road', under 'life is a journey'. Write up other conceptual metaphors that seem to find themes in the metaphors on the board. Invent them if necessary.

4 Explain how metaphor is a common part of everyday expression and go through any short newspaper or other text, getting students to underline the metaphors they find whilst pointing out those they do not notice.
5 Give students a list of conceptual metaphors that seem to bear more of a cultural imprint and feel less universal. For example, 'time is money' (Lakoff and Johnson 1980) has a stronger cultural footprint than 'time is a precious resource'. This is because the last conceptualisation reaches back to a primal need to hoard food and other resources. It also taps into a schema that is even more fundamental in the sense of being derived from bodily posture. 'Hoarding food' suggests making a pile or building *up* a heap. The schema of the heap, or of building *up* a store therefore taps into the image schema of vertical movement and bodily posture and the conceptual metaphor 'up is more', or 'up is good' (Lakoff and Johnson 1980). 'Time is money' expresses something of this schema, but in the discourse of materialism and its associated twentieth- and twenty-first century cultures. Here are some other examples from English:

- 'life is a sports match'
- 'life is a quest'
- 'life is a gambling game' (*ibid.*)
- 'business is war' (*ibid.*)
- 'machines are living things'
- 'ideas are products/commodities or fashions' (*ibid.*)
- 'relationships are physical forces' (e.g. electric)

6 Tell students to collect as many text metaphors as they can find that realise the above concepts. They should do this by reading as much as possible and listening as carefully to their own and others' conversations as they can.
7 Ask them to present their findings and to reflect on how a topic, for example, 'love', is perceived in their own language and culture.
8 Explore such areas as entailments and intentionality (see the introduction to this chapter).

Residues of behaviourist thinking and stimulus–response approaches to teaching often discourage more conscious explorations of language and meaning in the class. This tendency has not been helped by the misinterpretation of communicative language teaching (CLT) that treats grammatical approaches as a brake on fluency. However, an appreciation of meaning differences between languages and their cultural motivations can encourage a more conscious exploration of lexical and grammatical meanings, and how these differ between languages. In their turn these may help the student achieve a better manipulation of target language meanings.

Activity 19    Cross-cultural meanings
1 Compile a list of abstract words that represent key socio-cultural concepts, for example: friendship, family, love, home, politics, the work–life balance, the arts, thought, discussion and argument, driving.
2 In groups, ask the students to come up with statements for each word on the list as follows:

- In the USA (the Tl country) friendship is... They can complete this with a metaphorical complement (friendship is a trap) or a more literal one (friendship is a superficial relationship between two people).
- In my country, friendship is...

3 Mix the students into different groups of the same size and ask them to read their conclusions to their new group. The groups should discuss why they have said what they have, and provide supporting anecdotes where possible.
4 Ask each group to make a presentation on the meaning of one of the concepts in one country then in a target-language country.

## Different meanings for different languages

Lakoff's (1987) view was that the more abstract the meaning, the greater the chance of language causing cultural divergences in how that meaning was conceptualised. Grasping such areas of divergence between a target and first language are one of language learning's greater challenges. I have already noted how one of the least abstract and most fundamental areas where this may show is in the expression of movement. English verbs of manner express an aspect of fundamental distinction in how languages conceptualise movement. Whether or not English poses challenges to the learner in this domain does not relate simply to whether the learner's L1 is satellite- or verb-framed. As a satellite language, English also boasts a huge repertoire of expressions of manner. Examples of these verbs are as follows:

- creep – move noiselessly
- march – walk in time in military fashion
- plod (along) – walk with slow heavy steps
- saunter (off) – walk in a free, showy but directionless manner
- scuttle away – move off with a quick, noisy movement of the feet
- sidle (up to somebody) – approach somebody furtively
- slink (away) – move with a lowered profile and some sense of shame
- sneak (in) – enter without being seen
- sneak (up on) – approach without being seen or heard
- shuffle (around) – move with feet barely leaving the ground
- stroll (around) – walk in a free leisurely manner
- tramp – walk with tired and heavy steps
- wade (through) – walk with effort through water that is over the knee
- paddle (in) – walk through water up to the feet
- waddle – walk like a duck

(from Pourcel 2005: 163)

There are also motion verbs whose expression of movement is metonymically derived from the sound they make:

- creak (he creaked upstairs)
- clank (the faulty car clanked into the yard)
- thump (the speed boat thumped through the waves)
- thud (the projectile thudded into the wall)

and from the conveyance used:

- cycle
- sail

or from the action of using a conveyance or instrument of motion:

- drive
- ride
- trot/canter/gallop (for a horse)
- fly

- blast
- drill

or from the vertical motion that results from forward motion over a certain topography

- bump (bumped down the road)
- sway

or as a result of such states as injury and intoxication:

- sway (swayed through the field)
- stagger (as if hurt or injured)
- limp (more literally when something is soft and lifeless, also walk with a bad leg)
- hobble (a walk that results from foot injuries)

or as the metaphorical extension of a statically accomplished action:

- tear (generally used in the past tense with the preposition up or down as in 'I tore up the street') – move very quickly
- grind (move with effortful slowness as in 'I ground to a halt)

English verbs of manner can also encode the rapidity of movement:

- hurry (move or accomplish an action quickly)
- rush (move very quickly, with a greater implication of physical movement)
- speed (an implication of mechanically assisted movement)

Because these verbs express movement they can be taught by the type of E&M routine discussed in the last chapter.

Activity 20    Exacting movements
1 Using the list of verbs of manner just given, select three or four, for a given session, and write each verb on a piece of paper in the past simple tense with an appropriate prepositional phrase that leaves the complement of the prepositional phrase unspecified (for example, 'I sidled up to...'.). You can also do this activity with elementary students using common verbs of manner such as 'walk', 'run', 'ride' and 'drive'.

2 Give the papers to learners, then distance yourself from them as far as possible. Ask a student to read the verb on the paper, then you demonstrate the meaning by approaching them in the manner expressed. As you do so, repeat the verb inside a phrase that expresses what you are doing. For example, you sidle up to John and say 'I'm sidling up to John'. Give the student the paper and ask them to repeat what is written there, using the past tense. Then ask the whole class to repeat the phrase.
3 When the papers are given out, each student gives the paper to somebody at a distance from them by miming what is written on it. The class should try to guess the verb of manner that is being mimed, and the person who receives the paper should repeat the action until the class has found the right verb.
4 After repeating step 3 two or three times, put the verbs on the board, get the students into pairs and ask them to recount to each other a simple narrative using these actions and appropriate prepositional phrases. For example: 'I ran to John, walked to Jane, hurried to Susan and rode my cycle to see Paul'.

As a satellite language, English may require its learners to think more deeply about the meanings of prepositions and the use that is made of them. This is partly because English prepositions and their use in phrasal verbs and other phrasal constructions often seems highly conventionalised and largely inexplicable unless one explores their meanings through the larger metaphor of a space grammar and the image schemas of horizontal and vertical space, or movement within the same. Further, from a CL perspective, prepositions, or their inflectional equivalents in inflected languages, exemplify the strong use of spatial conceptualisations in grammar. Thus the seemingly irrational nature of the use of prepositions as between the use of 'to' and 'on' in such prepositional verbs as 'sidle up to' and 'creep up on' has caused advocates of the lexical approach to teach these as fixed or lexical phrases. However, these items are not phrasal verbs and can in fact construct with different prepositional phrases. Some can in fact express the large variety of paths along which motion is generally mapped. For example:

- I crept out of the room
- I crept into bed
- I crept over the boards
- I crept past the door

- I crept up to them
- I crept up on them

But others encode path as an attribute of manner:

- I sidled up to him
- He slunk away from her

And tend, as a result, to represent a less general and rarer meaning.

My broader point is that rather than approach prepositional phrases as chunked with specific verbs, one may provide the language student with a more productive use of them if one provides them with a better understanding of the phrase itself, then look at how this will or will not combine with certain types of verb meaning. Activity 21 attempts this by contrasting how 'up to' and 'up on' construe a scene differently when they complement motion events. However, the activity framework used can be used with almost any such contrast of prepositional meanings.

Activity 21    Furtive movement
1 Explain how one of the meanings of 'up' is to represent completion, as when a trajectory stops at the end point in 'I put the picture up'. You can use figure 6 to illustrate this, or you can use illustrative actions and objects in the class. Illustrate how 'come up on somebody' and 'come up to somebody' construe a motion event differently. The point is that 'up to' construes the person in motion as visible to the person they approach, or as approaching an object without stealth. 'Up on' (not to be confused with 'upon'), implies that the person being approached is surprised by what is perhaps an unwelcome intrusion 'on' their personal space. They are also perhaps 'down' in relation to the posture of the moving figure, implying an inferior, difficult or less prominent posture. Interestingly also, 'up on', construes the motion even from the perspective of the approached person. Thus one can 'come up on somebody', but one cannot 'go/walk up on somebody'. Perhaps this is because they have no prominence or are not fully visible to the approaching person.
2 Give the students a list of motion verbs, for example: come, go, move, walk, creep, tiptoe, crawl, run.

*Language, Culture and Linguistic Relativity* 105

Up is the end

go up to

up to

I came **up to** her and said hello.

The picture is up.

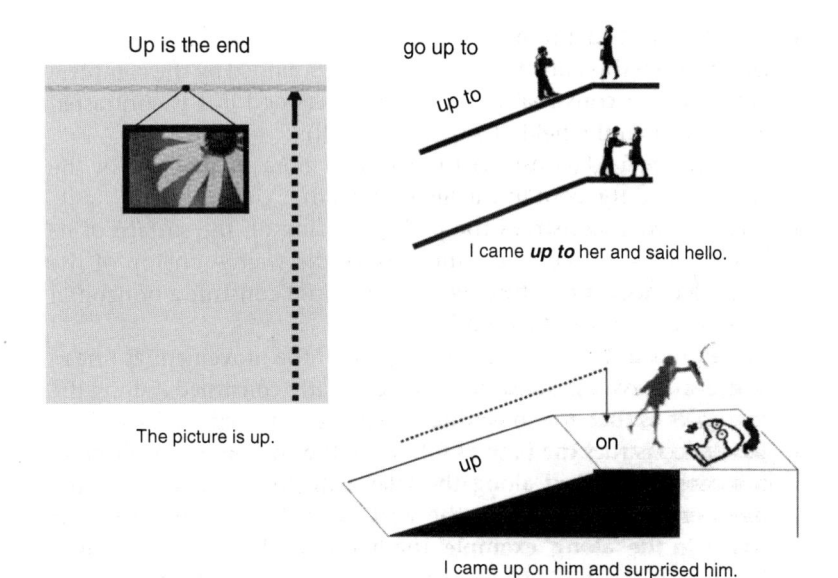

up    on

I came up on him and surprised him.

*Figure 6* 'Up to' and 'up on': furtive and prominent motion paths

3 Students use their understanding of 'up to someone' and 'up on someone' to decide which verbs can go with only one prepositional phrase, and which can go with both. They should do this by making appropriate sentences.
4 Ask for sentences and correct. Point out that 'up on' is not neutral as to manner. It implies a furtive path, and is therefore restricted to verbs that are neutral as to manner, verbs such as 'come', or verbs that express quiet or furtive movement, 'creep', 'tiptoe', or possibly 'crawl'. 'Up to' implies a visible approach and therefore can be used with a wider variety of verbs.

Langacker (1990: 53) uses the term *search domain* to reflect the basic experience of finding a figure in space, or in its ground. Motion paths, with or without an expression of manner, propose search domains as follows:

- to the house (an approach ending near but outside the landmark)
- into the house (an area able to contain the person who moves)
- out of the house (antonymous with the above)

- over the field (if the moving person does not actually leave the ground then this construes the ground as bounded by the complete movement; a construal that can be understood if it is contrasted with 'through the field' [Langacker 1990])
- through the field (construes the action as more encumbered by the ground, as if the corn in the field were tall)
- onto the roof (construes the path as ending on the surface of its destination – hence 'she jumped onto the wall' – on top of the wall – but not onto entities where we cannot construe a horizontal surface, as in 'onto the room')
- along the sea shore (construes the path of the movement as linear, so it must have a ground that can be linearly construed. 'Along the city walls' is therefore meaningful but 'along the city' is not)
- Beside (construes the path as following the contour of the ground: compare 'he walked along the lake' with 'he walked beside the lake', or 'he walked along the wall' with 'he walked beside the wall'.) In the 'along' example, the figure can be on the wall or at its foot. In the 'beside' example, it can only be at the wall's foot. Further, we can 'stand beside something' but not 'along it'. 'Beside' therefore construes the figure's spatial position in relation to the ground, letting the verb express the movement, or not. 'Along' construes a position as dynamic, or as changing
- under (places the ground temporarily over the figure)
- beneath (construes the ground as above the figure for longer than does 'under'. Compare: 'he walked beneath the bridge' with 'he walked under the bridge', where the first could construe movement back and forth under it)
- down (construes the path as an angled or vertical descent according to the type of motion: compare 'he dropped down' with 'he walked down')
- down to (construes the ground as being at the end of the descent)
- up the ladder (antonymous to 'down')
- up to the roof (antonymous to 'down to')
- at the station (when a motion path, it construes the ground as external but in close proximity to the destination. Thus in 'I arrive at the station', 'station' is construed as being external but close to the figure. In 'I arrive in the station', the ground is inside the station, or contained by it.)

Not only is the use of prepositional phrases essential to the expression of motion in satellite verb languages, it can also become the basis for how they use space to conceptualise abstract relationships between phenomena. Therefore, practising and understanding the expression of search domains in a language such as English underpins the control not just of how we locate our movement in space but of how we perceive the relationship between phenomena, as when we connect one object to another. Activity 22, below, elaborates on the common type of meaning-matching technique used on the pages above and can be recycled to help students master the very complicated conceptualisation of motion paths and their search domains in English. It also helps students grasp prepositional phrases not as collocation-based preferences between motion verbs and their paths (as between 'arrive' and 'at'), but as meanings which can construe one form of motion as having different paths (as in 'arrive on the runway, at the disembarkation point, and in the terminal building'). The word lists used by the activity can be edited to fit very different levels of learner.

Activity 22  Motion paths
1  Provide a list of prepositions that can head motion paths. You could use the list above as a source but should only work on some of the items at a time.
2  Get the class into groups of between four and six.
3  Give each group a list of nouns or noun phrases that could be used as the ground of a motion path. For example: 'surface of the lake, water, bridge, building, tunnel, field, wall, the ground, the hill, mountain, road'. Check that they are understood.
4  Give each student a list of motion verbs and check that their meanings are understood. For example: climb, go, walk, jump, flew; or make a more elaborate list with the examples given above.
5  The students make as many phrases as possible using the prepositions and verbs. Remind them that these must make sense and that a particular preposition cannot always take a particular noun as its complement with a particular verb.
6  The groups appoint a secretary who is supplied with pen and paper.
7  The groups make as many sentences as they can, using the first person, and fitting the verb, preposition and complement together, whilst the secretary writes them down. The complement can be elaborated in any way the group chooses; for example, 'surface' to 'on the surface of the lake'. The sentences must make sense: for example, 'I sailed over the surface of the lake', but not 'I walked along the surface of the lake'; or 'I swam under the surface of the lake' but not 'I sailed under the surface of the lake'. Note how a path

can make sense when a term is treated metonymically or metaphorically. For example, 'I drove through the mountain' ('mountain' is a metonym for the tunnel passing through it), or 'glided under the surface'.
8  Going round the class, build a chain story in the present simple or continuous tense by asking one group representative to read one sentence, then another to suggest a sentence that could be sequentially connected. For example 'I walk beside the walls. I come up to the road. I shuffle along it'. Each time a student suggests a continuation, ask them where they are and what they see when they look up, down or ahead, as if they were the narrator in the unfolding story. Check that their answer makes sense from the perspective of the chosen ground; if it does, check that they have understood how. For example, student: 'I walk along the wall'. Teacher: 'Look up! What do you see?' Student: 'I see the wall'. Teacher: 'OK, so you're walking along, beside the wall, not on it?'

Re-using this activity with different sets of motion verbs and prepositional complements will help learners conceptualise the English representation of motion. Step 8 of the activity argues that if students cannot mime the meaning they should imagine it, thinking of how their body moves in that conjured space and garnering a meaning from that. They can also create a kind of 'half-way house' between their mental and their immediate, physical, world by walking in the classroom whilst seeing and talking about it as if they were moving through an altogether grander space. I call this 'envisioning'.

## Conclusions

In this chapter I have broached two central and related concepts in CL: the first is the process of fashioning meanings, called conceptualisation. The second is the related assumption that language, culture and meaning are bound up with each other. Fundamental to CL is that meaning is treated as conceptualised and not perceived. Such conceptualisations must be shared among individuals because they support communication. This social need to share and conventionalise our common conceptualisations as meaning is largely a property of culture. In fact it is arguably a culture's defining attribute.

If culture and language relate closely, then linguistic meaning will not only be culturally shaped, but will also have a role in shaping culture. A further possibility is that language learning success entails a degree of integration into the target language culture, and language learning failure could also presuppose a failure to acquire that culture's modes of conceptualisation and hence a degree of cultural marginalisation. Of course, we are all endowed with the same cognitive architecture and therefore see the same forms and colours. However, meaning quickly departs from the security of how we experience the physical world. In other words, it builds quickly towards abstraction, establishing grammars to represent abstract relationships in space and time. Abstraction posits modes of conceptualisation that are less well secured by a world of objects and therefore it affords room for greater differences among the meanings that we use. The entailment is that cultures, as the archives of these shared modes of grasping the world, could operate with different abstract worlds, conventionalising these into different grammatical and lexical meanings. Therefore there is a sense in which learning a language involves acquiring new modes of common conceptualisation.

We have looked at some teaching activities that made students more sensitive to this weak relativity hypothesis, looking at such features as English's representation of motion with satellitic verb phrases, or at how English prepositions construe spatial relations. We have also considered the complication that in most modern second language classrooms, the target languages, their cultures, and their communities of use can no longer be located in neatly segmented geographical areas. Culture cannot therefore be treated straightforwardly as a specific set of customs which have impacted upon language in a particular way, providing particular discourses. An even greater complication is that English first evolved in tandem with a relatively remote and insignificant island community, then was spread across world to become bound up in the evolution of other cultures and their meanings. Therefore it is not just our perception of culture but also language which needs to be looked at from the dual cultural perspective of the globalised and the localised. In other words, many of English's conceptualisations are imbued with a local historical cultural identity but used in communities to which the identity of that locality means little. If understanding how meanings have evolved can help students manipulate them more successfully, however, then it does no harm to gain a better understanding of the context from which those meanings once emerged. In this sense, a language's culture need not be treated as a mode of contamination that impedes the student's ability to bend its meanings to their own communicative and cultural will. It should be treated more as a source of imagery, able to facilitate the process of semantic personalisation that lies at the heart of successful language use.

From a CL perspective it makes no sense to treat the international role of English as equivalent to a cultural limbo. No language is capable of being constructed as an acculturated mode of communication, since the very fact of communication leads us towards the processes of conceptualisation that differentiate one culture from another. The very fact of operating in a given language will in some sense entail a speaker's use of the meanings that this language has evolved to represent. This is itself an act of acculturation.

To capture the very complex relations between language and culture entailed by an international language, we therefore need to look at language and culture in ways that are more responsive to how these proceed from a dynamic that has shifted to an international context. With a crude Whorfian determinism being no longer applicable, we should instead think more about practice models of both language and culture. For this, we need Bourdieu's characterisation of a practice as a kind of embodied convergence between action, the social conventions by which an action is conditioned, and the individual use that is made of the same. Such practices create communities from how they share skills and discourses. An international language is like any other, in that it will be used by these communities in ways that advance their activities. What is different is the range of communities involved, how they exist in a new concept of space and rework our concept of time.

The pedagogical challenge is to understand such a language as emerging from a local culture to actually rework our concept of what a culture can be. The goal should be to produce learners who do not learn to live in one monolithic target language culture so much as to negotiate their way through numerous communities of practice that an international language brings into existence. Such a goal requires pedagogies that make the bodies and minds of their learners into areas of convergence between custom, gesture, meaning, and form.

# 6
# Conceptualisation and Construal

## Introduction

Fundamental to cognition is how we can conceptualise the same series of events in different ways. This ability is reflected in both the lexis and grammar of language. Consider sentences (32) and (33):

(32) I adore Rome!
(33) I love Rome very much!

At first sight, 'adore' and 'love very much' seem to make these sentences almost synonymous. However, each *construes* the expressed emotion somewhat differently from the other. 'Adoration' abases the subject before their admired object. 'Loving very much' simply makes Rome into the object of an intense emotion. The use of 'love' and 'adore' represent the same scene differently. CL calls these different ways of conceptualising a scene, *construal* (Langacker 1987). In CL there is no such thing as true synonymy because a different selection of words will achieve a different construal. Construal affects the grammar of the language and accounts for why we may select one form over another. Consider the following two sentences:

(34) Now the plane was over the cars
(35) Now the cars were under the plane

These two different sentences also depict the same scene. However, there are central differences in the way the depiction is construed. First, to reflect this difference of meaning, different prepositions are selected. Second, sentence (34) is about the plane whilst sentence (35) is about the cars. In sentence (34), the plane is perceived against the ground of the cars. In sentence (35) the opposite is the case.

Imagine if sentence (35) is said by somebody actually in the plane. It now represents a *construal operation* that Langacker (1987) calls *objectification*, because of how the subject observes themselves in their scene as if they were an objective entity and were situated among the cars or even were a car. In other words, they are *objectified* as if by an entity outside themselves and looking back. Construal operations are also the natural conclusion of an approach to meaning that is conceptual and enactive rather than perceptual and passive. They show the observer not as simply representing their world but as shaping an image of it, locating themselves in different vantage points and taking different perspectives.

In this chapter I will explore *construal operations* further, looking at how they make language reflect a given form of conceptualisation. I will show how, because construal operations often determine our selection of lexis and grammar, they can help teachers explain our use of a given form to their students whilst also structuring modes of practice in the same.

## Construal operations

Until this point, my discussion of conceptualisation has chiefly focused on metaphor, metonymy or figure and ground. Metaphor and metonymy have been topics of immense interest in cognitive linguistics because of how they are immediately identifiable in language as an aberration that contradicts many of the assumptions of formal linguistics. They are implicated in the development of new meaning and even of all abstract meaning, typifying what we mean by an enactive cognition through how they show meaning as developed from conceptualisation rather than perception. However, there are many other types of conceptual operation used to construe scenes in different ways. Croft and Cruse (2004) provide a useful account of construal operations that I summarise as follows:

- **Attention/salience:** selection, scope, scalar adjustment, dynamic attention
- **Judgment/comparison:** categorisation, metaphor, figure, ground
- **Perspective/situatedness:** viewpoint, deixis, subjectivity, objectivity
- **Constitution/gestalt:** including most other image schemas
- **Structural schematisation:** force dynamics: relationality

There is some overlap between these. Thus metaphor receives different degrees of emphasis among cognitive linguists (Dirven 2001) and most of the above types of construal operation create imagery and could be analysed as metaphor-making in some sense. Likewise, selection entails metonymy because one feature such as 'a sail' is selected to represent a larger entity. But metonymy is a hugely extensible rhetorical category and could also involve types of imagery that are sometimes considered metaphorical. However, these categories are useful to open a discussion about how we can help language learners grasp how their lexis and grammar reflect a given way of construing a scene.

## Attention and salience

The ability to focus on one aspect of a scene rather than another is critical to animal intelligence and hence to our survival. It allows us to identify a threat or to focus on a potential prey. It lets me write this book whilst ignoring the background movement of the trees and the sea outside my office. In language, almost any act of communication singles out one entity from another in this way.

## Attention, salience and enactive SLA

Hitherto our focus has been upon how conceptual operations shape the meanings of the languages that we have to learn. However, I would argue that the construal operations are relevant to how we grasp the language itself. A language, as an auditory or visual phenomenon, is conceptualised as part of the reality of which we are trying to make sense. To take a very simple example: learners facing the puzzle of input from a poorly understood or barely known language will gravitate towards familiar sounds. I remembered the Cantonese word for 'left' by finding some similarity between it and the English word 'jaw'. It is the enactive nature of second language acquisition and human cognition in general which ensures that we at first use a few known phonological mnemonics to pick some path through the otherwise meaningless noise of an unknown language.

The problem of second language learning does not come just from grafting second language forms onto first language meanings but from how we conceptualise a target language itself. For example, central to how we conceptualise a language is the issue of what we should attend to when deciphering meaning. Learners who are confronting inflected languages for the first time may not treat the final or inflected syllable of a word as salient in the way that has become second nature for native speakers of such languages. They may therefore operate with a more holistic concept of lexical form, and so fail to recognise the salience of the final morpheme itself. For example, Chinese learners of English have a first language that does not use grammatically marked final morphemes or *inflections*. French does have them but leaves some unpronounced. Speakers of these languages may therefore have less interest in the information placed at the end of an English word. A pedagogical approach is therefore simply to give *inflections* greater prominence. A possible way to do this is to adopt the CL premise that these morphemes are basically meaningful. Teachers can then show how the morpheme is not a schematic meaning added to a word but a word embedded in a schematic meaning. The root in fact makes the meaning of the inflection precise. For example, the determiners, 'some', 'a lot of', 'many', or 'several', occur either with uncountable nouns or plurals. If focusing on plurals, the teacher can present them not with a pluralised noun but with one or two of the common plural morphemes such as the voiced or unvoiced sibilant.

Activity 23    Teaching the plural morpheme
1  Illustrate the meanings of some plural English determiners that show quantity, for example: 'no', 'a few', 'several', 'a lot of'.
2  Write an 'I've got' construction on the board with one of your determiners and the plural morpheme, but do not provide a noun. 'I've got a few s'.
3  Students to say the clause without inserting a noun. Tell them they can only imagine the noun they are talking about. Small children or even adults may find this funny. To make it more so, get them to use gestures that seem to match the determiners, cupping the hands for 'some' or waggling the fingers for 'several', shaking the head and waving the finger for 'no'.
4  In pairs, Student B says the 'I've-got-some' construction by saying the appropriate determiner, making a gesture, saying the morpheme and imagining a noun. Student A simply repeats by inserting what they think is the imagined noun and its morpheme. Student B corrects.
5  Repeat on another day with nouns that take the voiced sibilant [-z] for '-es'.

Techniques where morphemes are made salient by being detached from their lexical stem can be used to practise almost any such form. CL does not recognise the traditional distinction between a grammatical and a lexical morpheme, as between the third person present -s, or -z in 'he does', for example, and the 'deverbing -er', 'a murderer'. Finally, this is because all morphemes, whether bound as in '-er' or free as in 'give', are treated as meaningful, and hence as simply operating on different points of the lexico-grammatical continuum. Grammar and lexis are thus part of a continuum of meaning, moving from the highly schematic to the more specific (Langacker 1990).

The lexico-grammatical continuum means that CL follows the generative analysis of a word such as 'singer' but for different reasons. In a more traditional analysis, the bound morpheme '-er' will be treated as the head of the word 'singer' because it determines its grammatical category. In CL the same conclusion is reached because the bound morpheme '-er' sets up a schema into which the more specific meaning 'sing' is inserted (Taylor 2002). Many students intuit the morpheme's symbolism when they make the mistake of interpreting '-er' as 'the person who performs the associated action', leading to such over-generalisation errors as 'you are a good cooker (cook)'. Students who make this over-generalisation are working with a reasonable assumption. In actuality the meaning of '-er' probably derived from an Anglo-Saxon root '-ere' that had this meaning, but in a typical process of grammaticalisation and concomitant schematisation it has now acquired a sense that is more generally agentive (Panther and Thornburg 2001).

By contrast the suffix, '-ee', as in 'employee', is generally construed as marking the patient of a process. The distinction becomes more difficult in intransitive processes, however, where one has an 'escapee' 'who escaped', and a 'sleeper' 'who slept', giving both an agentive complexion. In the case of 'sleeper' however, the action assumes that there is no other *participant* apart from the agent. A 'participant' in cognitive grammar refers to the other meanings that are assumed by the frame of a particular verb. Thus 'sell' assumes a 'seller', 'goods' and 'a buyer', even if these are not always stated. In the case of 'escapee', or 'retiree' there are other participants such as 'a prison' or 'work'. Thus in transitive sentences where there is no participant, the agentive morpheme will tend to be '-ee' rather than '-er' (Taylor 2002: 425).

The meaningfulness of these derivational morphemes should not be doubted, therefore, and can be found more straightforwardly in how some stems have a choice of morpheme. For example one can nominalise 'commit' with '-al', 'c-ion' or '-ment', and obtain different meanings:

- the process of completing the action – committal
- through a people-for-action metonymy this is the group that implements the action – commission
- having the quality needed to implement the action – commitment

The example of 'commit' and 'commission' shows how metonymic or metaphoric extensions are conventionalised as a prototypical meaning over time. Such processes can make the meaning of the derivational morpheme an unreliable guide to that of the word it helps create. Native speakers may assemble a root and a head to create a new word for a context only rarely, but this does not mean that one should not encourage non-natives to achieve greater lexical creativity and a broader vocabulary by experimenting with adding roots to final morphemes. An easy way to encourage this is through definition exercises where a defined word is gapped, and the root only given when it is rare or difficult to deduce.

Activity 24   Word building
1 Explain and illustrate the morpheme meaning, for example: '-ance' is undertaking or completing a process – thus 'avoidance' means the action of avoiding someone.
2 Construct an exercise where you provide students with the morpheme but not the word and they have to guess the word from the context and an attached definition. For example:

- Example: The _____ance of the play failed to satisfy us
- Definition: The doing of an action or operation

3 Ask students to try creating words using the morpheme, then to contextualise the created word in a sentence. The teacher should reject or accept their experiments.

I have attempted exercises that mix derivational morphemes and ask students to select the most appropriate one on the basis of meaning, but these create more confusion than they resolve, if only because the meanings of the morphemes are highly schematic and hence difficult to explain or grasp. They are more likely to bed down meanings through usage than explanation, and may anyway not be stored as independent meaningful items in the way that would be the case for elements such as '-ed' that are normally called 'grammatical'. However, some derivational morphemes such as the adjectival '-less' or the de-nouning '-ify' have quite accessible meanings and can be used to encourage creative classroom experimentation with word formation.

## Metonymy: attention and salience

We have discussed how metonymy is crucial to our perception of the world, allowing us to manipulate larger entities, interpreting a form by its function or a product by a producer. The construal operations *attention* and *salience* are crucial to metonymy. We call a car 'a nice set of wheels' because we make a *selection*, singling out 'wheels' as that vehicle's most salient aspect. We can do this because our culture has evolved conventions that treat one aspect of an entity as more important than another. Thus in the common alternative word 'hand' for 'crew man', the culture of use selects a hand as a person's essential attribute, for the person is recruited for manual work. In 'head' as in 'one hundred head of cattle' the criterion is the part of the animal that can be most easily counted.

A metonymy thus attends to one aspect of a category meaning rather than another, then represents the category meaning through this selected feature. Metonymy is thus built out of the conceptual operation of selection, a process that enters into the grammar. For example:

(36)  They played lots of Mozart (Langacker 1991: 189)

Sentence (36) treats Mozart as no longer a single countable person but as uncountable like the music that is being talk about. There is a product-for-producer metonymy (person for their music) where we attend to what they produce over and above who they are. This shift in attention and salience changes our grammatical interpretation of a word, causing us to debound Mozart or to treat him as a substance lacking linear definition, as opposed to a person with a bounded form (Croft and Cruse 2004: 50–1).

Gibbs (1994) and Lakoff (1987) point out how much descriptive language depends on metonymy by selecting a few essential elements in a scene to evoke the larger whole. When descriptions are over-detailed, they do not put enough trust in our ability to process metonymy. The description seems pedantic and tedious. We also use metonymy and metaphor together to select the key elements in a scene. Consider, for

118  *Cognitive Linguistics and Language Teaching*

example, this summary of the life of the failed scholar, Casaubon, by the English nineteenth-century novelist, George Eliot:

(37) With his taper stuck before him he forgot the absence of windows, and in bitter manuscript remarks on other men's notions about solar deities, he had become indifferent to the sunlight.

Finally, this whole extraordinary sentence is founded upon a series of metonyms of a scholar's failing daily routine. For example, 'taper stuck before him' evokes a larger picture of a man hunched over a candle in his study. At the time of writing in the mid nineteenth century 'a taper' was already an established function-for-form metonymy where it had come to mean, not the type of candle itself but the dimly burning light it emits. 'Windows' are here used creatively as a function-for-form metonymy, suggesting not a glass-covered aperture but the admission of daylight into a room. Because of 'the absence of windows', and hence daylight is forgotten, we learn that the passing of day and night have become irrelevant to the scholar's routine. 'Light' also has a metaphorical association with intelligence through the 'knowledge is sight' conceptual metaphor, giving such terms as 'bright' (or clever), 'lucid', meaning articulate, or 'illuminating' for thoughts that show us what we did not know. Without windows, light, and hence intelligence, or insight, is a concept from which this hopeless pedant is now cut off. We then have a metonymy where 'single items are used to evoke the larger set of items with which they have a schematic or mentally established association' (Lakoff and Turner 1989). Casaubon's scholarly effort is encapsulated by the 'bitter remarks' about others' notions of 'solar deities'. This metonymy carries the theme of light through the text. In trying to snuff out others' interests with his acerbic commentaries upon them, Casaubon reveals his indifference to all sunlight and hence to any knowledge able to illuminate his world. He thus creates his own darkness.

Many literature teachers will know how to help students access the larger themes encapsulated through such passages in a series of question and answer routines. For example, for sentence (37), above:

- A taper is a dimly burning light. If the 'taper' is 'stuck before him' what is it on? A window sill? A writing desk?
- Is it night or day? Do you know? Does it matter? Why doesn't it matter?

- Is he (Casaubon) appreciative of the work done by other scholars? What does 'solar' mean? Why does he focus on solar deities and not just deities?
- How is Casaubon's own dark mood changing his attitude to his topic?
- How is the idea of Casaubon becoming totally lost in his work, conveyed in this sentence?

Teachers can thus help students construct a larger subtext that embraces the greater themes of work around an aptly chosen sentence. Such exercises enhance vocabulary and help establish a greater measure of textual appreciation. In this example, the novel *Middlemarch* is very much about the unrealised ambitions and stultified dreams that are expressed by this sentence. The sentence can thus become a metonymy through which students can be helped to build and manipulate a larger knowledge frame of the book.

A simpler text such as that in Activity 25, below, provides a more straightforward series of metonyms from which lower-level students can start to build a descriptive discourse.

Activity 25    The room
1 Ask students to close their eyes and listen to the following text: She went into a room. There was some old furniture and a fire burning. A cat lay purring on the carpet.
2 Ask the class to listen again and note down all the nouns, starting with the most comprehensive category in the description, for example, 'the room'...
3 Working in pairs, students should describe what the first noun names and take notes. Thus for 'room' the students say how the room looked, what was in it, and where it was situated. They should detail the furniture and describe the kind of fire, whilst asking the teacher to supply unknown vocabulary.
4 Students should draft a longer description using their notes.

The text in Activity 25 shows how we use the metonymies to communicate a more elaborate and detailed scene than we have the time or inclination to describe. It also illustrates another process of construal where we narrow our *scope of attention* from one form to another, or from the room to its furniture, to a chair and to the cat. The activity has the merit of forcing students to build a larger vocabulary within the knowledge frames of the words that the text provides, itemising furniture for example.

## Scope of attention

Lakoff (1987) notes how we may zoom in and out of a scene. Thus when seeing a herd of cows we may simply see a herd or can zoom into an individual animal. Our language, by offering collective terms (herd) or pluralised but individuated entities (cows), reflects these differing modes of construal. Often we use the collective category (herd) to confine our *scope of attention* to its parts (cows). Thus when we say 'my house has two bedrooms', we use 'house' to narrow the scope to 'bedrooms', but also the determiner 'my' to narrow the scope of reference of 'house' making our reference to one such form and not to another. The possessive pronoun also creates what Langacker calls a 'reference point', in this case the speaker who owns the house, and a 'domain' projected out from them, locating the house (or any other noun) as theirs. When teachers use the type of question and answer routine just discussed, they can encourage students to construct descriptive passages that narrow their scope of attention, building vocabulary and its associated knowledge frames as they do so.

Scope of attention can be expressed by syntax and in English it posits an iconic order where our narrowing of the focus matches the order in which items are presented. Understanding scope of attention may therefore help students to construct sentences that are grammatically and lexically appropriate, reinforcing how we use determiners to ground nouns and narrow their scope of attention, then to modify them with relative clauses that elaborate upon the nature of this narrowed ground. They can then extend these sentences into a larger chain of discourse.

Activity 26   My what?
1 Teach a question and answer routine as follows:

- the teacher says 'my table has...' using countable nouns
- the student responds 'your table has what?'
- the teacher responds: 'my table has one leg'

2 Practise with other nouns.
After a few minutes practice, respond by asking: 'The book has four pages that...?' to elicit 'that what?', to get for example, 'that are difficult to understand'.

3 Stop here, or ask someone to repeat the entire sentence so far and extend with another relative pronoun in the same way as before: 'My book has four pages that are difficult to understand but which...'
4 Show how English does not generally sanction 'but which what?', but will use the relative pronoun as an interrogative, 'But which?', to get, for example, 'The book has four pages that are almost impossible to understand but which you can forget about'.

Such routines can form useful fillers in a lesson and can be used to recycle vocabulary in a way that respects the student's knowledge frames. They can be used to expand our lexical grip on such items as:

- a house and rooms:
  The house had a large sitting room and three medium-sized bedrooms.
- a car and its parts:
  The car had a flat tyre and a broken steering wheel.
- a book and its contents:
  The book has four chapters that describe Napoleon's advance on Moscow and only one that describes the retreat.

These sentences can also be used to practise the use of an adjectival phrase to narrow the scope of the noun to which it refers:

- Sandman and Groves had five departments, and *the largest* was the Sales Division on the first floor.

Some passages of academic discourse are also organised around this contracting scope of attention. Consider example (38):

(38) There was the birth of a new kind of politics, the politics of the pressure group. Thanks to the work of zealous activists armed only with pens, paper and moral indignation, Britain turned against slavery. Even more remarkably, the slave trade had been abolished in the face of determined opposition from powerful vested interests. The West Indian planters had once been influential enough to intimidate Edmund Burke and hire James Boswell. The Liverpool slave traders were not much less formidable. But they were simply swept away by the evangelical tide. (Ferguson 2004: 118)

122  *Cognitive Linguistics and Language Teaching*

The passage is describing the abolition of the slave trade in the British Empire of the early nineteenth century. It begins by giving us an overview of a new form of politics, that of the pressure group. The focus thus moves from a broad categorisation, 'new form of politics', to a slightly narrower one, 'the pressure group'. It then starts to look at what the pressure group was in this context, 'the zealous activists armed only with pens'. The focus is then narrowed still further onto the pressure group with a summary of its activities and the opposition that these aroused. There is a struggle with vested interests and the scope is narrowed again when these interests are described.

A diagrammatic representation of these types of discourse can help students grasp their structure. This technique is now quite common in EAP and produces instructional metaphors such as the 'hour glass' model of the paragraph where the structure is compressed from a general, or topic statement towards a more detailed elaboration then expanded again into a concluding generalisation. Figure 7 uses this technique to show a narrowing scope of attention, ignoring the expansion. Students of academic writing can arrange a text such as that given in the example into the shape shown, thus identifying how it narrows its scope. They can then reconstruct their own examples in similar, but blank, diagrams. Composing in the box is a powerful metaphor which

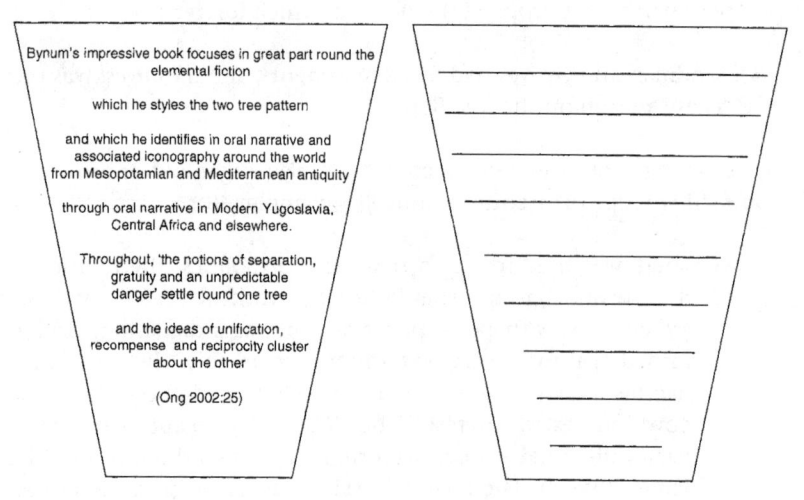

*Figure 7* Scope of attention in discourse: using diagrams to master discourse structure

can encourage the student to narrow their own discoursal focus and find constructions like the expression 'epitomised by' to express the reducing scope.

## Scalar adjustment

*Scalar adjustment* describes another method through which we change what we attend to in a scene. Talmy (1983: 238) explains this in the difference between sentences (39) and (40) (Croft and Cruse 2005: 52):

(39) He ran across the field
(40) She ran through the field

Sentence (39) perceives 'the field' in its entirety, whilst sentence (40) sees it as an entity that the subject is working through, yard by yard, and which can therefore impede progress. These differences imply a larger difference in how the scene is construed, with (39) offering a bird's-eye view and (40) an action more in close-up. Understanding how abstract relations derive from spatial ones can help students see the use of English prepositions as being more principled than may at first seem the case. The process of scalar adjustment can be used to make this clearer. Consider sentences (41) and (42), below:

(41) They walked through many towns and villages
(42) They worked through the problem in detail
(43) They went through the text line by line
(44) They thought through every possibility
(45) The bird flew over the field
(46) They skipped over the text
(47) They went over the plan in detail
(48) They thought over their future

Sentences (41) and (45) encode a scalar adjustment through a literal expression of space. Sentence (41) closes up on the scene suggesting that the 'towns and villages' mark, or even impede, the subject's unfolding progress. Sentence (45) perceives its trajectory as a complete entity. Space becomes our movement's enduring consequence. In examples (46–48), this concept of achieved movement is transferred into an abstract domain. The work, whether detailed or not, is framed as complete. In sentences (42–44) we retain a sense of an unfolding progression through that work, and of the work as something of an impediment to progress. This is why the expressions with 'over' retain the sense of a 'review', as of something already observed in its entirety, whilst expressions with 'through' tend to capture the sense of an effort subject to implementation.

Learners can be encouraged to give these distinctions a gestural representation to help establish the physical imagery from which they have evolved.

Activity 27    Through and over
1  Remind students of the prepositions 'over' and 'through'. Get them to say 'over' whilst extending the arm and arching it up and *over*, and 'through,' with the hand pushing effortfully forward, or the finger prodding its way through an imaginary obstruction. In this way use the expression and the gesture to reinforce each other:

'over' (rising intonation on the first syllable, fall on the second, extension of the first syllable o͡__ver)
'through' (effortful as if pushing against an obstacle).

2  Tell the students that they are going on a long journey on foot. In groups tell them to brainstorm for what they will go 'through' – for example, towns, villages, streets, gardens, fields, orchards, deserts, forests, etc.; and what they will go over – for example, mountains, hills, rivers, walls, fields.
3  Each recounts their journey using the two prepositions. If they say something that has a difficult meaning, point this out. For example:

'We went through a river'
So you got wet?

4  If they use a verb that can allow either preposition with a different construal but no radical change in meaning, for example, 'think through a problem' versus 'think over a problem', show them figure 8 below and explain how each preposition construes 'the field' differently. If possible get them to move effortfully 'through' space and more rapidly 'across' it.
5  In groups ask students to complete this cloze test where the missing items are paraphrased. Some of these can be done with both types of construal, though the added text in brackets tends to steer towards one more than another.

## Conceptualisation and Construal 125

- They walked _____ many towns and villages
- They worked _____ the problem in detail (looked at it closely and effortfully to solve it)
- They walked _____ to his house (his house was on the other side of the street)
- They skipped _____ the text (they did not really read it)
- They went _____ the plan in detail (they reviewed the plan completely then discussed something else)
- They went _____ the plan in detail (and they stopped at each point to discuss it)
- They went _____ the text line by line (and they thought about every word)

The cloze teaches how certain expressions evolve from certain ways of representing space, and so tries to bed down the modes of construal on which these expressions are based.

## Dynamic attention

Dynamic attention derives from how the movement of an object in a scene makes it salient. In language, we may construct imagery from this

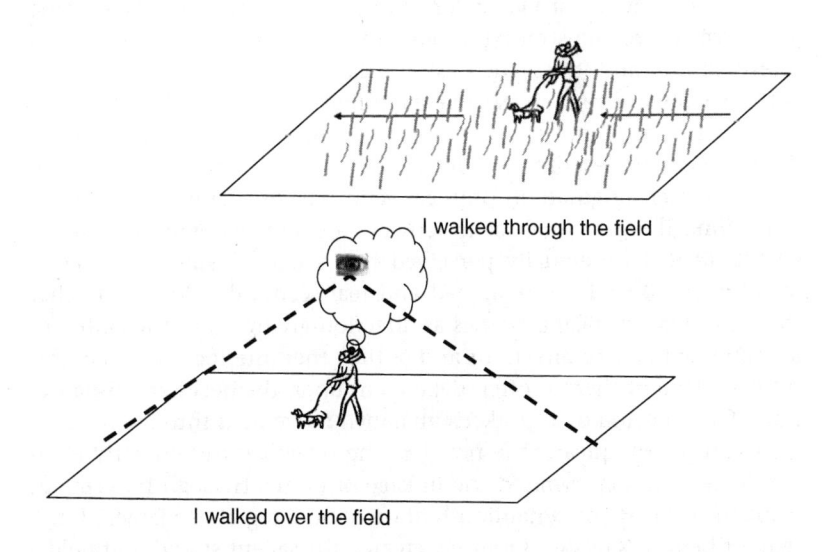

I walked through the field

I walked over the field

*Figure 8* Scalar adjustment: different construals with 'through' and 'over'

process by perceiving the static as mobile in order to draw together the attributes of scene. For example, we say that 'the road climbed the pass'. Dynamic attention is a common property of descriptive discourse, perceiving one feature as if in movement so that it stitches together the other mentioned items in the scene. Consider the following passage from Joseph Conrad:

> Neither did the telegraph line cross the mountains yet; its poles, like slender beacons on the plain, penetrated into the forest fringe of the foothills cut by the deep avenue of the track; and its wire ended abruptly in the construction camp at a white deal table, supporting a Morse apparatus, in a long hut of planks with a corrugated-iron roof overshadowed by gigantic cedar trees – the quarters of the engineer in charge of the advance section (Conrad 1994; first published 1904).

The passage uses the device of a telegraph line to link together various aspects of a scene, carrying the reader's eye from out of the larger landscape and narrowing the scope of attention onto a hut with the detail of a corrugated-iron roof over shadowed by trees. Students can be asked to construct such paragraphs prior to seeing them, from a series of visual or verbal features. These cues are themselves metonyms from which we construct our picture of a larger landscape. For example, one can provide a class with cards illustrating 'mountains', 'a plain', 'a track through a forest', 'a hut' and 'trees' then ask the class to connect them together with a single feature such as a telegraph line.

Teachers who doubt the technique's usefulness in encouraging the development of descriptive language should remember how imagination may itself originate in physical action, or in a 'simulation' of the same. 'Imagining a visual scene activates areas of the brain that would be activated if we actually perceived that scene (Kosslyn 1994, cited in Johnson 2007: 162). Imagined and real scenes develop each other through such practical activities as direction-giving. Thus the ability of a respondent to give directions and of the other interlocutor to successfully implement them is often dependent upon the necessary visualisation of a scene and of a speaker's imagined movement through it.

In Europe, the picaresque novel of the seventeenth and early eighteenth centuries epitomised the linkage of events through movement, using the property of dynamic attention to hold together a larger plot. A hero or heroine's physical journey created the salient strand that held a series of often improbable and sometimes thematically unrelated events together. Chain stories, where one student starts a story and another must continue it can be given a picaresque feel when focused on a journey. The journey stops the tale from drying up, since with new places come new events.

The linguistic manipulation of imagined landscapes may also furnish a basis for the organisation of more abstract types of meaning and their associated discourses. Arguably, we interlink arguments and develop ideas through a similar device, watching them as if they unfold a trajectory in space. The following activity should be used with the work on motion paths that was discussed in the last chapter. Just as the dynamic attention given to one element in a landscape can hold its disparate features together, so that given to the evolution of an idea will be an organisational principle in discourse, allowing other concepts to gather around like settlements about a new road.

Activity 28    The open road
1 Review verbs that can describe directional movement, 'run', 'pass', 'turn', 'bend', 'rise', 'descend' etc. Ask the class to imagine a road running through a landscape. Tell them how we can treat the road as an object that is itself moving with the following example:

'The road runs down bank turns to the left then passes over a narrow bridge'

2 In groups of four, one student starts to unfold the scene that they have imagined then another tries to continue by extending it with their own picture, trying to merge the different landscapes in a way that avoids repetition whilst continuing to expand a collective picture. For example, student 1 says: 'the road passes by a housing estate', and student 2 continues 'it turns in front of a supermarket then continues to the rail station'.
3 One person in the group presents an edited description that uses the movement given to the road to hold all the landscapes in the group together.
4 In groups, each student thinks of one practical idea that would help save the world. They discuss their various ideas, then edit them together to make one overarching strategy.
5 When they have the final idea, ask them to reflect on how this was developed. Still in groups, they write a short paragraph discussing the emergence of the concept they have put forward. They should

first state what it is, then discuss how it evolved. They could use expressions such as the following:

- The idea began as ...
- It was developed by (the suggestion that)
- It evolved into ... when
- It was extended to include ...
- Finally it reached the current form when ...

6  Each group should explain their idea.

The above exercise shows how we pay attention to objects, or, by extension, themes and ideas, because we make them salient by conceptualising them as if in motion. The larger issue of salience is one of the most central in CL and its pedagogical implications may be explored less directly in other activities under other headings. Finally, salience allows us to manipulate the multiple concepts that we assemble into categories, by making one of them more prominent than others, hence furnishing us with a type of cognitive handle.

Most fundamentally, the process of *scalar adjustment* shapes the grammar by differentiating the way verbs and nouns may grasp an event. Thus the verb 'fell' in sentence (49) suggests *sequential scanning* because it conveys a dynamic scene that unfolded episodically before the observer's eyes. The noun 'fall' in example (50) captures the event as if from high above, perceiving the boundaries of its end and beginning.

(49)  The king fell from power
(50)  The fall of the King from power
(51)  The fall of the King from power plunged the country into chaos

The perception of an event as bounded and complete therefore allows us to see it as a phenomenon that can itself initiate other actions, as in sentence (51). Our ability to perceive phenomena as dynamic, and others as static thus enters into the grammar as one of its most fundamental differences.

Often we use this distinction to construct discourse, scanning a process as a verb then bounding it as a complete entity that can impact another, as in: 'The Black Death reduced the population of Europe quite substantially. The reduction in population had some profound socio-economic consequences'. Teachers can help learners to build cause and effect chains around this property. Thus, the teacher prompts or the student uses their knowledge to suggest:

> 'A labour shortage meant the peasants began to move from one manor to another.'

And another student suggests a consequence:

> 'This mobility meant they no longer considered themselves owned by an estate'.

Teachers who want simpler, or less academic, examples can exemplify this chain through journey sequences. For example:

> 'We flew to Paris. The flight exhausted us and we over-slept. Our oversleeping meant we missed the plane'.

Such journey narratives can bed down schemas derived from connections in physical space so that they may later be used to develop more abstract and elaborate cause and effect chains.

## Judgment and comparison

*Judgment and comparison* involves three core modes of construal that have already been considered briefly: categorisation, metaphor, and, figure–ground relationships. I will now consider the nature and pedagogical implications of these in greater detail.

## Category formation

Different languages do not operate with exactly the same categories. This fact forms a key challenge for the learner both within grammatical and lexical meaning. As a form of conceptualisation, therefore, category formation is crucial to how different languages can register a cultural effect in the way that they represent meaning.

The psychologist, Eleanor Rosch (1975 and 1978) argued that categories were organised round 'a best example', or prototypical member. Thus, in American culture, the robin had far more of the quality of 'birdness' and was taken as a prototype of 'bird' whilst the 'penguin' was held to be an outlying category member. A difficulty with Rosch's theory is that it still did not account for the types of meaning that seem to stretch categories to breaking point. Also, she did not really tackle the question of how we form categories out of abstract entities when there is no observable prototype. Lakoff (1987) proposed a more elaborate radial category model which retained the idea of a set of meanings organised around a best example but postulated different types of relationship between this prototype and the other category members. Like Rosch, he also emphasised that the category boundaries were fuzzy, with one meaning merging into another. Thus category members could be metaphorically or metonymically extended from the central member, even until they became members of other categories. Because one member could be a metaphorical extension of one that was not necessarily a prototype, this meant that the category could include members which bore almost no apparent relationship to each other, as in the famous example from an Australian aboriginal language that gives the title of Lakoff's book, 'women, fire and dangerous things'.

For Lakoff (1987) the prototype was the only category member to which all others related in some way. The prototype could respond to a folk definition of the category through a sharing of features with other category members, thus insisting that all books had 'covers' and 'pages', for example. Yet, a prototype could also be a 'typical example' of the entity in question, positing that others were in some sense like it. Other prototypes could be constructed out of a positive social belief about what the category should be. For example, a mother might be less a biological category and more one that conformed to a social consensus about it being a woman who looked after children. It could also be antonymic to some consensus, like the category of 'criminal'.

## Category formation and language teaching

One way to help language learners explore categories is to produce texts that focus less on immediate communicative need and more upon the linkage of a given set of lexical items to a category. Such texts will be familiar to those who have used topic-based methods and materials. For example, consider the English concept of 'a building'. This concept embraces various structures that are used for various purposes. As types of building, these structures are *hyponyms* of the larger category, with a hyponym being the relationship between two words where the meaning of one is contained in the other. Thus zebras, horses and tigers are hyponyms of a 'mammal' category which is in turn a hyponym of 'animal'. Teachers can use hyponym charts to explore category relationships and ask students to engage with a text structured by hyponymy.

*Conceptualisation and Construal* 131

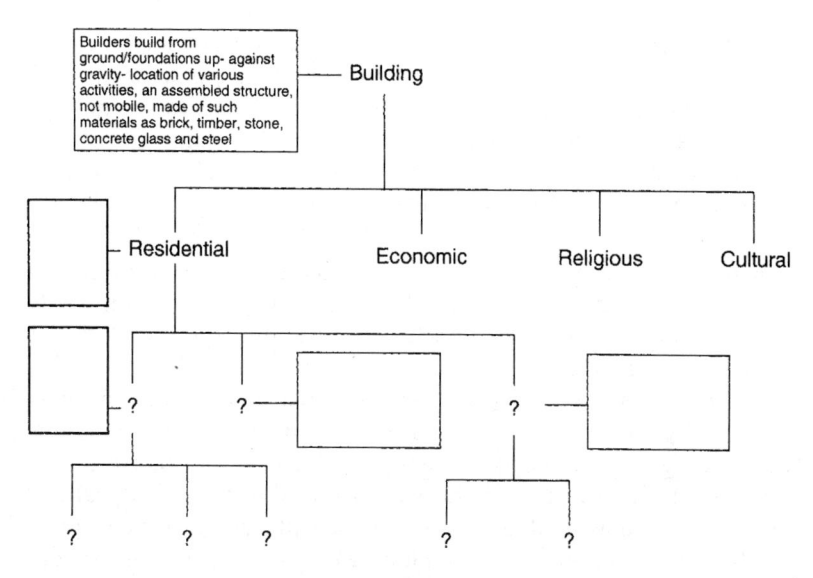

*Figure 9* The building: using hyponym charts to explore categories

Activity 29     Category building
1 Prepare a text such as that shown in the example text below, by trying to identify what is central to the described category structure, then mapping this onto a partially completed diagram such as that shown in figure 9. Include an example of a knowledge frame such as the one shown.
2 In groups of three or four, students read the text and complete the hyponym chart.
3 In their groups, students complete knowledge frames for some of the sub-categories given.

A building is a man-made structure. It can give people a home or be the location for cultural, religious or manufacturing activities. Buildings are made from various materials such as brick, timber, and stone, concrete, glass and steel. There are different kinds of residential buildings, for example, houses, cottages or blocks of flats. To the English, a cottage often suggests something rural, old and comfortable. The English picture of a house will change according to its situation. The phrase a 'country house' suggests quite a large expensive building with its own garden. A semi-detached house is something smaller that is attached to another house and is quite a modern structure. Terrace houses are rows of houses joined together and are common in English cities. A block of flats, or an apartment block, is also generally found in a city. Blocks of flats can be in huge high-rise buildings with lifts and dozens or even hundreds of flats inside them. Some buildings with flats can be smaller and may be created by dividing larger and older houses.

Such activities can be more than the rather arid type of information transfer and reading comprehension activity that they are traditionally used to stimulate. First, the attachment of knowledge frames makes them into an exercise in cultural exploration. The building category reveals the extensive knowledge networks that basic terms can incorporate. When students explore these frames further, dividing 'building' into a religious subcategory, of 'temples, churches and mosques', for example, the complexity of the word's meaning and of its cultural associations and associated contexts of use will start to become apparent. In a case used in a Chinese Hong Kong school, the concept of a mosque was almost unknown to a group, and their exploration developed a larger understanding of Islamic culture. Hyponym charts can also guide the reproduction of discourse structures that are built around hyponym relationships. Such charts and their associated texts can also keep pace with students' learning, rising into rarer and more abstract superordinate categories such as 'structure' for 'building', or descending into other more esoteric subcategories (hutch, hut, or shack, for example).

Such central categories as 'time', 'space', 'life' and 'death' are also a rich vein to mine, particularly by teachers interested in linguistic and cultural differences.

Activity 30    Seeing time
1 Ask the class to close their eyes and try to see 'time'.
2 Present students with a series of sentences that seem to represent time in different ways. For example:

- He used up all his time
- They arrived on time
- They were running out of time
- They got there just in time
- He wasted his time
- We must find some more time
- We are getting through the time
- It's time to leave

- Who knows where the time goes?
- What's the time please?
- We still have a long time

3 In groups of four to six, learners draw a diagram or picture representing each of the above ways of talking about time. Show them what you mean, by taking one sentence and illustrating it. For example, 'time' in the first example could be a 'heap' of coal that someone is shovelling into a furnace. They can divide the task any way they like and discuss it with each other.
4 The class decide which diagram/picture most corresponds to their representation of time. They put it in the centre of their table. They arrange the other drawings around it, near or far according to how far it corresponds to their idea of time, thus creating a category diagram of the meaning of time.
5 The groups use their arranged diagrams to explain their different ideas of time.

Holme (2004) described how one can help students grasp the radial nature of category meanings by researching how supermarkets may arrange products differently in different countries. Old-style department stores also form an intriguing glimpse into how we arrange categories. Most interesting is the rationale behind the store's spatial arrangement. Why, for example, are hardware and cooking implements often found in the basement, and toys near the top floor? The reason could be a combination of practical logic and cognitive processing. First, food needs to be kept near to street level to facilitate the delivery and disposal of a perishable product. Second, food and cooking implements are semantically contiguous. Finally, all of these reasons may be inappropriate. The problem could turn around 'weight'. Certain types of hardware, for example washing machines, may be better kept at ground level because of handling costs. Categories can be extended by metaphor and this may also play a part in planning the store. Toys are 'light', for example, in the sense of being unserious, whilst washing machines and tools have a functionality that makes them into a form of social ballast. Toys or electronics might also express a concept of reward, as if for a completed ascent. Students can conduct research projects where they locate the spatial arrangements of products and the types of items that a given category includes. Such projects lead to an exploration of lexical meaning through a study of some of the metaphorical entailments of store organisation, seeing 'light' as less serious for example. Such research can also be largely imaginative and computer- or classroom-based.

The department store may be an endangered relic of the consumer culture. It is rapidly being replaced by malls, specialist warehouses, and on-line purchasing. These newer ways of selling goods also offer different insights into category formation, and can be used as the basis of activities that are similar to the one above. Finally, though, department stores are not just monuments to fading forms of consumerism, but larger metaphors of the category-forming mind, and hence invitations to a virtual promenade through one of the core human conceptual operations.

## Metaphor

Quite simply, different metaphors posit different modes of construal. For example, sentences (52) and (53) show how time is construed differently as ground to be covered and as a moving object:

(52) They lived in a far-off time
(53) Time passed quickly

Metaphor is also bound up in several other construal operations such as categorisation or dynamic attention. As one of the most studied of construal operations, it is unsurprising that metaphor was one of the aspects of CL that was quickest to attract the interest of applied linguists and language teachers.

## Metaphor and language teaching

The applied interest in metaphor has broadly divided into four overlapping areas:

> *metaphor analysis* (Low 1999): the occurrence of metaphor in spoken and written discourse is analysed to show the systematic nature of the speaker's or writer's attitudes towards their topic and the cultural values that these display;
> the differentiation of first language and target language content;
> to create analogues that help explore and explain target language content;
> to foster the cognitive organisation, retention and correct production of second language grammar and lexis.

I will now consider each of these in turn.

## Metaphor analysis

Broadly, metaphor analysis is looking at how people construe a given topic. It exposes both their conscious and their reflexive construal of that topic. It can also provide insights into the affective, or emotional attitude that shapes their treatment of a subject, the cultural values by which these stances are nurtured, and the cultural attitude that they have helped develop (see for example, Cameron and Stelma 2004; Cameron and Deignan 2006). The dynamic nature of metaphor is implicit in how it construes its subject from the interaction of two or more sets of meanings. Thus if we take the metaphor 'if music be the food of love', the meaning will be constructed from how we engage 'music', 'food' and 'love', each with the other. In its turn this dynamic will reflect the larger negotiation of meanings that occur in any act of conversation or reader–writer engagement. Thus how 'food' and 'love' do or do not extract meanings from 'music' will depend on how the listener who engages with the metaphor will themselves construe these topics and the nature of the cultural resources that are employed.

Applied linguists have used metaphor analysis to look at how teachers and learners conceptualise their task or arrange their broader approach (see for example, Block 1997; Cortazzi and Jin 1999; Oxford *et al.* 1998; De Guerrero and Villamil 2002). Block (1992) explored how teachers and learners used different metaphors to construe the language learning task, implying that the teachers' approach may not be fully grasped by the students. Oxford *et al.* looked exclusively at the metaphors through which learners talked to their teachers. They found four conceptual metaphors that they expressed as 'the teacher as doctor', 'the teacher as a conduit (for information)', 'the teacher as a learning partner', and 'the teacher as nurturer'. These metaphors were analysed for their expression of broader social attitudes. For example, 'the teacher as nurturer' was identified with a broader understanding of the organic nature of learning and its association with a larger process of social growth.

Looking at a much larger sample than in these other studies, Cortazzi and Jin (1999) used metaphors to explore the different ways in which English and Chinese teachers conceptualised learning. Most interestingly, they used metaphors to explore how teacher trainees' attitudes can change during training and start to converge with the aims of the course, or the attitudes held by their trainers.

## Metaphor and target language differentiation

One of the earliest and most significant contributions in the area of using metaphor to specify language was Low's (1988) notion of 'a metaphorical competence' (Littlemore and Low 2006). This basically specified what students needed to know if they were to use the figurative portion of language more successfully. Low broke down 'metaphoric competence' into such features as being able to 'construct plausible meanings' with metaphor, or to differentiate between new metaphors and conventionalised or dead ones. However, from a CL perspective the use of the term 'competence' and the associated approach is problematic. First, a linguistic competence, of whatever kind, presupposes the storage of language in a different form from that in which it is produced. CL contends that linguistic knowledge is built by usage and that the forms retained reflect the way that forms are used. Second, the concept of one competence as opposed to another presupposes a strong demarcation between figurative and conventionalised language knowledge. Certainly the concept of conventionalisation is indicative of such a divide; but the CL contention is that even the interpretation of new or live metaphors is constructed from the schematic knowledge and semantic frames that underpin conventionalised use. The metaphoric competence model may be helpful for how it identifies the types of problem that metaphors pose to learners, however. In this respect it predicts metaphor-based activities that help students grasp the differences between their target language and their L1. Understanding such differences can help students towards a greater knowledge and hence control of the target language meanings themselves.

## The explanatory power of metaphor and analogy

There is a body of research that shows how metaphor and analogy can positively or negatively influence a language learner's grasp of concepts. In putting over new meanings, teachers must phrase them in the language that students already possess, and help the students relate new conceptual knowledge to that which the students already possess. An appropriate analogue can recast relationships and situations that are obscure in those that are better known. Essentially, teachers use analogy so that students can construe new knowledge through familiar circumstances and narratives.

Analogy and metaphor are difficult to differentiate, and probably overlap in many areas. When discussing Tomasello's (2003) views of second language acquisition, we noted his view of how infants generalised forms on the basis of analogy, perceiving the roles of agent and patient in one sentence to be analogous to those of another. Accordingly we found the core of a successful analogy to lie in a relational similarity between items rather than in a superficial similarity of features. This argument gives analogy a strongly relational complexion. Holyoak et al. (1994) looked at analogy from a perspective of both relational and featural similarity, however, arguing that the quality of the learning outcome can be affected both by strength of the similarity between features or relations of the analogy. Finding strong and apt analogies can be essential to a good outcome in learning, therefore, just as suspect analogues can lead to future conceptual distortion (Gentner and Gentner 1983). Two protagonists can also trade analogies like proverbial blows, claiming the one that proves their case to be more apt than the opposite.

The centrality of analogy formation to a successful educational experience should not be in doubt. Brown et al. (1986) showed that the successful learning of abstract concepts in both science and mathematics is often dependent upon successful analogy formation. Brown et al. (1989) found that the importance of analogy to young children's communicative ability was determined by the types of mental models that children had of a given problem. Goswami (2001) related the educational need for analogy to the fundamental processes of how we reason about reality that Chen et al. (1997) took back to earliest stages of learning, or even to infancy.

The way in which classroom analogies can positively affect learning has also been studied. Thus, Novick and Holyoak, (1991) argued that the ability to use analogy can, when encouraged, be transferred from one type of subject to another, hence promoting more successful learning across the curriculum. Although, the search for suitable analogues should perhaps be given greater emphasis in teacher training, Richland et al. (2004) have shown that the use of analogues is already common in US pedagogy and that they are most often formulated as a response to problems with conceptual understanding.

The use of analogues in language classes is probably also common. For example, teachers and text books make use of time-lines to illustrate tense structure. The situational approach also depends upon the capacity of the student to deal in analogy. The approach may now be regarded as 'dated' but is in fact the basis of many communicative approaches to teaching form. In the older method, a situation was selected to show how a structure was used. Thus in a situation, people tell the police what they were doing when the bomb went off, to show how a tense, the past continuous, can express interrupted time. In a communicative method, the situation may be disguised as a communicative function. For example, the past continuous is an 'expression of failed intentions' in such sentences as 'I was hoping to see you but you were out'. No matter how the situation is disguised, learners must use a sense of analogy to make these situational approaches work for them.

To avoid the sense that the meaning of a structure is wedded to a given context, students must search for an analogous context where the structure can be used. A central point to be developed in the next chapter is CL's proposal that we deal in complex categories of grammatical and lexical meaning. We therefore need to learn these meanings through usage in multiple contexts. To be successful we have to appreciate when those contexts are and are not analogous. Thus seeing the relationship between the exploding bomb and some scenario of a failed intention can be crucial to developing a strong sense of category-meaning for the past continuous.

Holme (2004) also explored how an analysis of a grammatical form can itself furnish visual analogies or metaphors through which students can be helped to grasp the meanings of such grammatical items as continuous aspect. Thus figure 10 stresses the meaningful nature of the '-ing' morpheme, illustrating this as a trapped and recurring action whose dimensions are defined by the space that the speaker occupies. The morpheme is detached from the verb to expose how it carries meaning, and bounds the verb meaning as a recurring action rooted in real-world events. The appropriate form of 'be' is treated as situating the subject inside the action. Such figures can form the basis of wall-charts that are used to collect a growing number of instantiations of these types of structure upon the classroom walls, furnishing learners with constant visual reinforcement. Such charts can be instantiated in E&M routines where learners perform actions that are analogous to the language they use. For example, they move and speak sentences such as: 'I am walking round the class' or 'running in the playground'.

## Using metaphor to learn second language lexis and grammar

In the previous section a metaphor was treated as explanatory on account of how it can be developed into an analogy. By implication, language was treated as possessing a principled subject content that

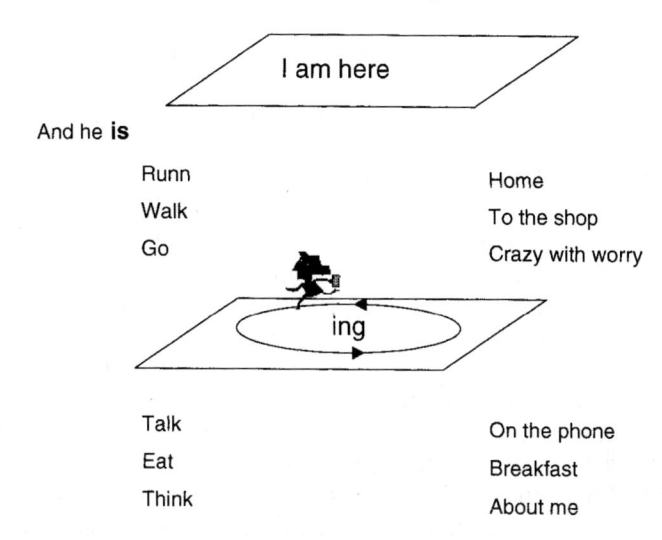

```
                    ┌─────────────────┐
                   /   I am here     /
                  └─────────────────┘
    And he is
              Runn                    Home
              Walk                    To the shop
              Go                      Crazy with worry
                         ( ing )
              
              Talk                    On the phone
              Eat                     Breakfast
              Think                   About me
```

*Figure 10* Visual analogues of the language content of English: continuous aspect

required explanation. In this section, metaphor is also seen as a way to elucidate meaning, but those metaphors are themselves responsible for the meanings that are studied. Thus, if grammatical relations and their abstract lexis are produced out of conceptual metaphors, then a given conceptual metaphor can link lexis and learning together whilst also furnishing key organisational principles in discourse.

For example, approaches to teaching languages for specific purposes often found it difficult to identify more than a few obvious and quite general elements that were specific to a scientific register. In a response to this problem, Henderson (1986) suggested that if one made students more aware of how metaphors helped build theories, or shape different theoretical perspectives, one could help them develop a more critical and analytical perspective. Lindstromberg (1991) and Dudley-Evans and St John (1998) also both asked whether one could find discipline- or register-specific conceptual metaphors to help students group the sub-technical lexis that might be useful to a particular discipline.

In another ESP study, Boers (2000) helped students to explore how metaphors might shape an author's attitude towards a particular topic in economic texts. One text concerned state subsidies to private companies, and what the authors thought of the merits of these. In an experimental group, two expressions, 'bailing out' and 'weaning off' were explored through their literal meanings. This exploration of literal meanings allowed the teacher to stress how 'bailing' was a temporary and somewhat desperate measure intended to stop a vessel sinking. In the same way one can construe 'wean' as resulting in an enduring detachment of an infant from its dependence on a mother's food and hence as a positive achievement. Such terms have acquired particular prominence in the discourses of 2008–9. It is thus of particular interest that not only did the experimental group show a significant difference in the ability to retain and use the terms over the control group but that their critical understanding of the text was also enhanced. The students of the experimental group were thus more aware of whether the author was for or against subsidies than the students of the control group.

Metaphor has also been found to help with general vocabulary retention. Boers (2004) found that grouping new vocabulary around the conceptual metaphors from which it had been derived would also help students improve their uptake of the same. A central strategy to take forward is that of teaching metaphorical expressions by exploring their literal roots.

Activity 31   Keeping it together
1 When introducing new abstract lexis or an idiomatic phrase, identify a conceptual metaphor in which the forms could be said to originate.
2 After identifying an appropriate metaphor, place it in the middle of the board and brainstorm for forms that derive from it, giving input of your own to help the process along. As you produce new forms write them on the board around the conceptual metaphor, thus producing a type of mind map. Either in speech, writing, or both, students try to come up with sentences that use the brainstormed forms.
3 Extend or try to elicit the mind map at a later date. If possible, keep such maps on your classroom walls and renew or extend them constantly.

Teachers using the above activity must make a judgment call as to which conceptual metaphor is both experientially consistent with the items being taught and maximally productive. For example, EAP students might come across sentence (54), below:

(54)   The roots of the concept lie in Darwinian evolution

They or the teacher could identify 'origins are roots' as the conceptualisation here. However, this would miss how example (54) relates to an expression such as 'a new type of discourse grew out of the popularisation of scientific method', where the reference is more to seeding or germination. Arguably, a more powerful metaphor through which to examine example (54) would be 'ideas are plants' (Lakoff and Johnson 1980). Another possibility might be, 'beginnings are beneath' which would incorporate the phrase 'lie in'. Others might argue that this conceptual metaphor is over-general since it misses the idea of germination and growth implicit in 'roots'. Finally, a problem with working with conceptual metaphors is that these point to overlapping conceptualisations and their associated imagery rather than to meanings pegged down by their linguistic formulation. When put into words, such imagery is like a long-buried and very ancient object that disintegrates when it is brought up to the light.

Metaphor as an organisational role in discourse was exploited by Holme (2004) and Holme and King (2000). In a series of classroom interventions they used conceptual metaphors to help students develop cohesion in types of paragraph writing that were useful for students of English for Academic Purposes. Thus the conceptual metaphors, 'knowledge is sight', and 'writing is thinking' were used to underpin the meta-textual part of the introduction to a student essay. Accordingly, student writers told the reader about what they would 'survey', 'look at in detail', 'elucidate', 'view from different perspectives', then 'come to see', or examine 'from a different point of view'.

Text (55) shows how conceptual metaphors can organise descriptive prose. In this paragraph from Melvyn Bragg' *The Soldier's Return*, the author reflects on his hero's social origins:

(55) When he was a boy...he had been aware, made aware, that he and his kind were the bottom of the heap. As a soldier he had served in the East, India as well as Burma, and seen untouchables and mutilated child beggars, and now he knew how deep the heap was; but as a boy in Wigton he was the lowest which was why Grace had been so resentful of his courtship of Ellen. (Bragg 2001: 101–102)

The text is built around the schema of vertical orientation and the 'down is less' conceptual metaphor. This is exploited by a less productive but common English metaphor 'society is a heap'. Teachers can exploit these metaphors of spatial orientation by asking students to rewrite the passage using an antonymous metaphorical structure. Thus using 'up is more' instead of 'down is less', one obtains something like example (56). This also helps build knowledge frames for words, with 'heap' having something of a derogatory sense as a social metaphor. This is because 'heap' construes its meaning from the perspective of what is beneath. 'Pile' by contrast looks at such meanings from the perspective of what is on top. In this case the exercise invites thought about how social hierarchies are culturally constructed and employ different modes of construal.

> (56) When he was a boy ... he had been aware, made aware, that he and his kind were at the top of the social ladder. As a soldier he had served in the East, India as well as Burma, and seen Princes and Maharajahs, and now he knew how high the ladder went; but as a boy in Wigton he was at the top which was why Grace had been so eager to encourage his courtship of Ellen. (adapting Bragg 2001: 101–2)

The exercise with metaphorical antonymy can invite an exploration of the knowledge frames that support the meanings of certain words. For example, 'heap' must change to '(social) ladder' because of it connotes something held together by gravity that will bury or weigh down those who linger beside it. 'Ladder', on the other hand, is an instrument of upward mobility and is thus a means of access to a new perspective or higher position. Using conceptual metaphor to unravel the discourse structures of such texts can therefore help students to engage more critically with them. For example, students can consider the language in which social hierarchies and social mobility is expressed in their own culture then contrast this with that illustrated by texts (55) and (56).

## Figure–ground conceptual operations, force dynamics and action chains

We have already noted how figure–ground is central to our conceptual system because it allows us to foreground one object in a scene, a figure, and make it a focus of attention Talmy (1978). Without this ability, we would live in conceptual anarchy where all the attributes of a scene vie for our attention. Langacker (1991) argues that this mode of conceptualisation enters the grammar in several fundamental ways, affording some quite different modes of construal. A sentence such as

(57) below typifies how movement makes an item into a figure. Langacker thus gives the name *trajector* to the most prominent item in the sentence, in this case 'the bicycle', and *landmark* to the ground, in this case 'the house'. Trajector–landmark relationships are construed by the basic force dynamics of one object striking another, or in a typical transitive sentence. Langacker (1987) expresses this in what he calls an *action chain*.

Broadly there are four kinds of action chain, and each can construe an event in a different way. Of the three illustrated in figure 11, the first is the most straightforward, expressing a straightforward transfer of energy from one object to another. As shown in figure 11, it is typified by a ball striking a window and breaking it and is expressed by the simple transitive sentence that describes this action. In this example, the trajector is 'the ball' and the ground is provided by the clause's object 'the window'. Broadly the relationships are profiled as one entity against another, as if in our spatial perception of a house (figure) standing in a garden (ground). Such schemas are surely universal and students will bring them from their first language, but it can never hurt to emphasise their many instantiations in English. For example, in cause and effect sentences, academic English will often nominalise both a causative process and the effect that results from it. In other words, each process is expressed as a bounded meaning that can impact directly upon the other. I show this again in example (57):

(57) The indundation of the delta caused massive crop destruction

When teaching, I have given material form to the action-chain metaphor by saying such sentences whilst banging one classroom object into another. Such demonstrations emphasise how such sentences treat processes as trajectors able to transfer energy to a landmark as in object to object (Holme 2004).

Action chains can also illustrate the reversal of grammatical roles between patient and subject that occurs in a passive sentence. This is shown in the second action chain in figure 11. In the second chain, the agent, or source of the charge, is unspecified. This chain is expressed through a passive. The diagram expresses how the passive does not construe a transfer of energy from agent to patient so much as the transfer of the charge itself. This gives us the passive's attributive meaning. A charge has transferred to the object (window) but the source is not expressed, leaving breakage as the window's attributed state. In the action chain

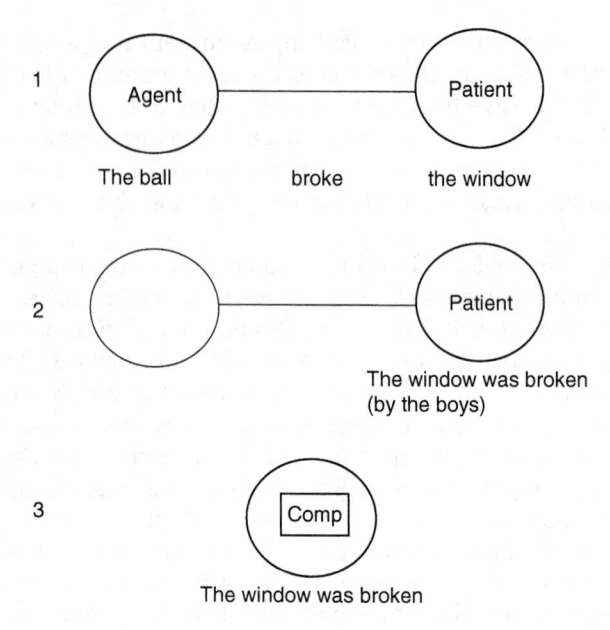

## 144  Cognitive Linguistics and Language Teaching

```
1    (Agent) ———— (Patient)
     The ball   broke   the window

2    (     ) ———— (Patient)
                  The window was broken
                  (by the boys)

3            ( [Comp] )
             The window was broken
```

*Figure 11*  Three action chains (Langacker 1987)

this is expressed by how the trajector is not properly profiled. Instead our emphasis is upon the attribution of a process to the landmark, thus reversing transitive participant roles. In the third chain we see a complement that completes the meaning of the designated process. There is an energy charge and the trajector, or figure, is grounded in the expression of a condition. The diagram reflects how it has not so much passed its energy to a complement but has effectively absorbed this into itself. Thus, here the sentence 'the window was broken' could be construed in the same way as 'the man was Spanish'.

(58) The window was broken often
(59) The window was broken and needed repair

This analysis of the English passive can help teachers avoid two pitfalls. The first pitfall is to treat the passive as a transformation of an active in a technique that was once reinforced by transformation drills where students were given active transitive sentences and asked to switch them to passives. Clearly, we use the passive to construe a scene in a different way, giving unusual prominence to the ground, or landmark. The second risk is to move too far the other way and treat the passive as a development of an adjective subjective complement structure of the kind shown in example (58); (see, for example, Lewis 1993, 1997). The concept of an energy charge may help to illustrate how passives and verb+adjective complement constructions construe a scene differently, as between examples (58) and (59).

A traditional test for the passive as opposed to an adjective–complement structure was to see if one could insert a 'by'-phrase without changing the meaning of a sentence such as (59). However, examples (60–61) makes plain that the 'by'-phrase may impart a stronger sense of attribution than agency.

(60) His face was swollen
(61) His face was swollen by an insect bite

The 'by'-phrase may itself deserve more pedagogical attention than it is sometimes given. Hoard (1975) argues that the 'by'-phrase is also meaningful and one can understand this from how the following sentences network together:

(62) The willow tree is by the river
(63) The sculpture is by Zúñiga
(64) Bragging by officers will not be tolerated (Langacker 1990: 139)

In example (62) we can see how the meaning of 'by' may be like that of other prepositions, and originate in a spatial relationship. The river is conceptualised as projecting a zone from itself in which objects are 'by' it as opposed to 'on' or 'away from' it. We can imagine how in sentence (63) this flexible concept of proximity comes to mean authorship. An artist is close to their work as they create it, so, they live in the conceptual space that is projected from it. To reach sentence (64) we need to understand how authorship connotes creative action. We are essentially the authors of our actions, so that agency can be expressed through the 'by'-phrase.

Many communicative and pedagogical approaches to the passive already stress how it is not so much a transformation as an alternative mode of construal. For example, teachers often introduce it through situations that emphasise:

- events whose agent is unknown (the occupants of a house returning to find it wrecked, or mysteries such as the discovery of a ghost ship);
- events where the agency is deliberately disguised, sometimes in a deliberate act of objectification, as in the description of a scientific experiment.

Perhaps more emphasis needs to be given to how passives and actives construe scenes from the perspectives of different participants. This scene switching is the objective of Activity 32, below:

Activity 32    Switched histories
1 Bring some old objects into the class, or pictures of these. You should have one for every four or six students.
2 Take one of your old objects and construct its history using the passive. This history can be entirely fictitious. For example:

> This bowl was given me by my grandmother when I was thirteen. It was made long before that in China, and was probably bought there by my great grandfather and shipped to London. He kept it in his house but it was stolen when they were robbed in 1905. Extraordinarily, the same bowl was found by my grandfather in a shop in the East London many years later. He bought it and it was then kept by my grandmother for more than fifty years.

3 Give each group a picture or object. They make up a story, tell it to the class then write it down.
4 Take the stories in and correct.
5 On another day, give the class back their stories and elicit whether they have constructed the story from the perspective of the object or another character.
6 In their story-groups, the students write down all the characters in the story, for example, thief, shop-keeper, grandmother, narrator, etc. They say why a person did what they did in the story, remembering that individual's motivations and character.
7 Each group writes the story from the perspective of one of the characters. Do not give them the object to reinforce this point. Tell them to put in details about the character. For example:

> 'one day somebody came to paint my great-grandfather's house. When the job ended, he realized he would have no more money

and would be hungry. He saw the bowl, knew it was valuable and decided to steal it...'

8 On another day, the groups rework each other's new versions from the perspective of the object.

## Perspectives and situatedness

Activity 32 reinforced how we can construe the same scene from the perspectives of different participants by using different grammatical constructs. Consider sentences (65) and (66):

(65) John pushed the door open
(66) The door was pushed open by John

Sentence (65) typically locates the narrator on the same side of the door as John. Sentence (66) affords a looser interpretation of the narrator's point of view but would generally situate them inside the room into which John walks. In sentences (67) and (68), the way in which the action is spatially situated is less important, but there is still an issue as to whether the author or the book is prominent. In (68), the figure of the author is prominent and thus creates the impression of a sequentially scanned, but completed action, or of a man who has completed the series of tasks called 'writing'. In (67) the impression is of a completed work, and therefore gives this book spatial prominence, placing it complete upon its metaphorical lectern.

(67) The novel was written by Tolstoy
(68) Tolstoy wrote the novel

Construal is therefore about the spatial imagery that underpins the words we select to represent a scene. As we showed in our opening example of 'over' and 'under', a way of construal is closely related to which prepositions we select to describe what is before us. Prepositions also carry these spatial relations into more abstract modes of thought, and structure how English represents an abstract topic. Consider examples (69)–(74), for example:

(69) I went into the field

(70) I went over the field
(71) I went through the field
(72) I went into the topic in some detail
(73) I went over the topic
(74) I went through the topic

Each prepositional phrase construes the same action quite differently. In example (69) the subject enters the field but reveals nothing about leaving it. In examples (70) and (71) an exit point is implied, but in sentence (70) the speaker's progress is less impeded by the space than in (71), because they are situated as being metaphorically above it.

The above construals are achieved by the speaker's adopting different points of view or perspectives. I show how this works through metaphor to construe abstract movement in examples (72)–(74). In example (72), the complexity of the topic is emphasised by the lack of an exit point. Sentence (73) can show a less effortful and more rapid review of a subject. Sentence (74) might imply a more effortful and detailed process of regurgitation.

The way we construe an entity in the world will affect the imagery and hence the meanings we derive from it when we use this to structure abstract thought. Arguably therefore, practising prepositions to construe concrete scenes such as landscapes or cityscapes can help students to make sound representations of abstract ideas as well.

Activity 33    Construal
1 In groups of four to six, the students appoint an artist who will sketch an unfolding scene. Remind the students of some or all the English prepositions or prepositional phrases that can express spatial relationships: for example, 'above, across, after, against, along, alongside, amidst, around, at, behind, below, beneath, beside, between, but, by, down, from, in, inside, into, near, of , off, on, onto, opposite, out, outside, over, through, throughout, to, towards, toward, under, underneath, up, upon, with, within'.
2 The groups of students close their eyes and envisage a scene in which there is a bird and a building.
3 Ask one group where the bird is. To get, for example, 'above the building' or 'on the building'. If they introduce another landmark with for example, 'on the roof,' say, 'where on the roof?', always extending the scene and asking for precision. Tell the learners that they are both an observer of the scene and part of it.

4  After the students in one group have answered the first question, the artist in every group draws how the scene has unfolded so far.
5  Ask one group, 'where are you?' If a member of the group says something that does not fit their construal, correct them. For example, they say: 'I am in the building' and you tell them, 'no, you're not, because you can see the bird above the building'. All the artists then draw themselves into their scene in a place that fits how they have construed it.
6  Add other items piece by piece and ask where they are. The different groups should thus listen to each others' responses and build a common scene.
7  Ask them to put another person into the scene and ask one or two of them to explain where the person is.
8  Ask one person in the group to switch points of view to that person and to describe the scene from their perspective.

In a similar activity one can ask one student in a group to imagine a scene then to envisage walking through it. The teacher stops them at a point in their mental perambulation and asks them where they are. They describe the scene from the perspective they've obtained.

The above activity can be metaphorically extended, carrying the concept of construal away from the clause and into discourse. Here, students are not just challenged by finding the language in which to express their analysis of a topic, but by the need to find an analytic perspective that is not entirely dependent on another authority. Students studying languages for academic purposes may produce the type of essay that provides an accurate and balanced summary of two or three different perspectives on a topic, but which ends with little more than a sentence at the end, where they give their opinion as to which view to adopt, but with hardly any sense of why. Generally this type of essay structure reveals a failure to adopt an individual perspective. Student writers may therefore summarise and balance three or four approaches to a topic quite well. But at the end of the essay they will do no more than throw in a few final comments as to which view they prefer. Before writing, such student writers should, instead, set out all the possible cases in note form and adopt one, modifying it in any way they think appropriate. When they start writing, students can then set out the various positions and finally use their adopted one to demolish the others. To achieve this type of structure, students need to construe another's better-researched opinion as their own. To manage this, one can chart a process of apprenticeship based upon a process of perspective-taking.

Thus in the first instance students may grasp a notion of construal by doing Activity 33 and trying to view the same scene from the perspective of different characters within it. In a second exercise they could try to view a historical or current event from the perspective of different protagonists. In a third phase, they could adopt one of the perspectives as an opinion as to how the event's outcome could be ameliorated or changed. In the fourth, they should gather other perspectives from their classmates and edit these into arguments that their own point of view will undermine. Each of these phases will require substantial practice and pedagogical input, but the outcome will encourage the adoption and extension of a point of view as the writer's own, not so much in the spirit of some rushed and final taking of sides as of the marshalling of evidence gleaned from an act of perspective-taking.

## Deixis

Deixis has been identified as a property of discourse for some time. The word, which is from the Greek for 'pointing', refers to how we structure an utterance in relation to where the interlocutors are (Lyons 1981: 170). The phenomenon of *epistemic deixis* (Croft and Cruse 2004) becomes very complicated in the way in which we may construe a fictional reality. For example, a novelist may insert themselves into the text as a first-person narrator, as in the opening sentence of Defoe's 'Moll Flanders':

> (75) My true name is so well known in the records or registers at *Newgate*, and in the Old Bailey, and there are some things of such consequence still depending there, relating to my particular conduct, that it is not to be expected I should set my name or the account of my family to this work. (Defoe, first published 1722)

The opening use of the possessive pronoun 'my' grounds the writer outside the text in some notional present where they are an observer of their own past. However, they are also a character in their own narrative and are thus observing their own construction of an alternative persona and making an implicit judgment upon that persona's actions. This alternative persona is to be given a pseudonym. Additionally, the character is shifted into other parallel texts, prison registers and trial documents. Thus they fictionally situate themselves as actors in others' narratives. Further, because the grounded persona is unreal, the

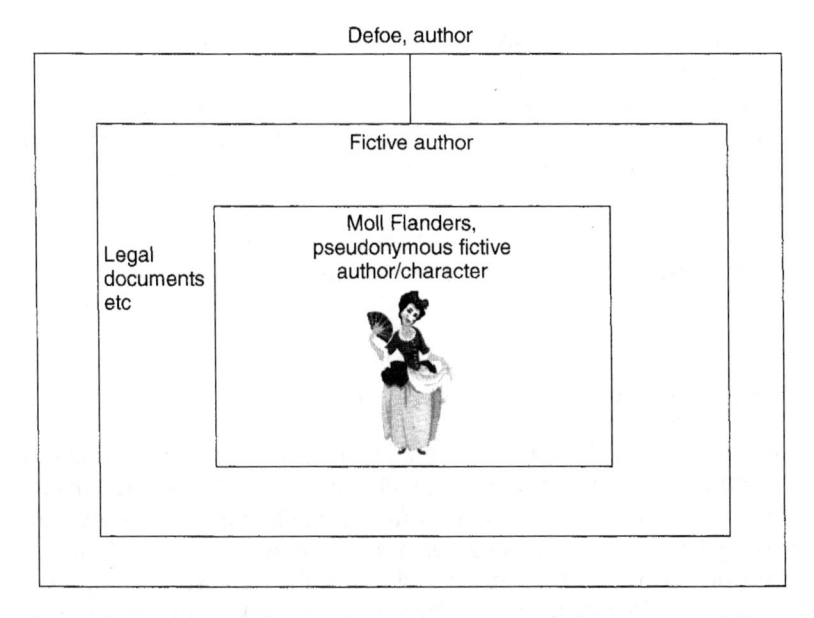

*Figure 12* Who is Moll Flanders? Epistemic deixis and the creation of different character perspectives

text points even further out to the author who is the actual narrator of events. The distance shown up by this last deictic shift is exaggerated by how the first-person character in the text is female and Defoe, the author, is male. Such an example illustrates how we operate with complicated layers of deixis grounding a text-created world in a parallel fictional realm. The events of a story are construed from the different perspectives that the author adopts within it. Students dealing with this type of text can be encouraged to attempt epistemic frames such as that shown in figure 12.

In an interesting transposition teachers can try asking students to construe events in their own lives from an adjusted perspective. In a sense, they can rework themselves as a kind of fiction.

Activity 34　　Someone else was there
1　In groups of four, ask students to note down four or five good or bad things about their character.
2　Ask students to remember some event in their life that they want to share, where they had to make an important decision. Tell them to recount the event to their group and to say how they responded.

3 Ask the group to analyse how the student's response to the event was or was not in character.
4 Ask them to re-imagine the student with one or two attributes changed, then to rework the student's response to the event as a fiction. They should write this down as a group story.

As the learners move outside of themselves to rework their life as fiction they achieve a different epistemic stance and should change their construal of events.

## Constitution/gestalt

Constitution/gestalt refers back to a mode of perception that has been a central subject of enquiry in psychology since the 1920s. Broadly the reference is to how we conceptualise whole objects, and that can best be illustrated by looking again at the much cited vase face diagram drawn by the Danish psychologist Rubin almost a century ago (Ungerer and Schmid 1996). When you first look at this drawing in figure 13 you will either see a vase or two heads looking at each other, but not both. The diagram illustrates the fundamental issue of cognitive linguistics, namely that we will constitute a given reality out of the information presented to us by our sensory system. Most people see this drawing one way until they find the other, then can move back and forth between each conceptualisation, but without finding both at the same time. However, since we know that both images are effectively present all the time, we can see how we ignore this and conceptualise what appears to be out there as one thing or another. In other words the meanings we think we perceive directly are being cognitively constituted.

To perceive the diagram as faces or a vase we have to *constitute* them as bounded, or drawn, against an unbounded background. We have already considered how our early experiences of reality form image schemas based on its presentation as shape and substance. Shapes are by their nature constituted from our unbounded conceptualisation of substance, as when we contain water in a sea. This concept of boundedness and unboundedness affects grammar in fundamental ways (Langacker 1987). We find it, for example, in the difference between countable and uncountable nouns, or in the use of the continuous tense to represent an action.

Rubin's vase

*Figure 13* Rubin's face diagram

Many teachers of English will recognise that the ways the continuous and simple tenses of English express time are overlapping and inconsistent. CL is not straightforwardly helpful here, as there is no straight fit between the way in which time is conceptualised and the meanings represented by the respective types of English aspect and their uses. Thus sentence (76) expresses a meaning that is episodic and continuing and is different from (77) in a way that is difficult to specify, let alone consciously operate:

(76) He's always eating chocolate
(77) He always eats chocolate

CL does tell us something about the meanings expressed by the English continuous and simple tenses, however. Langacker's (1990: 246–59) account is developed from Goldsmith and Woisetschlaeger's (1982: 80) distinction between what they call 'phenomenal' and 'structural' knowledge. Thus sentence (78) is phenomenal, or actual, because it expresses something that happens in the world, whilst (79) is structural because it generalises the described event as a theory about our existence:

(78) This engine isn't smoking anymore (actual or temporarily structural)
(79) This engine doesn't smoke anymore (structural [indefinite scope]) (Langacker 1990: 250)

For Langacker, the structural nature of example (79) is part of an image schema that has internalised a concept of cause and effect. This 'actual' and 'structural' distinction is encoded in other aspects of the grammar. For example consider sentences (80–84):

(80) A cat is stalking birds
(81) A cat stalks birds
(82) Cats stalk birds
(83) Every cat stalks birds
(84) Every cat is stalking birds (Examples derived from Langacker 1990)

Both sentences (81) and (84) are unlikely and example (84) is probably ungrammatical. Sentence (80) is bounded and phenomenal. Perhaps it is spoken by somebody observing the event through a kitchen window. Example (82) debounds 'bird' by treating it as a notional plural, or superordinate abstraction. It involves theory building, or making a hypothesis about the world. Theory building means that we treat the subject of the theory, 'cats', as a collective concept rather than as an observed and individuated phenomenon. It is therefore debounded and pluralised to represent all cases of cat.

In example (83) 'every' is also an unbounded reference, and creates 'cat' as a theoretical concept that applies to all such observed creatures. 'Every cat' is a theoretical convenience that is abstracted and unbounded. Accordingly 'every' is a determiner that concords with the theory-building nature of a simple tense but clashes with the particular, phenomenal meaning of a continuous tense.

English teachers may find it helpful if they contextualise the simple present more through its structural, theory-building meaning and less through its expression of habitual actions, though, as example (85) shows, these two types of meaning intertwine. In example (85), then, the simple tense expresses habitual actions and thus constructs a theory about what the individual does. The 'theory-building view' means that the sports commentary example given in example (86) can be treated as consistent with how example (85) uses narrative to expose the hidden structure of events. Example (86) uses simple aspect to engrave the described actions as an enduring sequence on the fabric of life:

(85) He reads a lot, eats little and goes out seldom
(86) He controls the ball with one touch, turns, and shoots

Simple tenses may therefore be better taught through texts such as examples (87) and (88), below. These texts make their appeal to ontological structures more evident than in the type of text book approach based upon a description of habits:

(87) That car uses a lot of fuel. It drives badly, looks ugly and is uncomfortable
(88) The house stands at the end of the street. The garden reaches down to the river and four trees hide it from the road

By contrast, teachers looking at continuous aspect, whether in the past or present, should relate this to simultaneous or recalled commentaries upon events, whether on film, in the classroom, or outside the classroom windows.

### Geometry

We also constitute objects according to *geometry*, or to how we construe their form in space. Thus the geometry of forms will change our perception of the relationship that pertains between them. For example, 'water is in a bowl' (Croft and Cruse 2004) because liquid must be contained and will thus find the bowl's property of containment, but 'dust will be on a bowl' because it sprinkles its surface. The geometry of the same object is thus conceptualised differently by a different communicative need.

Knowing whether entities contain or require containment is part of the knowledge frame of a word that requires more attention from teachers if they want students to select the pronoun that is appropriate to the relationship being expressed. Thus in a very simple exercise students can be asked to consider how they construe the geometry of a given entity so that they learn to use the appropriate preposition with it. This exercise also establishes when English does or does not use a schema of containment.

Activity 35    Container or surface
1 Make clear what you mean by the distinction between a container and a surface by using the examples of a plate and a bowl. Say 'food' is put *in* a bowl but *on* a plate. Then ask them to say whether the following are predominantly 'containers' or 'surfaces':

> house, car, book, desk, table, field, hill, room, floor, sea, sky, ground, skin.

2 When they argue over such items as 'desk' or 'sea', say much depends on what is being placed in or on it and on how its actions are construed. For example:

> 'a boat travels on the sea but we swim in it'.

3 Now ask them to place these entities in or on the other as appropriate.

> Dirt, water, information, papers, a house, a tree, a scratch, a cut, furniture, a bird, a driver.

Do not allow foolish sentences such as 'dirt on the hill', but do allow a mix such as 'a bird in the sky'; 'a bird on the table'. If they construe the situation in an odd way, saying for example: 'there's a driver on the car' ask what they mean with a question such as 'a driver on the car?' Also explain any radical differences of meaning that arise, as between 'information in a house' (for example from a document left there) and 'on a house' (papers saying how and when it was built).

A more difficult version of this activity can be done with more abstract concepts, or concrete concepts that are used abstractly:
For example:
  surface (ground):
    a downward slope, a different track, a way
  container:
    Decline, crisis, a new phase, a state/condition

And students can note that words derived through image schemas of path (track or road) are generally preceded by 'on', but that containment is construed as tending to the static, and hence uses 'in'. In related category development tasks students can exemplify the more general abstract terms such as 'crisis' with more specific subordinate forms, for example, 'car accident, house-fire, war, robbery' and will often find that their geometry is construed in the same way as that of the superordinate term (or as containment – in a crisis/in a car accident).

The above example is one of many where grasping shape geometry can help students decipher why a preposition is used for a given meaning. A larger issue with prepositions is how they also shape the construction, or meaningful combination, of words of which they are a part. Understanding the types of conceptualisation from which they evolve will therefore provide a more useful grasp of how to manipulate a given construction.

## Conclusions

Construal goes to the heart of how CL propagates a view of language and meaning that is conceptual and enactive rather than perceptual. The above discussion of construal and pedagogy, therefore, was not an attempt to summarise the topic then leave it aside but was rather a broader attempt to stimulate thought about how an understanding of construal operations can stimulate an interest both in certain types of form in English, and in the cognitive processes by which it is underpinned. Construal operations are generally analysed for their effect upon sentence grammar. However, I also showed how they can provide clues to more extensive discoursal structures. The imagery that these structures employed was also useful for inducting students into the structures' successful manipulation.

Conceptualisation is perhaps the feature which more than any other distinguishes a cognitive approach. When we advance to a discussion of meaning in the next chapter it will also do much to explain how a given combination of symbols adopts the form that it does.

# Part III
# Meaning and Usage

# 7
# Teaching Encyclopaedic Meaning

## Introduction

The analysis of language as a meaningful or symbolic entity would seem basic to any linguistic enterprise. But we should not forget that generative, and to a lesser extent structuralist linguistics attempted an analysis that looked more at structure and organisation than meaning. In cognitive linguistics, by contrast, the construction that pulls other meaningful items together is perceived as meaningful in itself. Accordingly, the CL assumption is that the central property of language is its symbolism. All modes of linguistic analysis treat words as symbols in some sense. Where the CL approach differs from some others, however, is first in how it describes a word's represented meaning, and second in how it perceives grammar as another form of symbolism.

CL treats lexical meaning as conceptual and thus as a function of experience. Human experience is self-evidently multi-dimensional, cumulative and social. The meanings that we derive from our experiences are first categories or networks of meanings that cannot be fully captured by a description of their essential features, or by a dictionary-type definition. The mental lexicon is not just a portfolio of words, their definitions and the appropriate grammatical marking. Meanings arise from how we experience an entity or a set of entities over time. They propose a mode of construal of that entity. Since our experiences occur within a culture, these meanings are culturally shaped. In its turn, the meaning of a word affects the development of the culture from which it first emerged. This is why CL treats a given meaning as *encyclopaedic*, or as encompassing a broad and culturally shaped spectrum of knowledge about an item. By the same token, a word is less the representation of a meaning and more an access point to this store of knowledge

(Langacker 1987). This knowledge store will integrate semantic knowledge with pragmatic knowledge, making no distinction between our grasp of a word's meaning and our understanding of how it should be used.

The above approach differs from that of formal linguistics where semantic and pragmatic knowledge are regarded as distinct. For example, a semantic definition of the English word 'over' would traditionally have been seen as built around a core meaning, perhaps of the path of an object's traversal. Such a definition could incorporate both sentences (89) and (90):

(89) The bird went over the wall
(90) The man went over the wall

This limited definition of 'over' as indicating a traversal meant that the task of constructing a plausible meaning for both examples (89) and (90) would have been left to pragmatics, or to the most relevant meaning that the context supplied. In CL, however, it is the word's attachment to an encyclopaedic meaning that makes this possible.

The idea of a conceptual and encyclopaedic meaning proposes that we approach vocabulary teaching from two broad and overlapping perspectives:

the meanings of terms are networked together, or conceptualised one inside another;
meanings exist in frames, or domains of knowledge about the category.

We can grasp the first point when we realise that to understand what a plant is we need to have knowledge of what is organic as opposed to inorganic. We therefore understand the meaning of the plant by situating it inside another category, that of the living thing, or organism. The second point can be understood when we remember that our understanding of so common a phenomenon as a tree must include whether our culture treats it as a resource, as an object of veneration and an abode of spirits, or both. Further, our understanding of trees must also be framed within that of the earth from which trees grow and the forests that their growth creates.

In this chapter I am going to think further how second language learners may need some induction into the encyclopaedic meanings that native speakers develop by dint of living in a given culture. Such an objective may raise the objection that learners do not need such an induction because they can simply transfer most of this knowledge from the categories that they operate in their first language. There are four points, however, that I will make in this respect:

- Meanings are not the same in all languages. Understanding encyclopaedic meanings can help learners explore the category differences between the languages in which they work. They can then operate second language meanings as themselves and not as if they were those of the first language.
- When teachers present a word's meaning as a larger knowledge frame, they are helping their students to express that knowledge and are hence developing a more general communicative ability.
- Knowing a word's encyclopaedic meaning can invoke the study of some of the contexts in which that word occurs. One word thus becomes a key to a broader study of meaning-making, helping the student organise lexical knowledge in a way that is friendly to their cognition.
- Grasping the encyclopaedic meanings of words, and particularly verbs and prepositions, can develop a grasp of the more extended constructions or combinations of words that are built around them.

With these points in mind, I will discuss how teachers can use the interconnected nature of word meanings, or their *sense relations*, to bundle lexis together in a manner we could term cognition-friendly. To do this I will first look again at hyponymy but will this time develop the concept through the notions of schematicity and inheritance. Another form of sense relation is meronymy and this will merit some attention as it is already a well-used device for organising vocabulary teaching. After some thought about how categories overlap I will turn to how we can use a more specific understanding of a frame, then consider a less-considered form of phonological sense relation. Finally, I will conclude with some points about the need to help students construct encyclopaedic meanings by seeing lexis in multiple contexts.

## Word networks: hyponymy and schematicity

In the last chapter we noted how category members exist in a hyponymic relationship. Thus cars and trucks are part of the category of vehicle. The higher the category in a hyponym hierarchy, the more abstract and the more schematic it is, and the lower, the less so. The more schematic categories do not always exist in all languages. The least schematic may not be identified by some languages, or even if identified they may not be known by all the native speakers of a language. Some people, for example, are challenged when asked to name some quite common flowers, whilst others will have problems with car parts. Generally we seem to gravitate to middle-range categories, talking about 'cars' or 'flowers' as opposed to specific instances of the same, or some highly abstract and inclusive term such as 'organism'.

The original Greek meaning of a 'schema' was 'appearance'. In Gestalt psychology, 'this was a visible shape or figure structured memory' (Stafford 2007). It presupposed forms or figures which were drawn from past experience and used to structure our present perceptions. One way to perceive schematicity in CL is as a quality of meaning or form that can group phenomena. The meaning or form will group phenomena because they correspond to its image and not to another (*ibid.*). Thus, if we take the case of an organism, we can see how our accumulated experiences of phenomena will treat them as living or lifeless. This image of life finds a relationship between entities as diverse as viruses, elephants and oak trees. The sheer diversity of phenomena that the image incorporates attests to its high degree of schematicity.

The concept of a hyponym relationship also gives us another cognitive concept, that of *inheritance*. We conceptualise a tree as a type of plant. This means we grasp 'a tree' as *inheriting* a plant's features, or the fact that it grows, and is organic but not animate. A notion of hyponymy is therefore likely to be part of an encyclopaedic meaning, for we do not fully understand what an entity is until we construe it as having inherited features from some superordinate category. Our knowledge of 'trees' for example would not extend far without the understanding that they are a type of plant.

Teachers can explore inheritance with learners by using the type of hyponym chart that was shown in figure 9 on page 131 to help students identify which features of a category are inherited and which are not. The following exercise can also be a useful way to give a meaningful context to the present simple tense in English whilst helping children of primary age to develop conceptual knowledge.

Activity 36    Passed down?
  1 Give students a set of categories that would be represented at the same level on any simple hyponym chart. For example: at a folk level 'plants' might give: flowers, trees, shrubs, vegetables and cacti.

*Teaching Encyclopaedic Meaning* 165

2  In groups, the students work out what features the category members share. These should be concrete inherited features: for example, 'leaves, roots and stem', or processes, 'grow from seed or bulb, photosynthesis'.
3  Still in groups, the students use the features to compose a definition of the superordinate category. For example:

> Plants have leaves, roots and a stem. They grow from seeds or bulbs through photosynthesis.

4  Each group reads out their definition and the others discuss its accuracy. For example:

> But cacti have no leaves... or do they?

The activity was tried at a folk level of definition but can be more technically focused. The objective here was not to understand plants but to build the vocabulary associated with a category, whilst also seeing how group meanings can be shaped by a superordinate one. This last objective will be shown to have more interest when we consider grammatical meaning.

### Word networks: meronymy

Meronymy is also an important principle in sense relations as it originates in our understanding of ourselves as an entity composed of parts and hence in proprioception itself. Further, our discussion of metonymy showed how this is prototypically a part-for-whole relationship, or the representation of one object through a meronym. Meronymy is also essential to our understanding of some abstract concepts. Our conceptualisation of the meaning of 'month', for example, depends upon our knowing that it consists of a certain number of days (Croft and Cruse 2004) and is itself part both of a year and of some larger stretch of time. To have more than a superficial understanding of an entity implies knowing something both of the parts of which it is comprised and the whole of which it is a part. Sense relations based on meronymy can also be crucial to the definition and understanding of terms. This is even more critical in the case of abstract concepts such as a 'month' where the meaning is almost entirely relational in nature. However, one should also reflect how meanings that are not obviously unitary, such as characteristics or qualities, may derive their sense from a recurring pattern of episodes. Thus, for example, our judgment that a person is stubborn may be accrued from a series of incidents. The more obvious forms of meronymy may be crucial to how teachers define entities that are obviously a whole composed of parts or parts of a whole. However, pedagogy may itself be a process that appeals to our ability to assemble parts from wholes. For example, when a word meaning is explored through a series of examples, teachers are asking their students to deal in meronymy by assembling instances into the larger compositional whole that constitutes a category meaning.

LSP (Languages for Special Purposes) teachers will be well used to teaching students terms with part–whole diagrams which may represent the organisms and artifacts that they confront in real life. Such diagrams are not only a useful way to organise lexis around a given topic but can also be used to create the discourses with which the function of a given entity is explored. Thus, students of anatomy can do category exercises with organs, deciding which part belongs to which, categorising the right/left ventricle or the mitral valve and aorta under the heart and the hepatic artery and gall bladder under the liver, for example. The categorisation of the parts may then help to structure the students' picture of the workings of the whole as when they recount how the left atrium drains oxygen-rich blood from the lungs and discharges it into the left ventricle. Interested teachers can also encourage students to be creative and to use parts to construct different wholes. Thus students of anatomy may gain a surer grasp of the function of a given organ if they are asked to engage in a Frankenstein-like experiment and use it to redesign the human being.

So we can use the meronymic charts that accompany the above types of activity to structure various types of texts. The example in figure 14 is somewhat more elementary than those referred to above and was designed for students in primary schools. The text describes the working of plants and is as much about the structure of the entity in question as about how the parts contribute to its larger function. The student, however, will first simply see the text as the exploration of the whole through its parts, by completing a category diagram. They can next reverse the procedure and use the completed meronym chart to help structure a short text about the workings of plants. As with category diagrams, such charts help students to organise lexis in a way that is conceptually effective whilst also making functional relationships of the parts of a whole into a principle that will help the organisation of discourse.

Many teachers will be well aware of the power of such exercises for teaching lexis and science. Some thought will show how we live in a

Always think about the patterns between words:

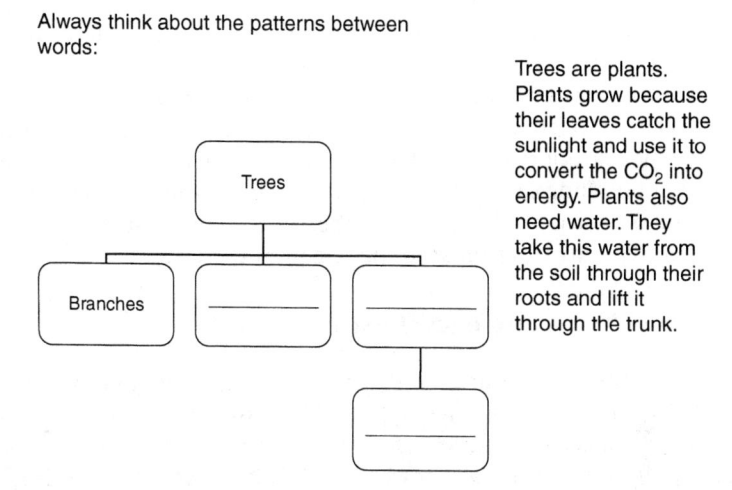

Trees are plants. Plants grow because their leaves catch the sunlight and use it to convert the $CO_2$ into energy. Plants also need water. They take this water from the soil through their roots and lift it through the trunk.

*Figure 14* Using meronymy for information transfer tasks

universe of interlinked forms, with each being a part of another. The question for teachers, then, concerns primarily the level of detail into which it is useful and conceptually plausible for students to break down the meanings they encounter.

## Crossing category borders

A moment's reflection on how we use categories will show that unless we are trying to construct a scientific analysis of a given entity we will operate them in quite a loose way. We will also create deliberate blends between them to produce hybrid forms that may be conceptually or physically useful. For example, a vehicle such as 'the people carrier', or MPV (multi-purpose-vehicle) arose from a blend between the van (on the chassis of which many of the first models were built) and the estate car, or station wagon. Students can be encouraged to build lexis through a design exercise where they work in groups to design new forms of furniture to which they give new names. Since most of such invention depends on blending extant forms and concepts to create a hybrid, students can analyse each others' plans and map their parts onto a meronym chart such as that shown in figure 14.

A teacher who works with one class in one room can wallpaper it with charts that show the meronym- or hyponym-based linkage between lexical meanings. Such charts furnish permanent visual reinforcement. In practice, however, it is generally, but mistakenly, only those working with primary-age children who have this type of facility, and even there such reinforcements must jostle for space with other project work. A more practical approach may be to create such charts in multi-layered powerpoint, linking each category with a hyperlink then using them for revision tasks where students activate their lexical information in design or descriptive activities similar to the one just described.

## Knowledge types and encyclopaedic meaning

An encyclopaedic meaning is structured around different types of knowledge. These knowledge types are classified as conventional, generic, intrinsic, or characteristic (Langacker 1987). They are also overlapping. Conventional knowledge is built up about a word by a community of native speakers and shared among them. It is knowledge which applies to the category as a whole, and thus excludes the specific understanding that the chair in your office is uncomfortable. Generic knowledge may also be conventional in that it will be shared in a community. However it is more likely to be culturally affected as it encompasses a more extended understanding of the term, asking for example, what a chair is made of and whether a specific instance is likely to be suited to work or relaxation. Intrinsic knowledge refers to the core characteristics of an entity, its shape, colour, or function, for example (if these are fixed). In the case of the chair it would be function, since the other factors are not *determinate*, i.e. making the entity what it is, but may be what is called *characteristic*. A characteristic form concerns knowledge that we normally associate with an object, a chair having legs, for example, but which may not always apply, as when it stands directly on the floor on a frame.

An awareness of these properties can help teachers construct straightforward question and answer routines to extend knowledge of a given item and build associated lexis. For example, one can build a variation of the word game 'animal, vegetable and mineral' where the class try to guess a category according to some of the properties of its encyclopaedic meaning. Their objective however should be not so much to name the category but to produce an extended description of it. For this reason, it is better if the item is not named even if correctly guessed until the class has built a greater understanding of the concept through their accumulated construction of its attributes. The activity can be structured in a way that builds a network of associated lexis.

Teaching Encyclopaedic Meaning  169

Activity 37     What it really is
1. Divide the class into two or three teams. Tell them that they are going to build knowledge about a particular item but that if they call out what they think the item is, they will be disqualified.
2. Divide the board into columns marked by: 'how we use it', 'how I use it', 'what it must have', 'what mine has'.
3. Think of the specific example of a category that is known or unknown to the class. For example, your house, a favourite chair, or book.
4. Ask the class to suggest sentences that describe what they think the object is. The sentences must fit one of the headings written on the board, for example it must be about 'how we use the category', or 'what is must have'. When somebody suggests a sentence, write it under the appropriate category. Help them with appropriate constructions, for example 'it is used for ...', 'yours has...'.
5. When the class has produced enough knowledge about the item to build a complete category description, ask them to describe it orally, in writing, or both, using the notes on the board.

## Finding the frame

The term *frame* (Fillmore 1977) also bears on our understanding of an encyclopaedic meaning. In Fillmore's view, the frame is critical to how we may or may not use a given word. Effectively it shapes the kind of syntactic forms into which the word can be inserted. Thus, for example, the frame for 'buy' assumes that there are various participant roles such as 'goods' which can be bought, money that must be paid and a seller who will receive it. This knowledge allows us to construct a range of meaningful sentences that have 'buyer' as their subject or which may use it as a possible object. Goldberg (1995 and 2006) reworks the insights of more traditional valency grammars when she proposes that clauses will largely shape their *argument structures* around the frame-semantics of the verb. Thus 'sell' presupposes participant roles such as a subject capable of this type of action and an object that can be the patient of it.

One consequence of the communicative method has been to discourage students from improvising on forms in a way that is not dedicated to the expression of a particularly relevant context. Looking at how verb meanings are framed can encourage such experimentation and hence help students to develop their understanding of how meanings fit together in ways that may or may not help them respond to future

170  *Cognitive Linguistics and Language Teaching*

*Table 1*  Using frame semantics tables to extend learners' lexico-grammatical control: 'sell'

| A seller | **sold** | something saleable | to a buyer | for a price |
|---|---|---|---|---|
| *The shopkeeper* | | *a toy* | *to the child* | *for a few cents* |
| *The government* | | *its integrity* | *to the oil giant* | *for a trifle* |
| *The supermarket* | | *the product* | *to the public* | *for a profit* |

*Table 2*  Using frame semantics tables: 'go'

| Someone/something (that can move) | **went** | from a place | to a place | by what means | on what |
|---|---|---|---|---|---|
| Susan | **went** | from London | to Madrid | by plane | |
| John | **went** | from Sha Tin | to Tai Po | | on horseback |

communicative needs. For example, departing from Fillmore's example, we can see that 'sell' sets up a frame that makes some meanings more likely than others. In tables 1 and 2 I have expressed the meanings presupposed by the frame of the verb, but in the most schematic way possible.

A filler activity is to simply invite students to see how many sentences they can create using the constructions and verb specified at the top of the table. However, they need to be reminded that a feature of English is that it can place almost any meaning into a subject position before a given verb (Tomasello 2003; Radden and Dirven 2007). 'A seller' therefore does not necessarily presuppose a human entity. Language, even in contexts that look for lexical precision, is hugely tolerant of non-literal meanings and a figurative interpretation of the subject's meaning will enhance the student's ability to expand its frame and still make sense. Such tables also practise how the construction of selling something to somebody will prefer (but not mandate) certain phrases, such as 'for+NP (noun phrase)' in the price slot.

There is no reason why this type of framing activity should focus exclusively on the common, generally irregular verbs. More advanced students who are operating in more specialised registers may find it useful to practise with verbs that have frames appropriate to the instantiation of these. For example, EAP students might find it useful to practise with verbs that can set up meta-textual clauses, such as, 'discuss, examine, consider, argue, claim', or those which unfold descriptions of developmental processes, such as 'develop, evolve, mutate or transform'. Such students can then experiment with appropriate prepositional phrases and thus start to build an appropriate range of verbs that can carry the academic text's more analytic function.

## Phonological sense relations

A less explored and conceptually less transparent connection between meanings can be found in their phonology. In CL linguistic form is not arbitrary and autonomous but motivated by language's prime function, which is meaning-making. Though heavily conventionalised over time, phonology may be iconic and onomatopoeic, or indexical in origin. Languages may bear the traces of these processes through sets of lexical sense relations that are phonologically based. Even if they are entirely coincidental, some rhymes seem to point back to a semantic connection between words, as in 'boat' and float', for example, or, more marginally, 'sunk, drunk', with these latter terms seeming to share some concept of immersion, or a reference to processes involving liquids. Such connections can hold together couplets that exploit the once well-recognised mnemonic qualities of rhyming verse, even if poetic merit is sacrificed to semantic transparency:

(91)  Upon the quiet river floats
      My old and over-laden boat
      When other craft in lakes have sunk
      Or are by stormy oceans drunk.

Teachers who want to use such poems to encourage more conventional forms of language use can make a prose narrative connection to this type of verse, and set up an oral or written composition task where the poem becomes a lexical source for a more straightforward text. Thus, after learning a poem such as that in example (91) above, students can, at another point in time be asked to recount or compose a boating story that includes each of the last words of the line.

Another more productive phonological mnemonic exploited in English, and more centrally in Anglo Saxon poetry is that of alliteration. Boers and Lindstromberg (2005) have explored the mnemonic effects of alliteration for learning lexical phrases with considerable success and such patterns may network words in ways that do more than merely search for a phonological relationship between their forms.

One of the most intriguing examples of how alliteration can underpin a sense relation is found in the English phonaesthemes, so-named by the structuralist linguist, Bloomfield (1914). These are words where the same initial constant cluster points back to some common meaning. They are not only interesting for how an underlying sense relation is captured by a phonological one but also for how they evidence the roles played by metonymy and metaphor in meaning-building. For example, the following words all have meanings related to the nose, either directly or by metaphorical association:

- snout, snoot (slang for nose, hence the more common adjective 'snooty' meaning snobbish, as in 'look down one's nose' at somebody), sneeze, snide, sniff, snarl, snigger, snot, sneer, snooze (sleep perhaps associated with quiet snoring), snore

Words such as 'snore', 'sneeze', and 'sniff', show directly how meanings are built from metonymy of actions associated with body parts, whilst 'snooty', and 'sneer' evidence further metaphorical development towards abstract states of disdain.

The 'gl-' group all have an association with 'light':

- glance, glare, glass, glaze, gleam, glimmer, glimpse, glint, glitter, gloom, glory, gloss, glow, glum

As in the first group, the association of some of the current meanings of these words with 'light' is less than clear. 'Glance' and 'glimpse' have a metonymic association with light since they are about seeing. Glance may derive less directly from a verb meaning 'slip' as in a 'glancing blow', and hence from the same root as the French word for 'ice', glâce (Etymological Dictionary Online 2007). Ice is itself translucent and 'glâce' is probably related to the same common root as the Germanic word 'gle' to glitter. The meaning of the Latin word 'gloria' which gave the English 'glory' was more associated with brightness and hence splendour (*ibid.*). Glum now refers to mood, but in origin was the same as gloom, which can still refer either metaphorically to mood or literally to (less) light. The association of the other words with light is clear.

A still larger group with a more schematic linkage are the 'fl-' phonaesthemes, all of whose relevant cases seem to express an association with 'lightness, ethereality or lack of substance'.

- flag (verb, to weaken or droop), flagrant, flail, flake, flunk, flop, flame, flap, flare, flash, flee, flicker, fly, flight, fling, flip, float, flock, flog, flood, flow, fluid, fluent, fluff

The metaphorical and metonymic of meanings again conceal some of the semantic associations between these words. For example, the word 'flagrant' as in 'a flagrant violation of their civil rights', has a historical association with flame because it derives from the Latin 'flagrare', meaning 'to burn'.

To use the relatedness of these words to help their learning and retention, I wrote the following poem and constructed an activity around it for older primary-school children. Again the objective here was a rhythmic repetition of the 'fl-' onset and not aesthetic merit:

(92) My boat now floats upon the streams
And streams will flow to sea
The lightning strikes and angry flames
Are flickering through the trees
Then hard rains stop the fire with floods
And float my boat amidst the forest.

This poem is written to foreground particular items of lexis rather than a larger meaning. One way to use such poems is to get students to recite them whilst tapping out their (generally) iambic meter, then to tap out the rhythm alone in unison with the teacher whilst inserting only the core item of lexis at the place where it occurs:

- / - / - / - flames

Younger learners can also embody the words through gesture, waggling the fingers to show 'flicker' or waving the hand palm down and moving it away from the body to show 'flames'.

In another technique, after a choral recitation of the poem, I have shown a powerpoint presentation that illustrates each line of the poem. One possible illustration is shown in figure 15. Two alternative captions are given. One marks the metre only, asking students to reconstruct the text. The other reproduces the whole line but with stressed syllables in larger type and the phonaestheme entered as its onset only.

Phonaesthemes are now non-compositional, by which I mean they are not identifiable morphemes that build words with their meanings. So it is a moot point whether modern English speakers work with even a residual sense of the semantic relatedness of these types of word. However, experimentation with native speakers has shown that they exert a priming effect (Bergen 2004). Thus, if subjects are primed with the phonaestheme's semantic area, lightness, light, nose, or whatever, a

174  *Cognitive Linguistics and Language Teaching*

⌣ /⌣ /⌣ /⌣ flames

The light<sub>ning</sub> strikes and ang<sub>ry</sub> fl__

*Figure 15*  Illustrating phonaesthemes set in a poetic metre

more likely result is the production of one of these words. If the effect exists, then this indicates that we work with a residual and highly schematic sense relation that teachers can tap into.

## Conclusions

Teaching lexis was never a straightforward process of finding mother-tongue equivalents then matching their meanings to the new L2 form. To build the encyclopaedic meanings that categories imply, learners need to track how words manifest different meanings in different contexts, then pull these together to build more extensive categories. Teachers should encourage learners to abandon vocabulary lists and replace them with word study sheets. After noting down new words they should start to build information about their respective categories over time. They should enter lexical maps where they build visual representations of lexical categories by clustering different meanings around a core prototypical sense. Concordancers can offer help here, but teachers may need to assist by conducting their own searches then editing the results into examples that extend rather than repeat a given context. For example, the adjective 'independent' has cognates in many languages but from a search of the Brown corpus one can find among the first 28 concordances the following very different types of usage, establishing a broad range of possible meanings, though all with a shared core:

i  A number of strong independent agencies, established in some cases with gov...
ii  For this reason, he appears as an independent and self-reliant figure, whose rugged indivi...
iii  "National Association of Schools of Art". Independent art schools granting degrees must, naturally...
iv  anitaire against the Soviets or posing as an independent, balancing power in between Russia and Germa...
v  A binomial experiment consists of **f independent binomial trials, all with the same probabili...
vi  ago, colonized, and stayed until Laos became independent in 1953 – the land had been even more delight...

In the initial case, the sense is 'free of government interference'. In the second, the reference is to a character type who makes their own way in the world. In the third, the reference is to a specialized freedom to grant academic degrees. In the fourth, the meaning encompasses a state's freedom of action. The last (vi) is also a reference to a state, but is more specifically a state's freedom from colonial rule. In meaning v, the reference is to a mode of experimentation where the results of one procedure will not affect another. One can argue that all of these meanings could be encompassed in a single core sense, such as 'unaffected by other phenomena', and that this sense is being adapted to a context. But the context is itself rarely that explicit. For example, meaning ii refers to a person's character and meaning vi to a condition which can only be fully understood inside the knowledge frame of colonialism. The knowledge for meaning vi is not immediately available from the context, but the meaning is immediately recognizable to any individual with a moderate historical awareness. Teachers may know how much of this knowledge about a word can be transferred from an equivalent form across languages. However, in some cases it clearly cannot be, whilst in others that knowledge may simply not be there. Teaching lexis, therefore, is not just a case of recycling words but of recycling words in variable contexts that in combination may at least start to set out the encyclopaedic nature of a meaning and which may also require elucidation and cultural or historical background. Finally there is also the issue of the other words with which a given term is likely to co-occur, and of the larger need to know how it will fit together with their meanings.

# 8
# Usage and Grammatical Meaning

**Introduction**

In CL, the nature of grammar is a subject of some controversy, as among, for example, the construction grammars of Lakoff (1987) and Goldberg (1995; 2006), the radical construction grammar of Croft (2001) and the cognitive grammar of Langacker (1987). However, all these approaches share some core views of what grammar is, how it is acquired and how it is used to shape utterances that we can understand. These views can be summarised as follows:

- A grammar consists of what Langacker calls symbolic complexes, or, meanings that combine others are thus themselves symbolic.
- The principles of schematicity and inheritance are fundamental to the nature of grammatical meaning.
- Both grammatical and lexical meanings are conceptually shaped as categories that construe a situation in a given manner.
- Grammar is acquired through usage, and, because usage varies from speaker to speaker, different individuals may possess different mental representations of the same form.

In this chapter I will first explore how these principles could be elaborated as the basis of a pedagogical grammar. To do this I will look more closely at the construction as the central grammatical form and will then consider how such forms are acquired through usage as a type from tokens. Next I will consider how this model impacts upon our approach to teaching grammar and language generally.

## Constructions

A construction is basically a meaning that combines others to create one that cannot be predicted from the combined parts (Goldberg 2006). A basic example is a prepositional phrase, and a very basic instantiation of this would be the preposition 'to', the definite article and the noun in the expression, 'to the house'.

If spoken alone, the word, 'house' and the phrase 'the house' carry more specific meanings than 'to'. We can understand this better if we consider the dialogue given in example (93):

(93) A: 'I'm going to... to...'
B: 'to the house?'

Speaker A shows how the word 'to' has a type of meaning that invites speaker B to insert a more specific meaning after it. It is as if the speaker is opening a space into which to insert a meaning whose exact nature cannot be immediately specified. Second, if we were to try to substitute the verb 'go' with another in this example, we would find that a quite restricted range of forms were possible. For example, we could not insert 'eat' or 'like'. This is because the word 'to' has set up schema of metaphorical or actual spatial direction and this restricts the type of verbs one can use with it.

A last point to note is that we are in fact using two constructions here. One is the NP, 'the house', and the other is the prepositional phrase 'to the house'. We can see that this last expression has been built from two pieces and hence places one meaning inside another. The first meaning grounds a thing, in this case a location or 'house'; the second specifies a direction or an image of a destination with the preposition 'to'. Thus we see that word meanings are incorporated into constructions and have their senses modified by them. Construction meanings are incorporated into others and are modified again. Language is like a series of lenses, where one meaning changes how the one beneath is seen, and this in its turn has the same effect.

Traditional grammars used a distinction between *open class* and *closed class* words. All languages must constantly evolve new words to symbolise the new meanings created by technological and social change. The larger lexicon consists of words that are 'open' to such innovation. They are therefore called 'open class' and constitute the greater part of the language. Closed class words, by contrast, do not readily admit new members. Closed class words are pronouns, prepositions, determiners and auxiliary verbs and are also seen as grammatical words. Traditionally, closed class words expressed a language's grammatical core, or the hard and fast structures that made it what it was.

CL retains the closed–open distinction but perceives the closed class as expressing schematic, relational meanings (Talmy 2000). Closed class words can even be called 'image-schematic' because of how they structure the relationships between lexical meanings according to the experiences of an embodied cognition. Thus prepositions express our 'vertical and lateral movement in space' or borrow this imagery to structure abstract relations. By the same token, determiners summate the gestalt bounding of an entity, as when we constitute it out of featural indeterminacy and nail down what we want to talk about and hold.

## Type and token

A perhaps even more significant point concerning constructions is illustrated in figure 16. This figure shows how a very basic construction such as an NP or 'the house' can be analysed at different levels of schematicity. The lowest level is highly restricted. 'The house' must generally be analysed as a reference to a specific building designed for habitation. As we have seen, the next level is much more productive. 'The + noun' can be instantiated in many ways. Another level is more productive still and sees the construction's meaning as the grounding of whatever is being

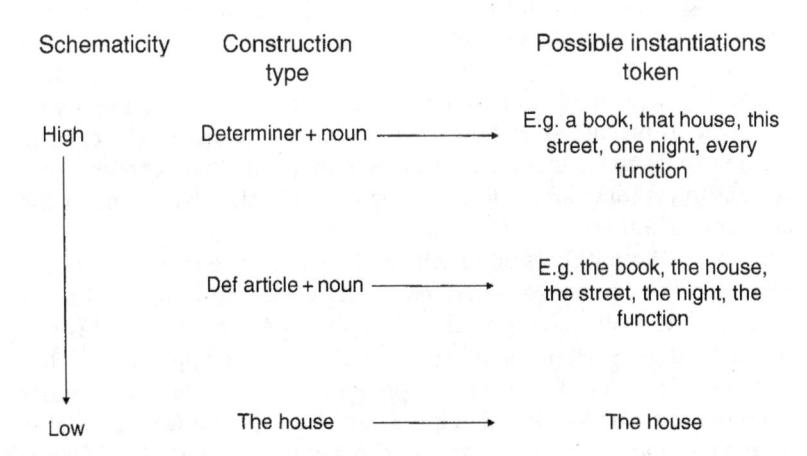

| Schematicity | Construction type | Possible instantiations token |
|---|---|---|
| High | Determiner + noun ⟶ | E.g. a book, that house, this street, one night, every function |
|  | Def article + noun ⟶ | E.g. the book, the house, the street, the night, the function |
| Low | The house ⟶ | The house |

*Figure 16* How a construction's productivity can increase in proportion to its schematicity

discussed. This is the wider meaning of a 'determiner+noun', allowing expressions such as 'a car'. Thus we can see how greater schematicity can allow greater productivity.

To explain this relationship between schematicity and productivity, I will explore two terms that CL has borrowed from lexicography, *type* and *token*. Originally the terms referred to words but now they apply to constructions also. For the lexicographer a *type* is the defined word that appears in the dictionary, whereas the *token* is a specific instance of its use. In the case of construction grammar, the 'type' is not a dictionary form, but the symbol, or construction, and meaning stored by the mind. 'Token' still remains the form that is used. We could hear and produce the phrase 'the house' so many times that we only store it as itself. In this case the stored type will match the uttered token. This is shown at the bottom of figure 16. At this level, the expression's schematicity and productivity are minimal. The form cannot recruit different words and its meaning will vary relatively little. However, there are too many nouns in the average English speaker's lexicon for each to be stored separately with, for example, a definite article and an indefinite article. Therefore to create noun phrases that refer to everything we want to talk about we will have to use a construction specified at a level of schematicity where there is a definite article but no specified noun.

As explained, in CL 'the+noun' is not a pre-specified grammatical structure in the sense of a pattern that is filled by different lexical forms. It is a symbolic complex whose meaning needs to be completed by the noun's more exact meaning. Generative grammarians suggest that the mind marks words according to their part of speech. This is essential so that words marked as 'verbs' could not follow a definite article. CL does not postulate a rule-bound system of this kind. In CL, placing a verb after 'the' is precluded by how it simply makes no sense. The definite article's indicative function is at odds with words that represent processes, unless these are first conceptualised as if they had some of the attributes of a thing.

If we recall our discussion of schematicity and inheritance we should remember how a category may be conceptualised through its inheritance of the features of one that is more schematic, thus 'trees' are understood as types of plant. This principle can be applied to a construction. Any word following the preposition 'in' will inherit features from the construction of which it is a part. Thus, even if we use a highly schematic noun such as 'thing' we can see how its meaning inherits features from the schema of containment when it becomes part of the construction 'in the thing'.

Some might ask whether we can accurately describe a construction using linguistic terms or parts of speech. Here we have to mark a difference between the categories that linguists use to describe words, and types of schema which actually guide their use. The precise status of grammatical categories such as 'noun' or 'verb' is still debatable in CL. A key feature of CL is that it is not reductive. This means that terms cannot be reduced to a grammatical category. For Croft (2001), parts of speech are purely epiphenomenal, or a deduction that is made about the relationships at play in a given construction. They are not real, or phenomenal in the sense of being used by the mind to build meaningful language. Croft's point is that 'no syntactic test will pick out' only and all of the entities 'that one wants to call verbs across all languages' (Goldberg 2006: 225). In Croft's position, the ways in which we describe a noun are generalisations based upon how nouns feature in a construction. They are properties that emerge from the construction itself and not from the nature of the parts that it assembles (2001). Croft's position has not gone uncriticised but unfortunately this is not a debate that I have the space to examine in detail. For our pedagogical perspective the key point is that we use schematic meanings to combine those that are less so. Teaching a grammar is therefore broadly about teaching what these meanings are and how they combine the forms that they do.

## Usage

Let us imagine that we have a couple who live in a house. The couple have a very specific reference for the word 'house', and are always saying such things as 'I've got to go back to *the house*' or 'I left my bag in *the house*'. Using a term borrowed from Konrad Lorenz (1957) there is some probability that these language users will *entrench* the construction as 'the house'. In other words they will store a type that matches their token. These learners store this construction ready-formed and do not have to assemble it. Then, let us imagine another couple who live in a flat and only rarely refer to 'the houses' of friends. This last couple might store 'the house' as more schematic and hence more productive meanings, or as something like 'the+thing'. In this way we can see how the type of language knowledge that we build is shaped by the form of usage we experience. Different forms of usage will produce different type–token relations. All speakers of a language do not therefore operate with the same grammatical competence. Rather they process the tokens of language through types of varying schematicity.

The concepts of type and token also tell us something about grammatical irregularity. In CL, irregularity is not defined according to an idea of deviance because there is no concept of a rule from which the form has deviated. Rather, irregularity must be described as a lack of productivity. Furthermore, there may be cognitive reasons that favour irregularity as a phenomenon.

In English, most irregular verbs have not been evolved by phonological processes within the recent form of the language but have been passed down from the Old English and the Germanic languages from which modern English arose. However, there is a detectable tendency for irregular verbs with a lower frequency to regularise. For example, 'wed' has quite a low frequency of use and we can already see a regular past participle beginning to establish itself as in the adjectival 'wedded bliss' (Lieberman *et al.* 2007). A CL analysis would reject Lieberman *et al.*'s conclusion that this is because the rule-governed nature of language is asserting itself. According to a principle of usage, irregular verbs are cognitively efficient because they presuppose a type–token match where the form that is produced is the same as the one that is entrenched. Where a common form must be constructed, as when we add a morpheme '-ed' to the verb stem to make a past participle, the process is cognitively less efficient. Storing rarer verbs as 'V+ed', however, is an effective way to use our cognitive capacity since we do not have to store a past tense form for every verb that we use. Therefore rarer verbs will regularise because this is cognitively less burdensome. But where the verbs are common, it is easier to keep them in a form where they are ready for use. Irregular forms must be stored as a type–token match, for there is no sense in which they can be constructed from other components. The converse does not always hold true, however. When a verb is regular, this does not presuppose that it is always produced from a 'verb+ed'. The same principle of usage will ensure that the past participle of a more common regular verb such as 'stop' will also be stored in the form in which it is used or in a way in which type and token match (Taylor 2002), though again, the extent to which this happens will vary from one person to another. This last point should make clear that I am not suggesting that verbs are irregular because they are common, rather, that irregularity is retained more successfully in a language's common elements because it is cognitively efficient to do so. As we can see from the increasing use of 'wedded', the converse will also hold true. The verb is rare and is therefore regularising quite rapidly. A point that I have made to second language students is that they should appreciate irregular verbs as a way to save long-term cognitive effort with some short-term investment of the same. Irregular verbs, once learnt, have the advantage of being cognitively 'ready-to-go'.

## Language learning as construction learning

The above discussion makes one very general point for those interested in second or first language acquisition. This is that, broadly, learners have to do two things:

- entrench words and their encyclopaedic meanings;
- entrench constructions and their encyclopaedic meanings.

From these points two others follow. First, the units or constructions that we write or utter are also the building blocks of language's cognitive organisation. Language, therefore, is no longer seen as divided between a *competence* whose stability makes it available for study and a *performance* that is too deformed by context and too changeable to yield a consistent, scientific description. Because second language learners will have a different exposure to different forms we cannot assume that one will acquire the same forms in the same order as another. Teachers should work in the expectation that one learner may treat a form as productive when another acquires it as a fixed phrase. At the same time there will be forms that have so little significance or emotional interest that they may not be acquired at all.

Second, teachers should think less about separating language knowledge into regular components governed by rule, and those that are irregular and hence impervious to scientific generalisation. Irregular forms identify some of the less productive features of a language but are treated as having 'equal value' when 'words', types of 'phrase' and 'clause' can all be treated as symbolic (Fried and Ostman 2004: 12). Teachers should therefore think more about teaching meanings of variable schematicity and productivity.

## Recognising constructions

A construction is any pairing of form with meaning use such that one aspect of the meaning use is not strictly predicted from the component parts (Goldberg 2006). This means, broadly, that if we list three items at random, 'house, room, wall', it is evident that although each is meaningful, and each has a semantic relationship to the other, they do not combine to create any meaning which individually they do not already have. However, if we take another three words, 'I eat chicken', we can see that when we bring them together in this order we can create a meaning that individually the words do not possess and which cannot be predicted from their individual meanings. There is first a syntactic relationship where an agent 'I' submits an object 'chicken' to a process 'eat', and second a semantic one where 'I' a human agent performs the human function of consuming an edible creature. We could call this a straightforward transitive construction because it has a meaning where one entity, an agent, causes a change of state in another. However, it is difficult to know how often such an open-ended construction as the transitive is actually used. As we noted when discussing cognitive frames, a verb such as 'sell' will presuppose that its agent is a seller and its object must be a saleable entity. Equally, 'eat' assumes an agent that is capable of consumption and an object that is edible. Therefore these verbs may restrict the participant roles to certain meanings within a given construction. In other words, clause length will pivot around the verb (Goldberg 1995, 2006). However, Talmy's point about the schematic nature of other closed class words should not be forgotten either (2000). For example, a prepositional phrase will do much to determine the type of verb and hence the other types of participant role allowed in a construction. Thus examples (94) and (95) allow very different types of verb because of the different types of spatial relation or space-based image schemas that are allowed.

(94) I _____ to the street
(95) I _____ on the street

A central, but by no means sole focus for teachers looking at longer constructions must therefore be verbs and prepositions.

## Teaching constructions

A construction can be an entity that is:

- filled, or where all of the words or morphemes are specified;
- partially filled, or where some of the words or bound morphemes are specified;
- where none of the words or bound morphemes are specified.

Usage and Grammatical Meaning 185

Further, the same combination of words can be analysed as a construction that represents each of these different categories. For example, if we say 'the house', we have a construction where all the words are specified. However, we might also call this 'the+N' and hence a construction where one word is specified. Finally we might have 'determiner+N or NP', where none of the words are filled. As explained, usage will be the main factor that determines which of these three forms a speaker uses.

I now consider how the filled category helps us conceptualise what a construction is. Next I will consider some general pedagogical principles when teaching constructions. Finally I will look more specifically at the challenges of teaching partially filled and empty constructions.

## Teaching filled constructions: idioms

Idioms typify what is meant by a filled construction. Idioms also make clear how constructions possess a meaning that supersedes the meanings of the elements they combine. They also show how a given expression can mandate some lexical items and preclude others. Consider this expression:

(96) We'll be tarred with the same brush

We say we will be 'tarred with the same brush' when we worry that our association with somebody will make us look guilty of the same wrongdoing as they. The idiom probably originates in the punishment where those held guilty of crimes were covered in tar and feathers. The tar would stick the feathers to the skin causing burning and irritation. As with all idioms, we cannot understand the combination of words used in this expression by knowing the individual meanings of the terms and decoding the syntax that combines them. Collectively the words have a meaning that differs from that which should be created as the sum of their parts. Applying 'tar' with a 'brush' does not seem to express 'being involved in others' wrong-doing'. This larger meaning is finally what belongs to the construction. The meaning of such idioms is so different to anything that can be derived from the sum of their lexical parts that they typify how constructions are symbolic entities, possessing a meaning that overrides those of their components.

As is implied by our discussion of 'tarred with the same brush', idioms are built from metaphors and these metaphors are often rooted in past practice. Exploring the roots of an idiom can thus provide an interesting glimpse into past cultural practices from which linguistic meanings emerge. The point is reinforced by Boers (2001) who found out that exploring the literal roots of idioms would improve their uptake. Asking students to find, then present, the story behind an idiom can therefore form a useful homework project.

Proverbs have a different interest. For example, our cultures derive a saying such as 'a rolling stone gathers no moss' by using their experience of the natural world to frame the observation that people who move around stay free from normal financial and social responsibility. This is a normal process of metaphor formation. Less common is how the proverb preserves the metaphor's source domain as a mode of expression that can describe some of the situations we encounter. It is a source domain looking for a target, in other words (Holme 2004). Accordingly, learners can be encouraged to engage in simple matching exercises where they try to work out proverbial meanings, then find an appropriate context.

## Teaching partially filled constructions: lexis, meaning and conceptualisation

Partially-filled and empty constructions are more difficult to identify than the fixed idioms just discussed as they require that we identify which words are mandated by the construction and which are not. Lexis is therefore central to the identification of such forms. Closed class words are more likely candidates for being fixed terms than others, but this principle can mean that we will miss expressions built around other types of lexis. Therefore to identify a construction's fixed terms we also have to evolve a notion of what it means. Finally, therefore, identifying the construction's lexis also means exploring its meaning. To understand the meaning fully, it may also help to know how it has been conceptualised. Central to teaching a construction, therefore, is the identification of its

- lexis,
- meaning, and
- conceptualisation

which gives the acronym, LMC.

Some might question why syntax is missing from the LMC acronym. However, my argument will be that syntax is not something that can be usefully abstracted from the construction and taught. When we teach a pattern in language, we teach it as a variable set of lexical combinations.

Once the lexis or the meanings restricting its use have been identified the syntax will be made manifest by these forms. In a construction that is empty or partially filled our teaching strategy will not be to specify the lexical gaps as grammatical terms, for these do not capture the construction's controlling meaning. Instead we will look for words that come closest to expressing the construction's meaning. For an example I will take the empty construction, the English ditransitive – or double object – construction.

The ditransitive is unfilled but probably best exemplified by the verb 'give' since this captures its core symbolism. Example (97) shows one instantiation of the construction whilst example (98) specifies it in a way that does more to make its central meaning apparent:

(97) I allowed them a little practice
(98) I gave them a new book

Clearly a syntactic specification of the construction as NP+V+NP+NP is unlikely to help students who want to use it procedurally. A better approach is to furnish a form that takes us closer to the construction's prototypical meaning. This is provided by the verb 'give' in example (98). So even in an empty construction, the prime task is to identify lexis central to that construction's meaning and hence to furnish learners with a productive prototype.

## Teaching partially filled constructions: bound morphemes, inflections and lexis

Filled constructions are self-identifying. There is no problem about finding out where they begin or end because if one cuts out one of their items of lexis the meaning will start to fall apart. Identifying the thousands of partially filled constructions used in everyday speech is a much more complicated task. Because any given sentence embeds one construction inside another, it is no mean task to determine simply where they begin and end. Further, it is not always clear whether words are a fixed part of the form or simply one way to express its larger controlling meaning. Yet the task must be begun if teachers are to help learners identify the productive units of language upon which a native-speaker repertoire will be based.

The above problem is made more complicated by how we talk of a construction as being partially filled, not just by words but also by bound morphemes. Thus partially filled constructions include forms that have:

- common bound morphemes but no common lexis;
- both common bound morphemes and lexis;
- common lexis but no common bound morphemes.

## Teaching partially filled constructions: bound morphemes

English constructions that are partially filled by bound morphemes will normally consist of the following kinds:

- one-word noun constructions where the morpheme is either a plural inflection or the genitive inflection (-'s);
- one-word verb constructions where the morpheme creates a past or present participle, marks the past tense, or signifies third-person agreement in the present;
- plural noun phrases, verb groups, or comparative phrases and clauses where the adjective takes the inflection -er or -est.

Highly inflected languages such as Russian, Polish, or even moderately inflected ones such as German will naturally furnish many more examples in both categories. Such languages are also more problematic when it comes to analysing a 'stem+inflection' construction as part of a phrase or clause, but this does not mean that their teachers should be drawn into an approach dominated by declension learning, any more than their English language counterparts. As both structural- and functional-based approaches have recognised, bound morphemes that symbolise case are used as part of the longer clause- or phrase-length constructions in which they occur. Grammar translation approaches to case seem to make implausible cognitive demands on students by arguing that they analyse the need for a given case, find the relevant declension in their mental grammar, search through it for the appropriate morpheme, then insert that construction into the correct place in another construction. Even treating this as an intermediate step towards proceduralisation in production and processing implies a somewhat contradictory strategy where the student is taken further from their goal in order to help achieve it. One approach to highly inflected languages might be to ask whether the inflection can be treated as determining the nature of a clause- or phrase-length construction as if they were a type of preposition. In practice, though, it can be difficult to postulate a phrase- or clause-length construction as having nominal inflections as its fixed forms, except within a specific declension. Consider the Polish negative and genitive shown in examples (99–102):

   (99)  Kot nie pije mleka (the cat doesn't drink milk – the cat not drink of milk)
  (100)  Agent+*nie*+process+object (something drinkable)+-*a*
  (101)  Kot mleka nie pieje (the cat doesn't drink milk – the cat of milk not drink)
  (102)  Agent+object (something drinkable)+-*a* + *nie* + process

One use of the Polish genitive is after a negative, as in the construction shown in example (99). This makes it temping to specify the construction to a student as possessing a fixed negative form 'nie' and genitive morpheme '-a' as in example (100). But this works only for one of the words that expresses a drinkable substance, 'mleko', or (milk). Among other objects that could realistically complement the verb 'pije (drink)' there is quite a wide range of genitive morphemes. For example, there is 'wod*y*' (water), 'sok*u*' (juice), 'wodk*i*' (vodka). Therefore to be fully productive the inflection can only be specified as a meaning and not as a form in the way shown in example (102). An additional problem is that highly inflected languages tend to allow different word orders, making example (101) another possible instantiation of this meaning, though with a slightly different construal. Teachers faced with such problems have two possible strategies. First, they can help students to master the words in a particular case as filled constructions, saying simply the genitive 'mleka' or 'soku' instead of the nominatives, for example. Second, they could practise building one or other of the negative constructions around these forms, perhaps changing some of the other terms such as the verb and the subject rather than the noun, whose inflected form is central to the construction.

In English, learning inflections as an element in a larger construction is only problematic in the case of verbs, with irregularity being the main problem. Here, though, some morphemes such as the past participle '-en' (broken, taken, shaken etc.) may be more generalisable than teachers often realise. There is therefore a case for teaching such forms as sets that share a common bound morpheme, then trying to hold these together in a common text. In the following example, verbs are taught and practised together because they share a common past tense irregular form, one which is anyway more salient in orthography and phonology. Students can play with text by seeing if they can insert different words into different slots. They can then discuss whether their version makes sense. The example given in text (103) has the answers written in but if it is set as a cloze, students will need the help of the teacher and peers to find a solution.

(103) School Report: learn, burn, spill, spoil, smell and spell
Daisy <u>learnt</u> little in technology last term. She <u>burnt</u> her pizza, <u>spilt</u> her tomato sauce on the floor and <u>spoilt</u> her partner's work. In her notes she <u>spelt</u> pizza as if it were an Italian city then wrote up recipes that <u>smelt</u> of everything she failed to cook. In this year, therefore, she <u>burnt</u> much, <u>spilt</u> more, <u>spoilt</u> most things and <u>spelt</u> it all wrong in work that <u>smelt</u> of her cooking.

Such texts can also be used to introduce the constructions that a given verb will create around itself, for example, 'Agent+spill+something *over* something/someone', or the intransitive, 'Subj+smell+*of* something'. This last can be explored as a contrast between examples (104) and (105):

(104) They smelt roses
(105) They smelt of roses

Putting verbs inside the constructions whose meanings they do much to tease out gives the verb a context of use that helps the learner grasp its meaning. It also improves the learner's control of the verb's inflected forms whilst fostering the recognition that verbs with similar meanings may occur in the same constructions:

(106) I noticed them go
(107) I heard her speak

If the 'make-them-do-something' construction is ignored, the form shown in sentences (106) and (107) will almost always occur with types of perceptual experience that can treat their object as being in motion, or conceptualise it as deserving of dynamic attention. Thus 'watched', 'observed', 'noticed', 'sensed' and 'looked at' all instantiate what Dirven and Radden (2007: 283) call a *perceptual event schema* but with a dynamic object. The prepositional verb, 'looked at' would therefore be excluded from the schema because it does not express our perception of movement. Thus teachers who are looking for ways to practise a regular past tense, 'V+ed' construction might consider setting it inside examples of this form. They can then group a set of regular verbs that all express the schema. The event schema can provide a thematic unity that approaches the lyrical. Example (108) shows how students can be asked to produce examples of the construction then assemble them into a poem.

(108) *Perceptions*
I did not see her leave
but in a darkened room
I sensed her move
and heard her shut
the door then from
the window watched her splash
along the rain soaked street.

Students can play further with such texts, rewriting them in multiple ways, and practising them as they do so. Thus learners can study the text and see how many versions of it they can create that make sense. They can do this using different examples of verbs that express a perceptual event schema ('see, watch, notice, feel, hear, sense'). They can also swap round words in the text, changing 'felt her move' to 'felt her shut', for example.

The category meanings of the English past simple and its conceptual foundations are generally relatively straightforward. The tense expresses bounded events. The event is therefore seen as if in its entirety or with a bird's eye view (Radden and Dirven 2007: 175). The category representation will be relatively straightforward because it can usefully be split between no more than three meanings. The first is when the event-time is temporarily separate from the speaking-time. The second meaning is so different that its relationship to the first may be missed. This is when the tense expresses an impossible condition, as in 'If your father found you here now he would get mad'. Speculatively, the relationship lies in an association between the past and a state of impossibility, perhaps because one cannot undo what has been done. The third meaning only applies to a handful of modal verbs but relates more clearly to the second, and is that of politeness. The relationship between the second and third meanings is vested in how indefinite meanings assume a tentativeness on the part of the speaker and give to the hearer an option as to whether they will fulfil the request or not. The past tense could therefore

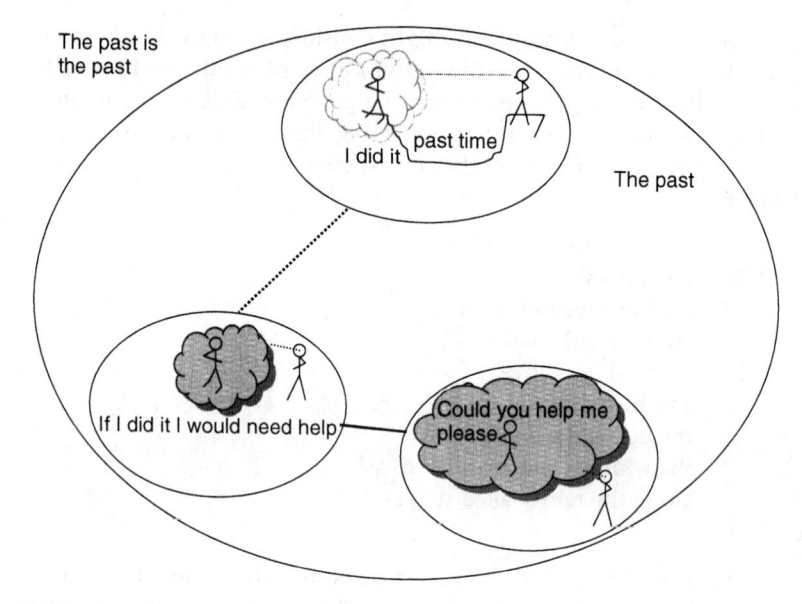

192  *Cognitive Linguistics and Language Teaching*

*Figure 17* Representing the English past tense as a category meaning

be represented to the student through figure 17, with each node forming a separate unit of study.

The figure stresses how the past makes actions into recreated or abstract phenomena, but the tenuous historical nature of the link between these uses of the same tense may cast doubt on the usefulness of treating them as a category at all. The category link between the narrative past and the impossible past is therefore treated as tenuous. The tense's prototypical meaning is not a difficult one to present and is already well supported by activities that stress its prototypical narrative function. Stories themselves are also a welcome medium for lexical expansion and further encourage a critical reader engagement which will in turn provide an arena for other types of language practice.

## Teaching partially filled constructions: lexis and morphemes

One construction that can have both a fixed morpheme and a word is the English comparative. Comparatives typically compare two noun phrases with a copula verb and a comparative adjective. The two noun phrases must have grounds for comparison and this will often arise from their having a category relationship, as between 'sailing boats' and 'power boats', for example, in sentence (109):

(109) Sailing boats are bett*er than* motor boats
(110) Sailing boats are *less* manoeuverable *than* motor boats

These constructions are often taught through the comparison of two entities such as two cities or two football teams. Clearly these scenarios set the construction in a realistic context and have several other merits. First they ask the student to choose the appropriate comparative, as between those that add '-er' and those that take the *scala*r 'more' in front of them. Second, they require the learner to select an adjective that can be *scaled,* avoiding expressions such as 'more unique than'. Third they require a comparative adjective that can find the grounds of comparison between the nouns in the clause. The more schematic the adjective the more it will be inclusive of the noun's larger category meaning. Thus 'better' in example (109) furnishes many more grounds for comparison than 'manoeuverable' in sentence (110).

Interestingly native speakers will quite often scale what is technically unscalable. In one famous case the error was deliberate:

(111) Some animals are more equal than others. (Orwell 1945)

George Orwell's assertion is technically meaningless. However, the sentence has become so meaningful that it has echoed down through the twentieth and twenty-first centuries. This is possible because this comparative construction (*more* adj *than* NP) confers a meaning upon the adjectives that it recruits, subverting their original prototypical sense. In other words, the construction imparts the property of gradability to a non-gradable term. We can also understand how the meaning of a word itself is prototypically an idealisation that will change when used in a construction. Exploring the basis of such meaning shifts can form an interesting activity:

Activity 38   The basis of comparison
1 Divide students into groups and tell each group to make as many comparative constructions as they can with the adjectives 'good' and 'bad'. Tell them to brainstorm, write down each example, and not to think too carefully about the sense of each sentence.

2 Exemplify two or three other comparative constructions, for example:

- less troublesome than ...
- not as demanding as ...

or the nominal:

- less trouble than ...
- not as much work as ...

3 Ask each group to provide their list of comparative sentences with 'good' or 'bad'.
4 Select any sentence from any group at random. Ask them to state the basis of the comparison by providing as many other comparative sentences as they can using the constructions you have just given them. For example:
Comparison:
   Dogs are better than children
Basis of comparison:
   Dogs are less troublesome than children
   Dogs are not as expensive as children etc.
Provide them with some of the lexis they need to extend the basis of comparison.

An interesting feature of this exercise is how the basis of comparison is in fact a development of the encyclopaedic meanings of 'good' or 'bad' in this context. The basis of comparisons thus stands in a hyponym relationship to the good–bad categories, bringing learners closer to the issue of how we construct adjectival meaning.

Another comparative construction that operates with quite a restricted range of meanings is generally conceptualised from what Radden and Dirven (2007) call a *cognition schema*, with verbs such as 'think, realise, wanted, hoped (for), know'.

(112)   He is wis*er than* I thought

This can be practised with scenarios where students are asked to remember when they got a wrong impression of somebody.

Activity 39     Pride and prejudice
   1 Brainstorm for the 'cognitive' verbs: 'think, realise, wanted, hoped (for), know, expect, imagine'.

2 Brainstorm for adjectives that describe somebody's character.
3 Ask students to remember somebody who they got wrong and to say why they did or did not like this person.
4 Ask them to make constructions using example (112) as a model.
5 Repeat the exercise with things they bought and subsequently found disappointing and/or places they visited or events they attended that were a let-down.
8 Provide the verbs, 'mean, intend, plan, and expect' then repeat with an idea that 'turned out better than planned'.

Activities 38 and 39 both show how teachers may need to place greater stress on exploring category meanings if they are to help students use constructions productively and correctly. My discussion of hyponym relations within encyclopaedic meaning introduced the principle of inheritance. Here, I argued that we conceptualise subordinate categories out of the inherited features of superordinate ones. Thus our conceptualisation of a tree would occur with the inherited features of those of a plant. This principle of an inheritance hierarchy is also crucial to how we extend a construction. Consider sentences (113) and (114):

(113) I knitted him a jumper
(114) I suggested him a new idea*

Sentence (113) was used by Goldberg (1995) to illustrate how the ditransitive can make us understand that a transfer of possession has occurred when the verb has no such meaning. Arguably it achieves this because it is part of what Sag and Wasow (1999) called an inheritance hierarchy. Thus 'knit' inherits a meaning of 'giving' from that of the construction itself. It can do so because there is nothing in its meaning that conflicts with the idea of transferred possession. Example (114) is asterisked because it represents a usage that would be unacceptable to most native speakers. In contrast to example (113), the sentence illustrates how some verb meanings are at odds with that of the construction and it is this which creates the impression of ungrammaticality. 'Suggest' puts an idea forward for uptake or rejection and implies that either process can occur. The meaning of 'suggest' thus runs counter to the idea of a transfer of possession that is inherited from the ditransitive construction. By contrast, the ditransitive can be used with the speech verb 'tell', as in 'I told him my idea', and this is exactly because the verb expresses a transfer of the message from speaker to hearer when some other speech verbs do not.

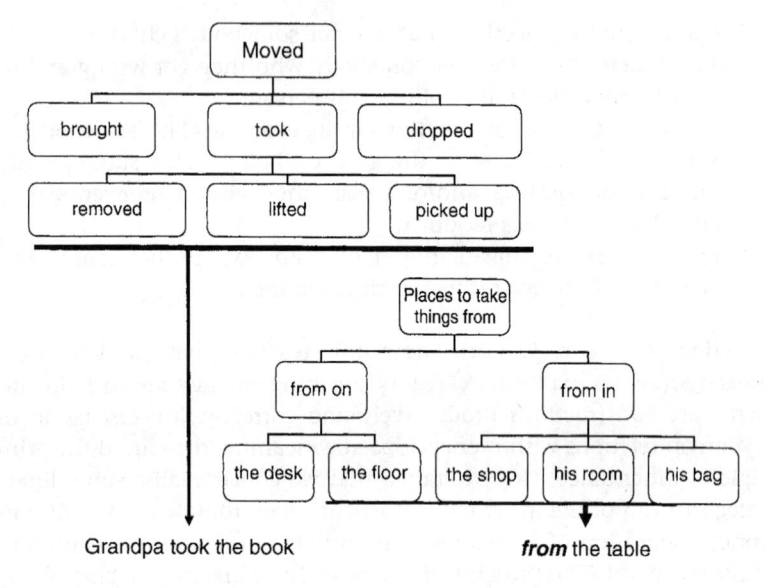

196  *Cognitive Linguistics and Language Teaching*

*Figure 18* Using hyponym charts to explore construction meanings

Teasing out these inherited features and helping students to develop a declarative, then procedural, knowledge of them forms part of the 'meaning' focus in our LMC approach to construction teaching. Thus, students can experiment with various alternative forms of a construction to test quite where the boundaries of its meaning lie. This approach can be helped by the use of hyponym charts.

In figure 18, I show how a hyponym chart can help students understand how a given schema shapes meanings that the construction allows. The student uses the chart to develop the appropriate inheritance hierarchy and to produce correct forms. Figure 18 uses a simple example to help extend their repertoire of verbs able to fit the prepositional phrase with 'from'. This provides a link between categorisation activities and expanding constructions.

Activity 40   Making constructions productive
1 Choose a clause-level construction relevant to your learners' needs.
2 Identify one or more words or phrases from the construction that have a meaning which is clearly restricted by the construction's schema. Try to think of some of the different words that can be

substituted for this item and arrange them in a category chart above it in the way shown in figure 18.
3 Remove most of the lexis from the chart and list it separately. Give a blanked chart, the construction, and the lexis to the learners.
4 In groups of four to six, the learners arrange the lexis in the chart and use it to produce as many valid versions of the construction as they can. They should speak or write the different versions of the construction.

The chart is used to feed appropriate terms directly into the construction, encouraging students to develop these as the subordinate terms of a schematic meaning.

A semantically complex English construction that combines lexis, or the auxiliary verb 'have', and a past participle morpheme such as '-ed' is the English present perfect. Our discussion of the tense and its use of deictic and complex time in chapter 3 revealed how this meaning can be problematic, particularly when it conceptualises event-time in ways that other languages do not. Most straightforward might be to consider the speech time as occupying a certain ground. Conceptually, when using the present perfect, the speaker is occupying the speaking time and extending it to include past or even future actions. In other words, the speaker is extending the temporal ground that they currently occupy to superimpose past and future onto their present. I illustrate this in figure 19. Figure 19 also makes the core point that a construction such as the present perfect cannot be usefully bundled as a single meaning that should be taught through one rule at one time. The category needs to be built up carefully over time, using different situations and contexts for each type of meaning. Some possible contexts are implied by the types of examples shown. Thus the way in which the present perfect of 'get' creates an act of present possession from one of past acquisition illustrates how the tense can superimpose deictic time onto speaking time. Very differently, the use of 'do' in 'I've done it before' reflects how the verb can set up an intermittent action along a given time line.

## Teaching partially filled constructions: lexis

When I address tense and aspect, I am using CL to help find new and more accurate ways of understanding forms that have already been identified and taught through meaning-based rules of thumb of varying accuracy. Of even greater interest are the types of constructions that may turn more on the presence of prepositions or preposition-like words. The

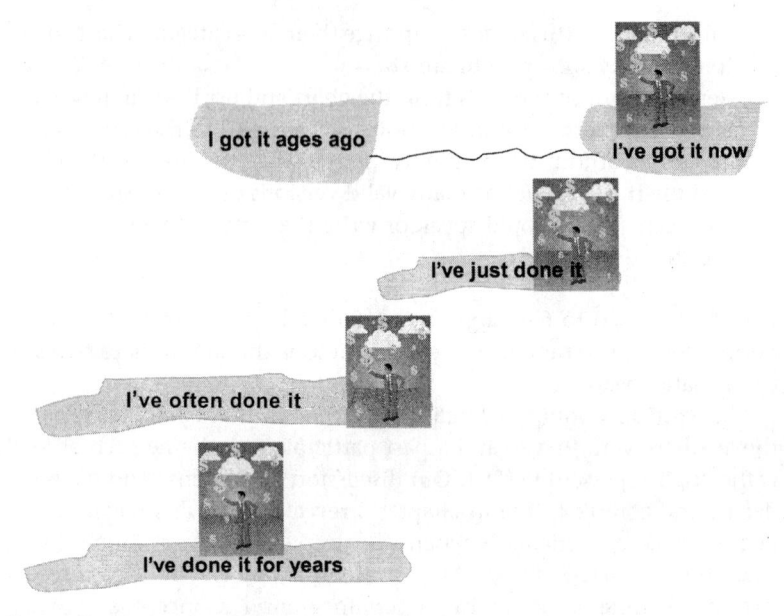

198  *Cognitive Linguistics and Language Teaching*

I got it ages ago
I've got it now
I've just done it
I've often done it
I've done it for years

*Figure 19* The present perfect: extending the time of speech

identification of such forms will greatly extend the repertoire of forms that teachers have to tackle.

One of the most difficult features of English is probably constructions that are built around prepositions. Consider the following sentences and the adjective + of +complement construction in particular.

(115) He thought me incapable of mastering anything
(116) Such people are capable ___ many things.
(117) Such people *are* _____ *of* doing much harm
(118) Such people *are* capable/certain/aware/glad/conscious/tired/sick *of* many things

For learners the difficulty of such forms rests in how different adjectives select different prepositions. A collocation-based method would treat the adjective and preposition as a chunk, or semi-fixed expression. There are three problems with this approach:

- 'in/capable of', or the collocation itself, is not a construction. We know this because 'of' is only added to 'capable' to show its relationship to a larger phrase. The collocation therefore has no productive use and will always be part of another form.

- The form is learnt as an adjective that requires a certain preposition rather than as a construction that requires a certain kind of adjective.
- Not seeing the construction means failing to see it as productive.

A construction approach would treat the closed class 'preposition' as the most likely fixed form, and the copula verb as another plausible candidate. The form that learners should be invited to substitute is exactly one of those a collocation approach treats as fixed, or the adjective itself. The construction's meaning seems to express the subject's enduring attributes. Thus one can contrast it with example (119), below, where 'with' suggests a complement which expresses the cause of the attributed state. Thus, 'I am angry *with* because you are the cause of my anger'. 'With' had an original meaning of temporary spatial proximity and originated in an Old English word 'wiþ' for 'against'. So the temporary presence of one feature becomes a cause of the condition attributed to another.

(119) I am happy/angry with you

In another example, of adjectival meanings in constructions being controlled by prepositions, sentence (120) shows that adjectives in a 'for' construction are constrained by an intentional meaning.

(120) I am eager/ready for many things

In these constructions, therefore, some alignment of the form with a meaning is possible. But two things must be remembered. First, in language, cultures conventionalise past acts of conceptualisation. By definition, conventionalisation adds to the pairing of form and meaning a certain arbitrariness. Second, constructions follow a general principle of category building, and their meanings cannot necessarily be captured as straightforward or consistent. The principles that bind one category member to another do not necessarily pertain to all its members (Lakoff 1987). Thus we know that birds fly, and generally construct our picture of 'a bird' from an inheritance of the feature of 'flight'. We must also accept that some birds are flightless and then look for another inherited feature to identify them as part of the category (Croft and Cruse 2004). By the same token, as an enduring attribute, 'capable of +verb+ing' may link more clearly to 'certain of+verb+ing' than to the more mental and less enduring 'tired of', though even in this last there is a category link with both 'tired of' and 'capable of' referring more to the subject's possession of the attribute than the attribute's stimulation of a changed condition in the subject. Yet bundling such meanings together may help successful retention and category construction even if the actual forms are in fact used as fixed phrases.

Although closed class words may *often* be a construction's only fixed terms, our previous discussion of idioms and fixed forms shows clearly how they are not *always* so. This also pertains when the construction is only partially filled. However, there is probably a tendency for constructions with fixed open class words to use the more schematic members of these classes. Consider the much analysed 'way' construction (Taylor 2002) in examples (121)–(124):

(121) I went a long way home
(122) I slept my way through University
(123) I studied my way to the top
(124) I took the steep way home

The fixed term, 'way' is the one closest to the construction's meaning. Like a preposition, it has a highly schematic meaning which conceptualises abstract relations first from a metonymy of 'path of movement is movement', then from a spatial metaphor of 'progress is forward motion' (Lakoff 1994). The construction is an interesting case also of how a meaning expressed through one of its elements will alter that of its verbs. 'Go' and 'sleep' would normally be categorised as intransitive. The construction overrides this, making transitivity itself into a feature that emerges from the construction. 'Way' can further confer the metaphor of 'progess as movement' upon verbs such as 'study' which is normally associated with a static process, and upon 'sleep' which may as a result be moved towards its sexual meaning. Teachers interested in putting across what is in fact quite a productive and expressive form can help students to develop the construction from a transitive movement-based meaning shown in example (124), through the odd but movement-based form shown in sentence (121). Activity 41 takes the 'way' construction as an example but is more interesting for how it exemplifies a general principle of identifying a construction then testing it to find the limits of its meaning.

Activity 41    Testing constructions to destruction
 1 The learners repeat the constructions: 'I took the long way home' and 'I went the long way home'.
 2 To get control of the constructions the learners can work in pairs and change them to interrogatives, building dialogues as follows:

A: Did you go the long way home?
B: No I went the short way.

3 The teacher writes the construction on the board and challenges the class to insert verbs that make no sense of it. Each time the class suggest verbs the teacher tries to adjust the construction to make sense of them. For example:

Learner: I bought the long way home.
Teacher says and writes: I bought my way out of trouble.

4 The learners write down the correct forms as they go.

Such activities assume some quick thought on the part of the teacher but are useful for showing how category meanings can be extended in unexpected ways.

## Teaching unfilled constructions

Unfilled constructions are empty of specific lexis but not of specific types of meaning. Predicting which lexical meanings will be congruent with those of a given construction is not always straightforward, however. Further, a given verb in an empty construction will impose constraints upon its participant roles, thus creating a more limited and less productive meaning within the empty construction's broader schematic meaning. Further, the construction's meaning is subject to the same process of metaphorical and metonymic extension as other categories.

Nakajima (2002) argued that a construction such as the ditransitive appears to have so many meanings that it cannot in fact be called a construction at all (cited in Goldberg 2006: 28). For him, this made the case for an autonomous syntax. Thus sentences (125)–(127) do not at first appear to inherit anything of the ditransitive's alleged prototypical presentational meaning:

(125) Mina guaranteed Mel a book
(126) Mina refused Mel a book
(127) Mina cost Mel his job

but we can in fact show that these sentences have inherited some features from the schema of transferred possession, though through a process of metaphorical of extension or other sense relation (Goldberg

1995, 2006). In sentence (125), the 'guarantee' makes an implicit future transfer of 'the book' from one person to another. Sentence (126) negates the possibility of transfer and hence extends the basic meaning through an antonymic relation. Example (127) uses the conceptual metaphor of transfer, or giving, to express causation. I make this metaphor explicit in sentence (128), where 'cause' is expressed through the metaphor of 'a gift':

(128) She gave him life (caused him to be born)

Accordingly, Goldberg (1995: 38) sets out the ditransitive as having multiple meanings. But all of these retain the core sense of a transfer of possession of one entity from agent to object.

Empty constructions such as the ditransitive were traditionally referred to as complementation patterns because of how they were defined by their arrangement of complements or, in the case of the ditransitive, by its double object structure. A summary of basic English complementation patterns will provide the following unfilled constructions:

*Intransitive*
You work very hard
She spoke slowly

*Transitive*
The children struck them
The manager said it was impossible

*Ditransitive*
I gave them the message
We cooked her a good meal

*Complex Transitive (resultative construction, Goldberg 2006)*
I have made him mad
I folded the paper flat

*Copula*
The children are crazy
She is the laziest

Most English curricula will cover these constructions in their early stages, recycling them through other combinations. But no matter what the students' level, teachers can always provide useful practice in these forms by furnishing an example, then asking students to see if they can or cannot fit a given set of verbs into the pattern, for example, with the resultative I have used:

drive, force, flatten*, strike, shake, sleep*, hammer, march*, call,

rejecting the verbs marked with asterisks.

Next, we can take an example where the verb creates a common construction and see how we can make this productive by substituting other parts of speech:

(129)  You drive me crazy/mad/insane/wild

The students can look at possible adjectives that can be substituted for 'crazy'. This can invite some discussion of adjectival meanings. For example, a student may produce sentence (130), which is asterisked as wrong. It is only possible in the resultative with 'make', shown in example (131), and here only marginally so. 'Made me look foolish' is probably the more common construction, perhaps because, unlike 'crazy', 'foolish' is construed as an enduring, though more placid, state, and hence as one whose characteristics can only 'look' to be forced upon us.

(130)  You drive me foolish*
(131)  You made me foolish

The encyclopaedic meanings of the plausible adjectives can also be explored. Thus one can look at how 'wild' can mean 'wild with love' or 'wild with rage'.

Further, when the students search for a meaning they may change the pattern slightly:

(132)  You drive me round the bend/up the wall

But this could show how this construction may not actually be straightforwardly about an object, 'me', and an adjective, object complement, 'crazy'. The complement is here a prepositional phrase, 'up the wall', but is a fixed form which is substitutable for an adjective.

In this way teachers can use filled or partially filled constructions to experiment with the unfilled forms in which they nest. They may find that students enjoy what is effectively a type of language play. Further, at any point a given instantiation can be contextualised within an appropriate scenario or dialogue.

As students develop their play with these constructions or start to apply them creatively in their own work, teachers can also note that the penalty of maximising a construction's productivity is the risk of extending the possibility for error. Consider example (133):

(133) They have to work very hard to just exchange for a bowl of rice
(author's data)

Ostensibly the error rests in the adjunct 'to...rice' and not in the main intransitive construction, which appears to be correct. In effect it is a failure to see the need for another construction that combines the main clause and the adjunct:

(134) They have to work very hard just to buy a bowl of rice

This construction could be described as:

(135) They have to do one thing *(just) to* do another

Often, then, what may seem to be a lexical error is better corrected at the constructional level. When teachers correct lexis by providing the appropriate constructional meaning through a schematically worded example, such as (135), they can then make this into a basis for practice and expansion in the way just outlined.

This example and the foregoing discussion make three important points. First, when students move past the elementary stage of language learning, their errors are unlikely to occur in basic unfilled constructions. This is probably because these core forms are combining others that may have lower rates of usage and closer lexical specification. These are the types of form on which teaching should be focused. Second, less schematic errors may often be perceived as lexical rather than constructional. In fact this is often a misunderstanding. A given meaning will require a certain construction and in its turn impose certain lexical requirements. Thus, the inappropriate, 'exchange for a bowl of rice' in example (133) is symptomatic of a larger failure to express this concept of 'exchange' as 'doing one thing just to get another'. Teachers should thus think more about how errors perceived as lexical may actually be a consequence of either an inability to find a larger construction, or of a failure to understand how to fit a construction's meaning with the appropriate term. Third, when correcting a construction, teachers need to think carefully about how to specify it and how to provide learnable and generalisable prototypes to make correction productive. They have to strike a judgment here between maximising the form's expressivity and so giving the student greater potential for error, or minimising both.

## Routines for more advanced students: lexis, meaning and conceptualisation

The control of a language entails control of countless constructions. The more advanced the learner, the more likely it is that construction learning will veer away from productive forms to those that operate with quite specific meanings and are appropriate for a limited range of contexts. The range of forms that competent language learners are going to require is therefore likely to defy prescription. Teachers therefore need procedures to help their students explore the constructions that they encounter in texts, may recognise at some level of understanding, but cannot use productively. In other words, they need to help students develop sufficient autonomy to explore and test constructions on their own.

## Encountering constructions

*Noticing* has acquired considerable significance as a term, both within cognitive psychology and second language acquisition. In cognitive psychology, the noticing hypothesis suggested that learning must be a result of some conscious attention being given to a target item. Noticing theory was used in SLA research to support the view that form will not be acquired subliminally from second language input but must be consciously 'noticed' and interpreted by the acquirer in order for it to be taken up into their language system (see for example, Ellis 1995).

In CL-directed pedagogy, however, the uptake of a form is primarily dependent upon its usage, and usage is more likely to occur after a form has been given some conscious attention. The issue therefore is not one of trying to identify the processes that students actually employ when they encounter a new form; the issue is how to help them pay attention to forms in a way that will help them foster their usage. 'Usage' should further mean exploring the form as a productive type, so that the learner's language can make a more successful response to their expressive needs. The learner must therefore frame their encounter with a second language as one where they are constantly asking, not whether they understand what they hear and read, but whether they have the capacity to make productive use of it. Learners should notice what they cannot use, not what they do not know.

## Finding useful forms

The first step is deciding where the form begins and ends, or what part of a text may have productive interest. Consider example (136) below. This was encountered when teaching a group of Hong Kong sixth-formers (ages approx. 17–18 years) how to write their own newspaper. To give them models for their own writing I was looking at various genres of article. These articles were sources of constructions that provided a means through which the learner could both reproduce the type of text under consideration whilst also expanding their general repertoire of forms. The article popularised some research findings:

(136) A new study shows an interesting link between exam success and the number of hours a day that a student studies.

How one isolates constructions from a longer text or identifies them as noticeable is very much a question of judgment. One criterion is to consider what Taylor calls a meaning's 'conceptual independence' (2002: 226–7). Conceptual independence refers to how well a term can stand as an independent meaning. Clearly nouns and verbs will have greater conceptual independence than such parts of speech as adjectives or determiners. If we say 'the' we expect another meaning to follow. If we say 'Home!' we could in certain contexts treat the meaning as complete. But a given part of speech is itself variable. A command, 'Stand!' is immediately interpretable but the word 'Put!' or even the phrase 'Put your clothes!' has almost no meaning at all (Taylor 2002: 226–7). The concept of conceptual independence can help teachers reject as candidates for study such forms as the collocation, 'link between', in example (136). They might opt instead for the entire noun phrase 'a link between one thing and another'.

In this case I first directed learners towards the clause itself, as the item likely to have the greatest conceptual independence. The clause was a basic transitive and ostensibly showed no particular problems. It could be expressed in the simplified form shown in example (137). Although straightforward, the clause expressed a specialised topic and we therefore experimented with this as a more limited construction that

*Table 3* Using a substitution table to explore a transitive construction

| The study   | shows     | something |
|-------------|-----------|-----------|
| The paper   | looks at  |           |
| The article | exposes   |           |
|             | finds     |           |
|             | discovers |           |
|             | uncovers  |           |

dealt with how studies, documents or texts showed certain things to be true or untrue:

(137)   The study shows something

The transitive construction was therefore tested with different verbs that would retain this metatextual sense. For this, we improvised the type of substitution table shown in table 3. In this table, a schematic but controlling form of the construction is placed at the top. The students then insert possible terms in the appropriate slots beneath and decide on whether or not their terms make sense. The class worked in groups on finding different versions of this main clause, building the substitution table shown in table 3. Using the table, the class also discussed whether one subject was more appropriate for a given verb. For example, I pointed out that articles tended to expose scandals whilst scientific papers found things out. To steer the choice of verbs I emphasised the visual nature of the metaphor by sketching a light shining on a connecting link. For revision this image was reworked in the form shown in figure 20. The visual metaphor elicited the first verb 'look at'. The class then expressed 'the link' as an entity that was uncovered or brought to light with 'find/discover/explain'. When a student pushed the process further by proposing a 'speech' verb 'say', I pointed out that this changed the construction from sentence (136) towards a form where the object had to be a subordinate clause, as in example (138):

(138)   Scientists said that there was a link between X and Y

Speech verbs express processes that frame their object as the speech event itself or as summaries of the same ('I said something'). 'Sight' verbs, on the other hand, express processes that can capture their object directly ('I saw the book'). 'Tell' and 'hear' also have further complexities that I did not examine at that time. 'Tell' can take a ditransitive. Notoriously, learners often overgeneralise the ditransitive to 'say', as in 'I said him the truth'. If they do this as a result of reflection, as opposed to straightforward pattern-generalisation it is probably because they do not understand how in English 'say' describes the process of an individual making an utterance, not that of the utterance's perception by another. 'Say' is not congruent with the ditransitive's meaning of transferred possession as from speaker to hearer, unlike 'tell' which construes a message as received.

When it came to breaking down sentence (136) into other smaller constructions, it was immediately clear that the relational nature of the relative pronoun meant that the subordinate clause lacked conceptual independence. Therefore, example (139) did not itself constitute a usable construction:

(139)  ...that a student studies

The noun phrase and its defining relative clause did look usable, however. This construction could have been analysed as a partitive noun phrase and a defining relative clause, giving an unfilled form of the kind shown in examples (140)–(142):

(140)  the amount of time we need to get there
(141)  the bag of sweets that you carried in your pocket
(142)  a gust of wind that blew away the roof

However, this partitive construction was also ignored in this class because of time constraints and an interest in the complete sentence itself. The fourth construction that might have had some interest was 'hours a day'. This might have been processed as a filled form, but also exists at a more schematic level as a partially filled one, expressing not just a space–time relationship but a general ratio:

- miles/kilometers an hour; feet a second; publications a year; thoughts a minute

All these forms were set out in the handout shown in figure 20, but only examples (143) and (144) received any extended class time.

*Usage and Grammatical Meaning* 209

| This study shows | a link | between one thing and another thing |

| A new study shows an interesting link between exam success and the number of hours a day that a student studies |

| An interesting link between exam success and the number of hours a day that a student studies |

| The number of hours a day that a student studies |

| Hours a day |

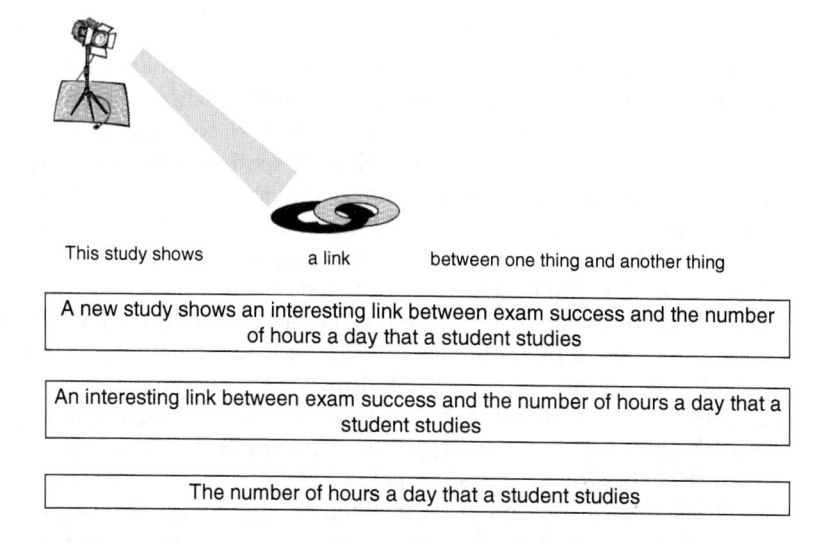

*Figure 20* Construction conceptualisation: between one thing and another

(143) A new study shows an interesting link between exam success and the number of hours a day that a student studies.

(144) an interesting link between exam success and the number of hours a day that a student studies

After working on example (143) I redirected our attention to example (144). The presence of two closed class words made it easy to identify this construction as the partially filled one shown in table 4.

There was some uncertainty over how to specify the co-ordinated nouns. At first I was fixed on this academic or metatextual context and steered the brainstorm towards 'trend' as the most schematic word that

*Table 4* Using a substitution table to explore a partially filled construction

| **a connection** | *between* | one trend | *and* | another trend |
|---|---|---|---|---|
| a link | | passive smoking | | cancer |
| a correlation | | the amount you eat | | how long you live |

was able to capture the type of correlative meaning encountered. This ignored the expression's more literal origin in such instantiations as 'a tunnel between Hong Kong Island and Kowloon Peninsula'. The more concrete example might have helped the students to conceptualise the form. However, in this case, I was keen both to let the textual meaning of the clause as a whole predominate whilst also to find a more abstract superordinate term for 'link' instead of the more concrete subordinate term, 'tunnel'. This did not cause the students problems.

Croft (2001) has produced systems of notation for describing constructions. However, my objective here was to help students tabulate an example which would help them to maximise the productivity of the form whilst also appreciating its constraints. My interest, therefore, was in finding concrete and usable examples of the construction, not in its linguistic description. The only borrowed element from Croft's notation is the use of italics to show fixed terms.

Deciding on the proform best qualified to summarise the agent's meaning was only slightly problematic in this and some other constructions. The decision to specify the agent as human accorded with a human sense of the self as the prime actor in any situation, but it risked discouraging students from exploring the multiple types of meaning that a figurative grasp of meaning will allow to occupy the role of actor, missing how students need to recognise that in English, 'studies can show facts', 'buses come along three at a time' and 'planes arrive on time'. However, 'someone' was used as prototypically agentive. Options for the object are generally more obviously constrained by the verb's meaning. Therefore object complements were often expressed by the proforms, 'someone/something', on the grounds that it would be obvious how these could and could not be instantiated in table 3. The procedure can therefore be summarised as follows:

Activity 42    Identifying and exploring constructions
 1 The teacher trains students to notice expressions that they can decipher but not use and which might be useful to them.
 2 The teacher removes the expression from its context and breaks it down into other interesting constructions, if these are present.
 3 The teacher selects the construction or constructions they want to work on and with the class looks for a way to express this in a more general form. They put this form at the top of a substitution table of the kind shown in table 3.

4 The students work in groups on completing a substitution table with different versions of the construction.
5 The groups swap their examples through dictations or presentations.
6 The students are asked to select the example of the construction that was most meaningful to them. They use this as a prototype and write it into the centre of the prototype chart shown in figure 21. For homework, the students complete the chart with other examples.

The construction shown in figure 21 is another example from the same text, and uses a student-generated sentence in the way described. The use of the prototype chart relates closely to the technique of semantic mapping. Semantic maps have a demonstrated effectiveness in L1 vocabulary building (Anderson-Inman and Ditson 1999). In the technique, students build visual maps of vocabulary that has a semantic association with a key concept. Thus, when talking about the weather, they may focus a series of adjectives on the word 'weather', such as 'hot,' 'muggy' or 'misty'. In this case however, the focus is upon visual category representation when the category meaning is constructional rather than lexical.

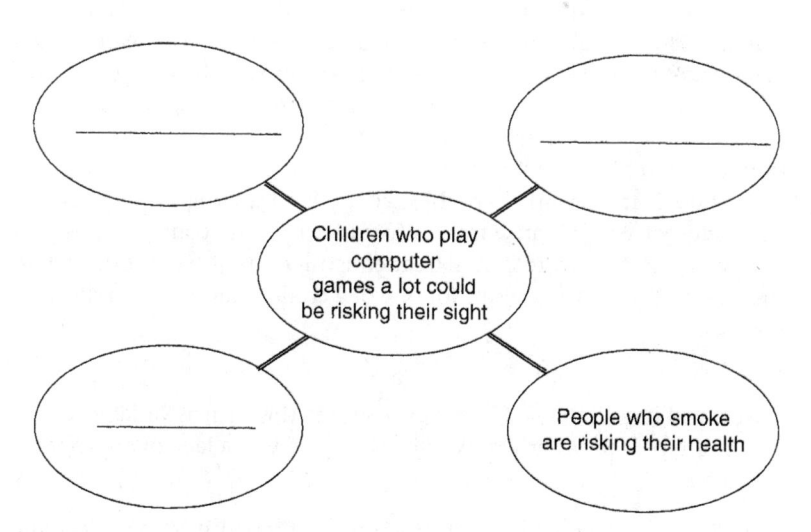

*Figure 21* Using a prototype chart to explore constructions

## Conclusions

If teachers understand grammatical forms as constructions they may develop a securer understanding of what we must learn before we can successfully process and produce a language. A view of language learning as construction learning will quite radically re-work our conception of what learners do. Language teachers may not previously have encountered the idea of an unfilled construction and its suggestion that language uses meanings that have no lexical expression to combine others that do. More familiar, however is the concept of a grammar controlled by the obligatory presence of certain lexical items or meanings. Nattinger and DeCarrico (1992) argued that theories of second language acquisition and pedagogical grammar had failed to account for the numerous fixed or semi-fixed lexical combinations that make up much of our discourse. They therefore concluded that these elements were acquired whole, and had to be taught in the same way. Nattinger and DeCarrico further argued that a dependence on lexical chunks should be interpreted as a stage in the acquisition process, one which, according to Wong-Fillmore, evolved 'directly into a creative use of language' (1976: 640).

'Chunking', or a strategic attachment to fixed lexical phrases, was also observed in generative SLA theory. In the generative research context, a dependency upon chunking constituted an early acquisitional stage where the acquirer did not yet possess the rudiments of a grammatical system with which to analyse language input. The learner thus depended on fixed lexical chunks. Acquisition was thus seen to move in a phase from the reproduction of these larger blocks towards their analysis as abstract forms which are susceptible to greater generalisation (Mitchell and Myles 1998: 98).

In the CL framework hypothesised here, chunking among second language learners will arise from difficulties in using constructions productively. In other words, they treat constructions as fixed forms when they are not. They will do this for one or a combination of the following reasons:

- they will have had insufficient exposure to the form as variable tokens of a type – in other words, they will have had a lack of appropriate usage;
- they will have failed to grasp the form's different tokens as symbolically or analogically related, or as members of a single category;

they find security in a fixed form, and risk in their treatment of it as a productive type whose constraints may not be fully grasped;

they simply lack the lexis with which to reword the construction.

A failure to use the appropriate form for a given meaning should be rationalised differently at different stages in the learning process. For beginners, the lack of lexis will be critical. Learners will be unable to recognise a construction as the new token of a type if they do not have the lexis needed to notice it. As learners move further into a language they will encounter forms that are less productive. However, less productive does not mean unproductive. To make a correction usable, teachers need to focus less on the word or words in which errors show up and more upon the misrepresentation of a larger constructional meaning that may be its cause. When new constructions are provided, however, the learner's uptake of them will still be minimal if contexts of further use are not also proposed and other tokens left unexplored. Additionally, students must themselves learn to notice the forms that a given spoken or written text is making available to them. They need to use a text not simply as an opportunity for reading and listening practice but also as an opportunity to ask themselves whether they are capable of making productive use of the forms that they encounter in it. Finally, they need to notice what they do not know.

In the previous section I recounted some classroom experimentation whose objective was to identify classroom techniques that would advance this process of construction-noticing and exploration. In the intervention discussed, the constructions were sometimes recycled by asking the students to produce short texts that were of a similar type, or at least similar in content to the ones where they encountered the construction in the first place. In a project-based topic this was not difficult to arrange. Further, it encouraged some spontaneous use of the constructions in less controlled but thematically similar contexts.

After a teaching intervention of the type specified, I tested the students' control of the taught construction through a cloze test involving examples to which they had not been exposed. In relation to a control group that covered the materials from which the forms were derived, but without exploring the forms in any depth, there was a significantly different improvement in uptake. In fact the control group tests showed that a straightforward exposure to the forms in their input produced no uptake at all. This result is unsurprising, as it simply confirms the consensus that form-focused instruction has a positive effect (Buczowska and Weist 1991; Cardelle and Corno 1981; Carroll and Swain 1993;

Carroll *et al.* 1992; Eckman *et al.* 1988; Gass 1982; Herron and Tomasello 1988; Master 1994; Robinson 1996; Robinson and Ha 1993; Scott 1989; Scott and Randall 1992; Seliger 1975; Tomasello and Herron 1988). Of greater interest was how the procedure used also had a significant impact on the students' writing accuracy when measured against the control group. But perhaps more significant still is how taking class time to explore form, and adopting a construction-based approach to its identification, will result in significantly improved uptake.

# Part IV
# Conclusions

# 9
# Towards a Cognitive Linguistics Syllabus

## Introduction

In this book I have set out some core findings of CL and tried to show how these can affect how we go about language teaching. My approach to the language teaching syllabus has been linguistic in the sense of treating a language as a topic whose meanings merit active exploration. I have advocated the exploration of language content, first to build what was once called the explicit knowledge that precedes proceduralisation, or automatised processing (Anderson 1980, 1983), and second to make a given item into a topic for practice. Such an approach means that a syllabus will vary greatly from language to language and cannot be simply a list of the communicative functions that a given age-group of international learners are deemed to need.

My objective in this part of the book, therefore, is to distil some key principles that syllabus designers should take into account when accommodating the ideas put forward here. To do this I will first argue that a CL approach proposes the rejection of a view of the language syllabus as either process or product. Next I will summarise some of the book's preceding content to show how a CL approach to language teaching can underpin the way we go about syllabus design. Finally I will distil some core principles to guide syllabus writers, but will not attempt to produce an actual syllabus: such an exercise would have little validity when the resulting document should respond to different linguistic, cultural, institutional and curriculum constraints.

## Product and process

Since Wilkins (1976) first proposed an analytic–synthetic distinction in the approach to second language syllabus design, views of the syllabus have either been categorised as a specification of what needs to be learnt or of what has to be done to learn it. 'Analytic' referred to how the learner was required to identify the elements of language they had to acquire, whilst the syllabus designer concentrated upon specifying the types of activity that brought them into contact with those elements. In contrast, 'synthetic' referred to the distillation of the elements of a language and the associated skills that were thought essential to its control (*ibid.*). Eclectic approaches have tended to draw together different ways of specifying language content but have done less to reconcile these fundamental differences in approach.

Throughout this book my argument has been that language is fashioned by how cognition shapes experience, and experience cognition. The form that language adopts reflects how it is used and acquired. If we go beyond language to knowledge itself, then the same principle applies; the product is a property of the process. The product's form is a reflection of the embodied mind and its interactions with the world. The principles that structure grammar emerge from our movements through the world and from the visual, auditory and tactile imagery that such movements provide. My core pedagogic principle is the reinvestment of linguistic form in this imagery of space and movement, and hence the description of the linguistic 'product' as a facet of the learning 'process'.

## Language teaching implications

Languages do not evolve in a structural vacuum. Their evolution is a response to how they are used and transmitted from generation to generation. As with any evolutionary process, the shape or form that emerges cannot be analysed as the 'best solution' to a problem but is rather the aggregation of a series of adaptive responses. Treating language as social does not entail its reification as some configuration of forces that shapes cognition. Cognition is enactive: it is neither the product of social forces nor the repository of our unmediated common perceptions. Our reality arises from how cognition is embodied. The mind carries the imprint of the body and the body is an instrument of mind. The mind is not some perfect perceptual organ that simply reflects what is out in the world. Our perceptions are governed by our existence as a sensory organism that moves amidst its reality. Cognition and the world meet in the body and our experiences emerge from that meeting place. Languages, therefore, do not simply symbolise a common reality in different ways. They symbolise the different meanings that evolve from collective experience, then will themselves extend the perimeters of the same.

To assert that different languages and cultures use different meanings is not the same as saying that these differences cannot be analysed, explained and shared. These meanings are created from the experiences of a common cognitive and bodily architecture. In fact, it is the enactive nature of cognition and its derivation from a common anatomy that gives to experience the common empathies through which divergences in meaning can be understood.

Experience arises from movement. Much infant experience arises from movement and object manipulation. Movement is also what Peirce (1931–1958) would have called our semiotic *material*. Movement creates human symbolism, first as gesture, then as sound and gesture combined. Even our writing systems, which seem to epitomise symbolic stasis, or meaning captured for all time, are in actuality only meaningful when the eye moves across them. They are also gesture held captive as the scratching of a stylus in clay or the assemblage of microdots on a computer printout. Thus, we move to experience what we will signify and move to affect that signification. Language and movement are thus interdependent.

Learning another language is both about matching new forms to known meanings, and about finding new meanings for unknown forms. The meanings themselves are categories of varying complexity. The categories are embedded into frames that carry significant degrees of cultural knowledge and understanding. Centrally, therefore, a language lesson should unfold as an episode of semantic exploration and symbolisation. In differing combinations, language classes should:

> re-embed linguistic form in the imagery and movement from which it emerged and through which meanings were acquired;

> engage the learners in the explicit analysis of form and meaning, helping learners identify the constructions that will carry the meanings they want to convey;

> establish a forum of usage that will help students acquire constructions as variable tokens of a type.

## Re-embedding linguistic form in the imagery and movement from which it emerged

The human use of sign has evolved from movement into speech. There is growing evidence that second language learning can be advanced when teachers acknowledge how movement structures meaning and is fundamental to learning. From infancy we learn to move and move to learn. The language syllabus should recognise how we conceptualise meaning from movement, by helping students use movement to attach new forms to meaning. It can help learners embody the symbolism of a new language by giving its gestural signification. It should set down mime routines to elicit form and help students to conceptualise its meaning. The extent to which we remain willing to explore our bodies as a semiotic and conceptual resource will vary with the individual, their age and their culture. But broadly we need to abandon a premise where pedagogy is interpreted as suppressing the infant's predisposition to move. Instead we should think how to reorganise the infant's need for movement into the formidable semiotic resource that it is able to become.

By this token, the syllabus should recognise that acquiring new sets of sign–meaning relationships is not simply a sterile exercise in grafting definitions or translated meanings onto new forms. The syllabus should provide the episodes through which we can explore the spatial relations in which so much meaning originates, whether through physical movement or diagrammatic and pictorial illustration. Acquiring literacy, whether in characters, syllabic symbols, or letters, has rarely come to be understood as a passive exercise in shape recognition, and is generally poorly achieved if it is. To teach reading we also teach writing. Just as writing helps children embody the symbols of literacy, so bodily movement, gesture, and the imagined projection of the self in their environment can help second language students embody new forms of linguistic symbolism.

## Engage the learners in the explicit analysis of form and meaning

First, CL's rejection of Chomsky's nativist position informs the basic position of this book. The book's view of language as a general feature of cognition is not compatible with the generative stress upon a universal grammar. The Chomskyan position has recently moved a little towards the cognitivist one by acknowledging that the language faculty should include a structured inventory of lexical items (Larsen-Freeman and Cameron 2007: 118). However, generativism marks out a very different starting point with its continuing insistence on a central language faculty in the brain, with structures that are unique to it. By contrast, in describing first language acquisition, Tomasello (2003) describes the processes required as broader facets of cognition. The processes are the ability to recognise intentions, form categories, pay attention to what is new or different, and achieve joint attention with an interlocutor. All of the capabilities identified by Tomasello as part of our broader cognitive endowment are essential not only to the acquisition of language but to its continuing use. They are further used in other forms of learning and in the uses of cognition that characterise our daily navigation of our reality. Therefore, for second language learners there is no issue about whether these abilities are still available to them or not. Instead, a mature second language learner differs from their infant first language counterpart along the following two dimensions:

- the measure of conscious control of their learning strategies that is afforded them by their first language;
- their ability to transfer, contrast, or suppress the set of meanings that come with the acquisition of the first language's symbolism.

The first point takes us into a difficult area. It begs the larger question of how far we can mediate our own thought processes or engage in the conscious implementation of the same without language. Such issues cannot be resolved here. However, it is evident that without language we cannot represent the forms we encounter in a manner that makes them available for sustained analysis. For the post-pubertal learner this is no longer the case. Thus, whilst the infant may be innately predisposed to pattern-seeking, the adult can represent that capacity to themselves, giving it an analytic form. Learner-training, whether implicit in the process of formal knowledge acquisition itself, or consciously constructed, must also positively affect our ability to use these strategies.

Greater conscious control over one's learning can also imply a meditated decision as to whether one pays particular heed to a pattern or not. In the domain of usage, it could involve the rote learner's decision to promote their uptake of a given item through the domain of private speech by repeating it to themselves, perhaps in tandem with gesture or related movement. By 'conscious control' we can also mean the learner's development and deployment of a metalanguage to help their analysis and subsequent control of a form. Central to any pedagogical model, therefore, is the awareness that a first language affords to learners the ability to analyse the second language. Teachers need to acknowledge that the first language can both assist the analysis of form in the second and impede its uptake with interferences from different meanings and patterns. When a class in an analysis of form includes the exploration of appropriate contexts, it will, almost inevitably, promote usage. In fact any analysis of the form itself can lead to experimentation with different lexis to find the constraints of its meaning. The exploration of a form holds it in the learner's line of sight, perhaps promoting its retention and even its proceduralisation.

Nonetheless, central to my position is how a language grammar *emerges* from our ability to establish the formal and semantic relatedness of one group of words to another, or to perceive each as part of the same pattern. Fundamentally, all symbolism depends on the assemblage of a sign from perceptible constituents. A word is an assemblage of phonemes and a construction is an assemblage of words. Both involve pattern recognition of one kind or another. Evidently, recognising a phonemic pattern as a repeated word is very different from grasping a repeated sequence of meanings as a construction. Morphemes and words establish patterns through sense relations. In a transitive construction we recognise some words as being plausible agents and reject others. A linguistic pattern is not, therefore, a series of similar sounds. However, when present, certain common repeated elements, such as determiners or auxiliary verbs, are helpful in establishing such schematic meanings. Thus determiners cue a word as representing the type of meaning linguistics ascribes to a noun even without that word's specific sense being understood. In this way a pattern can be established even from a relational meaning between symbols whose individual senses are not always grasped.

Larsen-Freeman (1997) noted Zipf's (1935) observation that 'there is an inverse relationship between the frequency occurrence of a word and its frequency rank so that relatively few words occur often whilst others are comparatively rare'. Within first language acquisition we can also note how infants replicate this pattern to a greater degree. First, they will use a few verbs to fulfil many quite complex semantic roles. In other words they are stretching the resources of a limited symbolic system (Tomasello 2003). Thus, verbs like 'give', 'get', or 'is' are being overused. However, this act of category-stretching may also help learners to uncover construction meanings. Category-stretching schematises the category concerned, extending it into a broader compositional meaning. If we take the verb 'give', for example, we can see how when grasped as part of a ditranstive this can be used to represent meanings as different as the transfer of 'permission' (give permission) or force (give a blow). We can also note how the learner's extension of the meaning through usage may assist their exploration of that of the ditransitive of which it is a part. The repetition of a construction with the same verb may lead to an impression of the chunking that characterises the first stages of acquisition, but if it is achieved across contexts it may also help bed down the construction as a category of meanings that can later be given a more precise instantiation with different verbs. Thus the type is being extended into a complex category representation that may at some later point be fractured into clearer subordinate meanings by the acquisition of other forms. Zipf's law may thus uncover one of the clues to acquisition.

In the second language case, new forms, whether lexical or grammatical, are being grafted onto meanings that already exist. In one sense this provides something of a cognitive shortcut, as the second language learner is not faced with the painstaking task of creating a new category system. In another sense this gives the process a greater complexity, because the meanings of the new and old languages will not provide a perfect match, whilst the extent to which words arrange themselves into analogous patterns will vary. Thus learners may construct new second language patterns by analogy both to those of the first and the second language, making the production of correct forms somewhat hit and miss. Old language meanings may also be attached to new forms in a manner that distorts the use of the form. A further difficulty is that these first language meanings may be rooted in quite deep modes of conceptualisation. The need to reconceptualise meaning may then form a further barrier of resistance to the acquisition of a different system of symbolisation. Another unpredictable factor rests in the relationship of the languages being discussed and how far their lexis and grammar are related, or cognate. This is not simply a question of how much lexis a learner can construct as analogues from first language cognates. It also involves questions of how well a learner notices second language forms. Thus speakers of highly inflected languages who are learning the same may be predisposed to noticing case, and hence to reproducing one or multiword constructions with inflected meanings, even where these are phonologically dissimilar. By contrast, native speakers of even mildly inflected languages such as English may tend to over-pronounce the final consonants of Chinese languages, perhaps because they are used to finding semantic information encoded in these. Chinese speakers of English, on the other hand, may not only find final consonants and consonant clusters difficult to articulate, but may also fail to notice their symbolism. By the same token, speakers of languages that use determiners may find pattern identification harder when faced with systems that do not have these parts of speech.

The blending of first and second language patterns and meanings adds a further element of 'complexity' to a process that is already made unpredictable by its usage-based nature. The unpredictable nature of SLA has led emergentist scholars to characterise second language learning according to precepts of dynamic systems, or chaos theory (see for example, Ellis 2005; Ellis and Larsen-Freeman 2006; de Bot et al. 2007; Larsen-Freeman and Cameron 2007). A dynamic systems approach has tried to account for how phenomena, such as the world's climate, are in some ways unpredictable because of how they are a product of a large number of interacting systems. When these systems are represented as static entities, or through a snap-shot view, something of their essential nature is lost. To understand them, therefore, we need to capture their dynamic nature and grasp how, because they are constantly feeding variables into the greater systems they compose, we may simply be dealing with a systemic unpredictability. Central to this understanding is how emergent systems, whether of biological organisms or societies and their languages, may be more than the sum of their parts. Accordingly, one cannot account for language as an internal, idealised model that comprises the principles and parameters responsible for our productive use. Language use may combine its elements in ways that a static version of grammar cannot fully predict. One must therefore turn generative theory on its head and treat grammatical principles as emergent from their usage in the manner just typified. One consequence for Larsen-Freeman and Cameron (2007) is the rejection of acquisition as a useful term to characterise how students construct second language knowledge. Because the result is never a static competence, or knowledge, a language cannot be characterised as acquired. Instead they prefer the term 'development', a word that also expresses how native speakers will also use language in different ways with different degrees of knowledge.

A function of education is arguably the development of both the native and non-native speakers' symbolic repertoire. Education is therefore not simply a matter of grafting new lexis onto a stable grammatical system or the acquisition of a grapholect, or dialect associated with written language. Learning the grapholect is clearly central to the educational process but could itself suppose the development of a greater grammatical and, hence, conceptual resource.

Lantolf and Poehner (2005) recognise the complex nature of language knowledge in their call for dynamic assessment. In this type of procedure, students are tested prior to and after an intervention that teaches them how to pass a test. The student's learning potential is then quantified as the difference between the test results. Dynamic assessment has clear procedural implications, where test questions can be designed in such a way that students have the potential to raise the bar of the assessment that is being made. Effectively, the complexity of the test could increase in response to the student's ability to cope with it. The quality of the students' performance would not just be assessed by deciding how well they responded to a given set of questions. Instead, the test would take into account the questions that the students' right or wrong answers motivated them to ask, thus considering how well they would use the test to extend their future knowledge. In this way the assessment not only focuses on what the students know at a given moment in time but also appraises their larger ability to learn.

Learning outcomes do serve a motivational need, however. Many learners need the syllabus to mark a sense of progression or to furnish a navigational chart through a complex and dynamic system. A similar argument can be used to justify textbooks even when these falsify the nature of what has to be learnt by reducing it to a series of context-bound examples and textual prescriptions. There is a need for a compromise where pedagogical expertise sets down a language content framework and students can then be free to negotiate a more precise syllabus within the parameters that this provides. By building class-dictionaries, and personal inventories of constructions, students develop a record of their learning. A syllabus can then be evolved, less as an internal and external, and more as a pre- and post-document. The pre-document would be a broad-brush set of topics, themes, texts and activity types that frames the student's further exploration of language. The post-document would be an inventory of the language knowledge that emerged. The act of the syllabus' co-construction will then also become a way to revise and re-contextualise the forms that have been recorded.

One can argue, also, that lower-level students require greater linguistic prescription. Learners cannot derive an inventory of useful constructions from text-based activities when they do not have the knowledge to tackle the texts and associated tasks in the first place. Elementary language knowledge can be classified as dynamic for how it represents a variable interplay between native language meanings and forms and differing degrees of interest in the new language system, not to mention variable motivations and degrees of susceptibility to the language learning task. But the enduring metaphor of learning as a 'course' should remind us that we need to conceptualise learning as a spatial progression that is marked out by a route map.

Beginners want the sense that the teacher knows what they, the students, need to know. Such knowledge will soon include which constructions are most used in the building of others, and which longer constructions are central to the discourse in which the learner wants to engage. Teachers should encourage students to find a construction's prototypical meaning, first setting down examples using the lexis that is most congruent with this. Thus they will build their example of the ditransitive with 'give', for example, and the resultative perhaps with 'make'. Learners should be concerned less with finding the lexis that makes forms immediately relevant to their communicative needs and more with that which clarifies how they can be used across contexts. The early over-use of a few schematic verbs can then promote the uptake of the construction as a more productive meaning.

More advanced students should first learn to 'notice' the forms that help advance their communicative ability, and second, should ask how they can find greater opportunities for their practice. But advanced students also want to be comforted by a sense of direction and progression. This is something they must partly do for themselves by post-constructing their lexico-grammatical syllabus as they encounter, explore and collect forms. The course designer's objective is then to recycle the contexts that will promote those constructions' re-use.

## A forum for usage

The broader need to foster usage should encourage classroom activities that have communicative goals. However, building encyclopaedic meanings, whether of lexis or constructions, proposes that teachers do not just foster usage by working outwards-in, or from context to language form, but inwards-out, or from words and their constructions to varying modes of use. The choice of a 'high-surrender value' communicative syllabus (Brumfit and Johnson 1979) is more based upon the perception of learnt language as having an immediate context of use. This is not the circumstance of the average school language curriculum. Where learners are in an EAL situation, or resident in their target language community, they will have strong awareness of their needs. A syllabus that meets these needs will also promote greater usage, since what is taught will be immediately used, and what is read and heard can be carried back into the classroom.

A much more questionable enterprise is the construction of syllabi that opt for an attempt to meet the communicative needs of a category of person, often too broadly defined, who may be a long way from any realistic context of use. For example, 'European' teenagers cannot be imagined as a homogenous entity, destitute of all cultural individuation and idiosyncratic need, who all share some common communicative objective. Such approaches can lock students into the tedium of a communicative stereotype with which they have no affective affinity and repel them into a taciturn lack of interest. The international identity of English cannot be summated in the homogenisation of its users' communicative needs, nor does it amount to a process of deculturation where myth, fairy tale (modern or old), story, play and film are wrenched out of the syllabus and replaced with an anaemic pretend-reality that convinces nobody and bores all. Instead, our sense of an embodied language should stimulate enactment of meanings in dramatic episodes or scenarios of both historic and contemporary concern. Language in the schoolroom is not a vocational instrument but a dynamic, acculturated entity layered with the analogies of lost communities and unfolding creativity of its multiple forms of usage. To understand a language grammar can be used to gain an insight into this vehicle of collective imagination and intellectual mediation.

## Sequencing

Language content will be more closely specified in the early stages of a CL syllabus because nothing about the language's constructions is known. However, the need to provide an inventory of constructions should not discourage the syllabus designer from setting out the types of activity through which they can be taught. Rather the activities should be aimed at trying to foster a broader understanding of the construction's meaning and so consider how to evoke the imagery from which that meaning has been derived. Thus transitive constructions can be exemplified with examples that express the transfer of an energy charge, as through one object striking another, whilst those that are idiomatic in nature can be taken back to a more literal understanding of how their metaphors have been derived.

A beginners' and elementary syllabus must therefore recognise:

> the need to teach a language's common constructions, first as fixed clauses and phrases, then through usage as variable tokens of a type;

> how learners will first operate the common clausal constructions as chunks, with restricted lexis and particularly verbs – one can kick

against this or run with it; but running with it can still mean making constructions productive by opting for examples whose wording takes the student closer to their schematic meaning;

the embodied nature of meaning by encouraging movement and gesture;

the spatial imagery from which much grammatical meaning is conceptualised – not just reinforcing relational meanings through diagrammatic analogy, but also through pictorial and cinematographic imagery.

Even at the outset, language learning can be not only a creative physical response to meaning but also to how a form is used, finding in a few verbs a string of multiple meanings. For example, 'be' constructions, whilst retaining a general copula relational meaning can express existential possibilities ('I think therefore I am'), an identity, ('I am John'), or by extension, an enduring attribute ('I am old'), then by extension again, a temporary state ('I am happy'). It can also be a locative ('I am in Spain'), or by extension again a descriptive condition ('She is in blue today'), then build up to how a present continuous is the assumption of a condition as a process ('She is wearing jeans').

Thus, when context and communicative need are not pressing, pedagogical sequences can be implicit in the way in which we can extend the meanings of certain forms, as, for example in the shift in usage of the copula verb.

As the more common constructions are mastered and their meanings are explored with a more elaborate lexis, learners will move away from a syllabus constructed around linguistic prescription towards one steered by linguistic encounters. But many points remain the same.

First, forms must be recycled to ensure their retention as multiple tokens of a type through recurring usage. Thus part of the function of the language class is to provide the contexts in which constructions can be re-used. This does not mean that specific situations will always be devised to elicit specific constructions, for such a procedure does not always meet with success. Rather, contexts should ensure an affectively involving and hence motivated language use. The mere fact of requiring students to communicate in contexts of increasing cognitive complexity will force them to fall back on their expanding repertoire and encourage teachers to help their search for the correct form. However, form itself must continue to be taught, even as the identified constructions show diminishing productivity and more specialised areas of use.

Second, error correction is the essential sequel of usage, but correction should entail expansion and exploration of a given meaning rather than a scatter-gun attempt to target too many distorted forms. Textual inputs should increase to support student interests and potential interests. The phrase 'potential interest' refers to the traditional attribute of education, where teachers do not simply pander to relevance, or to the learner's own compass of interest, but lead them into new topics.

Third, the bodily enactment of meanings should remain as an ongoing strategy to assist the (re-)conceptualisation and internalisation of new forms. The use of E&M routines is not limited to the type of command and carry-out routines that are sometimes erroneously over-associated with TPR. English verbs of manner, for example, take the student beyond the intermediate stage ('slouch' and 'stumble', for example, are hardly common schematic verbs). When E&M routines extend into drama and film, with students responding to directorial instructions, or starting to understand the significance of 'move' and 'speak' scenarios, then teachers will be providing them with an ever-expanding resource for learning. Even the more academic objectives found in an EAP or ESP source can sometimes be served by scenarios where students act out their critiques of each other's work as if in an imaginary class. All such activities offer the prospect of holding together the language of such areas as logical connection and contrast by mapping it back onto the spatial imagery from which it was derived. Even the discussion essay is finally a distillation of the dialogue found in the older platonic genre, and arguments can often be better explored and elaborated if looked at first through routines of discussion and debate. The debate can be held with speech and gesture, then the voices distilled as a text that balances arguments.

Fourth, learners must come to treat all contact with the target language as an opportunity to extrapolate and learn constructions. The techniques that teachers adopt to identify, explain, and generalise constructions and their meanings should be the strategies that learners need to fully exploit the learning opportunities afforded by all their contact with the target language. The treatment of pedagogy as an apprenticeship to autonomy is even more important to the model of language learning put forward here, because it proposes first that there is simply too much grammar to teach, and second, that the manner of the learner's uptake of it will be a function of the use they make of it.

Finally, the language that is being learnt is neither a dynamic system nor a set of unchanging algorithms. Both metaphors attribute to it properties of autonomy it does not have. Language is not, like a weather system, a convergence of forces that act in a manner that is independent of all agency. Although systematic in its expression of a common symbolism, it is unpredictable in its responsiveness to human volition. Evidently, one of the objectives of human language is to make human autonomy and creativity subservient to the collective need for comprehensibility. Language use has an implicit creativity and a need to tailor common meanings to an idiosyncratic interest. This fact may threaten to destabilise the system. But it is language's inherent flexibility, not its instability, which allows it to absorb the new category extensions that result. The study of linguistics is finally about the search for how language achieves semantic constancy without disrupting its sense of autonomy or freedom of choice. It is not a search for meanings characterised by dynamic disruption but for the convergences that produce studiable patterns and enduring meanings. Language learning is less about releasing the learner on a stream whose mingled significances reduce them to hapless flotsam, and more the assemblage of a semantic resource for their future creative engagement with the contexts that they will encounter.

# Bibliography

Adger, C., D. Christian and O. Taylor (1999). *Making the Connection; Language and Academic Achievement Among African American Students.* McHenry, IL: Delta Systems.

Anderson, J. R. (1980). *Cognitive Psychology and Its Implications.* New York: Freeman.

Anderson, J. R. (1983). *The Architecture of Cognition.* Cambridge, MA: Harvard University Press.

Anderson-Inman, L. and L. Ditson (1999).'Computer based concept mapping. A tool for negotiating meaning'. *Learning and Leading With Technology*, 26: 6–13.

Andrews, L. (1998). *Language Exploration and Awareness.* Mahwah, NJ: Lawrence Erlbaum.

Argyle, M. (1975). *Bodily Communication.* New York: International Universities Press.

Asher, J. (1979). *Learning Another Language Through Actions: The Complete Teachers Guide Book.* San Jose, California: AccuPrint.

Aske, J. (1989). 'Path predicates in English and Spanish: a closer look'. *Proceedings of the Fifteenth Annual Meeting of the Berkeley Linguistics Society,* pp. 1–14.

Bates, E. (1976). *Language and Context.* New York: Academic Press.

Bergen, B. K. (2004). 'The psychological reality of phonaesthemes'. *Language,* 80, 2: 290–311.

Bertenthal, B. I. and J. J. Campos (1990). 'A systems approach to the organizing effects of self-produced locomotion during infancy'. *Advances in Infancy Research,* 6: 1–60.

Black, M. (1962). *Models and Metaphors.* Ithaca, NY: Cornell University Press.

Bley-Vroman, R. (1990). 'The logical problem of foreign language learning'. *Linguistic Analysis,* 20: 3–49.

Block, D. (1992). 'Metaphors we teach and learn by'. *Prospect,* 7, 3: 42–55.

Bloomfield, L. (1914). *An Introduction to the Study of Language.* New York: Holt.

Boers, F. (1996). *Spatial Prepositions and Metaphor: a Cognitive Semantic Journey along the Up–Down and the Front–Back Dimension.* Tübingen: Gunter Narr Verlag.

Boers, F. (2000). 'Enhancing metaphoric awareness in specialised reading'. *English for Specific Purposes,* 19, 2: 137–47.

Boers F. (2001). 'Remembering figurative idioms by hypothesising about their origin'. *Prospect,* 16, 3: 35–43.

Boers F. (2004). 'Metaphor awareness and vocabulary retention'. *Applied Linguistics,* 21, 4: 553–71.

Boers F. and S. Lindstromberg (2005). 'Finding ways to make phrase-learning feasible: the mnemonic effect of alliteration'. *System,* 33, 2: 225–38.

Bourdieu, P. (1977). *Outline of a Theory of Practice.* Cambridge: Cambridge University Press.

Bragg, M. (2001). *The Soldier's Return.* Edinburgh: Hodder and Stoughton.

Brinton, D., M. A. Snow and M. B. Wesche (2003). *Content-Based Second Language Instruction.* Ann Arbor: University of Michigan Press.

Brown Corpus [accessed in January 2008]. (http://www.lextutor.ca/scripts/cgi-bin/wwwassocwords.exe)
Brown, A. L., M. J. Kane, and C. H. Echols (1986). 'Young children's mental models determine analogical transfer across problems with a common goal structure'. *Cognitive Development*, 1: 103–21.
Brown, A. L., M. J. Kane, and C. Long (1989). 'Analogical transfer in young children: analogies as tools for communication and exposition'. *Applied Cognitive Psychology*, 3: 275–93.
Brown, P. (2001). 'Learning to talk about up and down in Tzletlal'. In M. Bowerman and S. Levinson (eds.) *Language Acquisition and Conceptual Development*. Cambridge: Cambridge University Press, pp. 475–543.
Brumfit, C. and K. Johnson (1979). *The Communicative Approach to Language Teaching*. Oxford: Oxford University Press.
Buczowska, E. and R. M. Weist (1991). 'The effects of formal instruction on the second-language acquisition of temporal location'. *Language Learning*, 41: 535–4.
Byram, M. (1989). *Cultural Studies in Foreign Language Education*. Clevedon: Multilingual Matters.
Byram, M., V. Esartes-Sarries and S. Taylor (1991). *Cultural Studies and Language Learning: A Research Report*. Clevedon: Multilingual Matters.
Byram, M. and M. Fleming (eds.) (1998). *Language Learning in an Intercultural Perspective: Approaches Through Drama and Ethnography*. Cambridge: Cambridge University Press.
Cameron, L. and A. Deignan (2006). 'The emergence of metaphor in discourse'. *Applied Linguistics*, 27, 4: 671–90.
Cameron, L. and J. Stelma (2004). 'Metaphor clusters in discourse'. *Journal of Applied Linguistics*, 1, 2: 7–36.
Cardelle, M. and L. Corno (1981). 'Effects on second language learning of variations in written feedback on homework assignments'. *TESOL Quarterly*, 15: 251–61.
Carroll, S., Y. Roberge and M. Swain (1992). 'The role of feedback in adult second language acquisition: error correction and morphological generalizations'. *Applied Psycholinguistics*, 13: 173–98.
Carroll, S. and M. Swain (1993). 'Explicit and implicit negative feedback'. *Studies in Second Language Acquisition*, 15: 357–86.
Cary, M. and R. Carlson (1999). 'External support and the development of problem solving routines'. *Journal of Experimental Psychology, Learning, Memory and Cognition*, 25: 1053–70.
Chen, Z., R. Sanchez, and T. Campbell (1997). 'From beyond to within their grasp: analogical problem solving in 10 and 13 month-olds'. *Developmental Psychology*, 33: 790–801.
Chomsky, N. (1965). *Aspects of the Theory of Syntax*. Cambridge MA: MIT Press.
Chomsky, N. (1985). *Knowledge of Language*. New York and London: Praeger.
Chomsky, N. (1995). *The Minimalist Programme*. Cambridge MA: MIT Press.
Church, R., B. Ayman-Nolley and S. Mahootian. (2004). 'The role of gesture in bilingual education: does gesture enhance learning?'. *International Journal of Bilingual Education and Bilingualism*, 7: 303–19.
Conrad, J. (1994 [first published 1904]). *Nostromo: A Tale of the Seaboard*. London: David Campbell.

Cooper, D. (1986). *Metaphor*. Oxford: Basil Blackwell.
Cortazzi, M. and L. Jin (1999). 'Bridges to learning: metaphors of teaching, learning and language'. In L. Cameron and G. Low (eds.) *Researching and Applying Metaphor*. Cambridge: Cambridge University Press, pp. 149–76.
Craik, F. I. and R. S. Lockhart (1972). 'Levels of processing: a framework for memory research'. *Journal of Verbal Learning & Verbal Behavior*, 11, 6: 671–84.
Croft, W. (2001). *Radical Construction Grammar: Syntactic Theory in Typological Perspective*. Oxford: Oxford University Press.
Croft, W. and D. A. Cruse (2004). *Cognitive Linguistics*. Cambridge: Cambridge University Press.
Culicover, P. W. and R. Jackendoff (2005). *Simpler Syntax*. Oxford and New York: Oxford University Press.
Deacon, T. (1993). *Man: The Symbolic Species*. London: Penguin Books.
de Bot, K., M. Lowie and W. Verspoor (2007). 'A dynamic systems theory approach to second language acquisition'. *Bilingualism, Language and Cognition*, 10, 1: 7–21.
Defoe, D. (first published 1722). *The Fortunes and Misfortunes of the Famous Moll Flanders*. Project Gutenberg. (http://onlinebooks.library.upenn.edu/webbin/gutbook/lookup?num=370, [accessed 01/2008]).
De Guerrero, M. and O. S. Villamil (2002). 'Metaphorical conceptualizations of ESL teaching and learning'. *Language Teaching Research*, 6(2): 95–120.
Derrida, J. (1997). *Of Grammatology*. Baltimore, MD: Johns Hopkins University Press.
Dewey, J. (1896). 'The reflex arc concept in psychology'. *Psychological Review*, 3: 357–70.
Dewey, J. (1897). 'My pedagogic creed'. *The School Journal*, LIV, 3: 77–80.
Dirven, R. (2001). 'English phrasal verbs: theory and didactic application'. In M. Putz, S. Niemeier and R. Dirven (eds.) *Applied Cognitive Linguistics*, 11: 3–28 (Berlin and New York: Mouton de Grutyer).
Donald, M. (1997). 'Precis of origins of the modern mind: three stages in the evolution of culture and cognition'. *Behavioral and Brain Sciences*, 16, 4: 737–91.
Dudley-Evans, T. and M. J. St John (1998). *Developments in ESP: A Multidisciplinary Approach*. Cambridge: Cambridge University Press.
Duffelmeyer, F. (1980). 'The influence of experience-based vocabulary instruction on learning word meaning'. *Journal of Reading*, 24, 3: 5–40.
Eckman, F.R., L. Bell and D. Nelson (1988). 'On the generalization of relative clause instruction in the acquisition of English as a Second Language'. *Applied Linguistics*, 9: 1–20.
Edelman, G. (1992). *Bright Air, Brilliant Fire*. New York: Basic Books.
Eeg-Olofsson, M. and B. Altenberg (1994). 'Discontinuous recurrent word combinations in the London-Lund Corpus'. In U. Fries, G. Tottie and P. Schneider (eds.) *Creating and Using English Language Corpora*. Amsterdam: Rodopi, pp. 63–77.
Ellis, N. (2005). 'Dynamic Systems: the interactions of explicit and implicit language knowledge'. *Studies in Second Language Acquisition*, 27, 2: 305–52.
Ellis, N. and D. Larsen-Freeman (2006). 'Language emergence. Implications of applied linguistics. Introduction to the Special Issue'. *Applied Linguistics*, 27, 4: 558–89.

Ellis, R. (1995). 'Interpretation tasks for grammar teaching'. *TESOL Quarterly*, 29, 1: 87–105.
Etymological Dictionary Online (2007). http://www.etymonline.com/ [accessed 2008]
Evans, V. and M. Green (2006). *Introduction to Cognitive Linguistics*. Edinburgh: Edinburgh University Press.
Fadiga, L., L. Fogassi, G. Pavesi and G. Rizzolatti (1995). 'Motor facilitation during action observation: a magnetic stimulation study'. *Journal of Neuropsychology*, 73: 2608–11.
Fauconnier, G. and M. Turner (1997). *Mappings in Thought and Language*. Cambridge: Cambridge University Press.
Fauconnier, G. and M. Turner (1998). 'Conceptual integration networks'. *Cognitive Science*, 2, 2: 133–87.
Fauconnier, G. and M. Turner (2002). *The Way We Think: Conceptual Blending and The Mind's Hidden Complexities*. New York: Basic Books.
Fillmore, C. K. (1977). 'Scenes-and-frames semantics'. In A. Zampolli (ed.) *Linguistic Structures Processing*. Amsterdam: North Holland, pp. 55–81.
Fillmore, L. W. and C. Snow (2000). 'What teachers need to know about language'. http://www.cal.org/ericell/teachers.pdf.
Fodor, J. (1985). *The Modularity of Mind*. Cambridge MA: MIT Press.
Fried, M. and J.-O. Ostman (2004). 'Construction Grammar: a thumbnail sketch'. In M. Fried and J.-O. Ostman (eds.) *Constructional Approaches to Language*. Amsterdam and Philadelphia: John Benjamins, pp 10–84.
Gallagher, S. (2005). *How the Body Shapes the Mind*. Oxford: Clarendon Press.
Gallese, V. (2000). 'The acting subject. Towards the neural basis of social cognition'. In T. Metzinger (ed.) *Neural Correlates of Consciousness: Empirical and Conceptual Questions* Cambridge, MA: MIT Press, pp. 325–33.
Gallese, V. and A. Goldman (1998). 'Mirror neurons and the simulation theory of mind reading'. *Trends in Cognitive Sciences*, 2: 492–501.
Gass, S. (1982). 'From theory to practice'. In M. Hines and W. Rutherford (eds.) *On TESOL '81*. Washington, DC: TESOL.
Gattegno, C. (1971). *What We Owe Children: The Subordination of Teaching to Learning*. London: Routledge, Kegan and Paul.
Gentner, D. and D. R. Gentner (1983). 'Flowing waters or teeming crowds: mental models of electricity'. In D. Gentner and A. Stevens (eds.) *Mental Models*. Hillsdale, NJ: Lawrence Erlbaum, pp. 99–129.
Gentner, D. and A. Markman (1997). 'Structure mapping in analogy and similarity'. *American Psychologist*, 52: 45–56.
Gibbs, R. W. Jr. (1994). *The Poetics of Mind: Figurative Thought, Language and Understanding*. Cambridge: Cambridge University Press.
Gibbs, R. W. Jr. (2005). *Embodiment and Cognitive Science*. Cambridge: Cambridge University Press.
Gibbs, R. W. Jr., D. Beitel, M. Harrington and P. Sanders (1994). 'Taking a stand on the meanings of "stand". Bodily experience as motivation for polysemy'. *Journal of Semantics*, 11: 231–51.
Goldberg, A. E. (1995). *Constructions: A Construction Grammar Approach to Argument Structure*. Chicago: University of Chicago Press.
Goldberg, A. E. (2006). *Constructions at Work: The Nature of Generalisation in Language*. Oxford: Oxford University Press.

Goldin-Meadow, S. (2003). *Hearing Gesture: How our Hands Help Us Think*. Cambridge, MA: Harvard University Press.
Goldin-Meadow, S. and C. Butcher (2003). 'Pointing toward two word speech in young children'. In S. Kita (ed.) *Pointing: Where Language, Culture, and Cognition Meet*. Mahwah, NJ: Lawrence Erlbaum, pp. 85–107.
Goldin-Meadow, S., H. Nusbaum, S. D. Kelly and S. Wagner (2001). 'Explaining math: gesture lightens the load'. *Psychological Science*, 12: 516–22.
Goldsmith, J. and E. Woisetschlaeger (1982). 'The logic of the English progressive'. *Linguistic Enquiry*, 13: 79–89.
Gómez-Pinilla, F., V. So and J. P. Kesslak (1998). 'Spatial learning and physical activity contribute to the induction of fibroblast growth factor: neural substrates for increased cognition associated with exercise'. *Neuroscience*, 1, 26: 53–61.
Goswami, U. (2001). 'Analogical reasoning in children'. In D. Gentner, K. J. Holyoak and B. N. Kokinov (eds.) *The Analogical Mind: Perspectives from Cognitive Science*. Cambridge, MA: MIT Press, pp. 437–70.
Grady, J. (1997). 'Foundations of meaning: primary metaphors and primary scenes'. Ph.D. thesis, University of California, Berkeley.
Graham, C. (1988). *Jazz Chant Fairy Tales*. Oxford: Oxford University Press.
Graham, C. (2001). *Jazz Chants: Old and New*. Oxford: Oxford University Press.
Haith, M. and J. Benson (1997). 'Infant cognition'. In D. Khun and R. Siegler (eds.) *Handbook of Childhood Psychology, Volume 2*. New York: Wiley, pp. 199–254.
Hall, H. M and T. Y. Austin (2004). *Content-based Second Language Teaching and Learning: An Interactive Approach*. Austin, TX: Allyn & Bacon.
Halliday, M. A. K. (1993). *An Introduction to Functional Grammar*. London: Arnold.
Halliday, M. A. K. and C. M. I. M. Matthiessen (1996). *Construing Experience Through Meaning: A Language Based Approach to Cognition*. London: Continuum.
Halliday, M. A. K., A. McIntosh and P. Stevens (1964). *The Linguistic Sciences and Language Teaching*. London: Longman.
Heathfield, D. (2005). *Spontaneous Speaking: Drama Activities for Confidence and Fluency*. London: DELTA Publishing.
Heider Rosch, E. (1972a). 'Probabilities, sampling and the ethnographic method: the case of Dani colour names'. *Man*, 7: 448–66.
Heider Rosch, E. (1972b). 'Universals in color naming and memory'. *Journal of Experimental Psychology*, 93: 1–20.
Heider Rosch, E. and D. C. Olivier (1972). 'The structure of the color space for naming and memory in two languages'. *Cognitive Psychology*, 3: 337–54.
Heine, B. (1997). *Cognitive Foundations of Grammar*. Oxford: Oxford University Press.
Henderson, W. (1986). 'Metaphor in economics'. In M. Couthard (ed.) *Talking About Text*. Birmingham English Language Research: Discourse Monograph, vol. 13, pp. 109–127.
Herron, C. and M. Tomasello (1988). 'Learning grammatical structure in a foreign language: modelling versus feedback'. *French Review*, 61: 910–23.
Hoard, J. E. (1975). 'On the semantic representation of oblique complements'. *Language*, 55.
Hodges Nelson, L. R. and L. R. K. Finneran (2006). *Drama and the Adolescent Journey: Warm-ups and Activities to Address Teen Issues*. Portsmouth: Heinemann.

Holme, R. (1996). *ESP Ideas: Recipes for Teaching Professional and Academic English*. Harlow: Longman.

Holme, R. (2002). 'Carrying a baby in the back: teaching with an awareness of the cultural construction of language'. *Language Culture and Curriculum*, 15, 3: 210–23.

Holme, R. (2004). *Mind, Metaphor and Language Teaching*. (Basingstoke: Palgrave Macmillan).

Holme, R. (2007). 'Socio-cultural approaches to second language learning: the contribution of cognitive linguistic theories'. In R. Allanen and S. Poyhonen (eds.) *Language in Action: Vygotsky and Leontievian Legacy Today*. Cambridge: Cambridge Scholars Press, pp. 203–22.

Holme, R. and J. King (2000). 'Teaching through metaphor: towards a learner-friendly language'. In P. Robinson and P. Thompson (eds.) *Patterns and Perspectives: Insights into EAP Writing Practice*. Reading: Reading University CALS, pp. 117–30.

Home, R. and A. Chik (submitted). 'Making your own film festival: using film for teaching and teacher training'.

Holyoak, K. J., L. Novick and E. R. Metz (1994). 'Component processes in analogical transfer: mapping, pattern completion, and adaptation'. In K. J. Holyoak and J. A. Barnden (eds.) *Advances in Connectionist and Neural Computation Theory, Vol 2: Analogical Connections*. Norwood, NJ: Ablex, pp. 113–80.

Holyoak, K. J. and P. Thagard (1995). *Mental Leaps: Analogy in Creative Thought*. Rowley, MA: MIT Press.

Hymes, D. (1971). 'Competence and performance in linguistic theory'. In R. Huxley and E. Ingram (eds.) *Language Acquisition. Models and Methods*. London: Academic Press, pp. 311–55.

Imai, M. (2000). 'Universal ontological knowledge in the construal of individuation'. In S. Niemeier and R. Dirven (eds.), *Evidence for Linguistic Relativity, Vol. 1*. Amsterdam and Philadelphia: John Benjamins, pp. 139–60.

Imai, M. and D. Gentner (1997). 'A cross-linguistic study of early word meaning: universal ontology and linguistic influence'. *Cognition*, 62: 169–200.

Jaques-Dalcroze, E. (1988 [first published 1919]). *Rhythm, Music and Education*. Salem, NH: Ayer Company Publishers.

Jeannerod, M. (1994). 'The representing brain: neural correlates of motor intention and imagery'. *Behavioural and Brain Sciences*, 17: 187–245.

Jenkins, P. (1992). *Pierre Bourdieu*. London and New York: Routledge.

Johnson, M. (1987). *The Body in the Mind: The Bodily Basis of Meaning, Imagination, and Reasoning*. Chicago: University of Chicago Press.

Johnson, M. (1989). 'Image schematic basis of meaning'. *Récherches Sémiotiques, Seniotic Inquiry*, 9: 109–18.

Johnson, M. (2007). *The Meaning of The Body: Aesthetics of Human Understanding*. Chicago: The University of Chicago Press.

Johnson, M. F. (2007). *The Drama Teachers Survival Guide: A Complete Tool Kit for Theatre Arts*. Colorado Springs: Meriwether Publishers.

Kachru, B. B. (1990). *The Alchemy of English: The Spread, Function and Models of Non-Native Englishes*. Urbana and Illinois: University of Chicago Press.

Kahnemann, D. and A. Treisman (1984). 'Changing views of attention and automaticity'. In R. Prasuraman and D. R. Davies (eds.) *Varieties of Attention*. New York Academic Press, pp. 29–61.

Kay, P. and W. Kempton (1984). 'What is the Sapir-Whorf hypothesis?'. *American Anthropologist*, 86: 65–79.
Kellerman, E. and A-M. Van Hoof, (2003). 'Manual accents' *International Review of Applied Linguistics*, 40, 3: 251–69.
Kelly Hall, J. (2002). *Teaching and Researching Language and Culture*. London: Longman.
Kennedy, J., P. Gabia and A. Nicholls (1991). 'Tactile pictures'. In M. Heller and W. Schift (eds.) *The Psychology of Touch*. Hillsdale, NJ: Erlbaum, pp. 263–99.
Kirsh, D. (1995). 'The intelligent use of space'. *Artificial Intelligence*, 73: 31–68.
Kita, S. (2000). 'How representational gestures help speaking'. In D. McNeill (ed.) *Language and Gesture*. Cambridge: Cambridge University Press.
Kosslyn, S. M. (1994). *Image and Brain: The Resolution of the Image Debate*. Cambridge, MA: MIT Press.
Kövecses, Z. (2005). *Metaphor in Culture: Universality and Variation*. New York: Cambridge University Press.
Krashen, S. D. (1981). *Second Language Acquisitian and Second Language Learning*. Oxford: Pergamon Press.
Krashen, S. D. (1985). *The Input Hypothesis: Issues and Implications*. London: Longman.
Krashen, S. D. and T. Terrell (1983). *The Natural Approach: Language Acquisition in the Classroom*. Hayward, CA: Alemany Press.
Kurtyka, A. (2001). 'Teaching English phrasal verbs: a cognitive approach'. In M. Putz, S. Niemeier and R. Dirven (eds), *Applied Cognitive Linguistics Language Pedagogy*, volume II, pp. 29-54. Berlin and New York: Mouton de Grutyter.
Labov, W. and J. Waletzky (1967). 'Narrative analysis'. In J. Helm (ed.) *Essays on the Verbal and Visual Arts*. Seattle: University of Washington Press, pp. 12–44.
Lakoff, G. (1987). *Women, Fire and Dangerous Things: What Human Categories Reveal about the Mind*. Chicago: The University of Chicago Press.
Lakoff, G. (1994). 'Conceptual metaphor homepage': http://cogsci.berkeley.edu/lakoff/metaphors/ [accessed January 2008].
Lakoff, G. and M. Johnson (1980). *Metaphors We Live By*. Chicago, IL: The University of Chicago Press.
Lakoff, G and M. Johnson (1999). *Philosophy in the Flesh*. New York: Basic Books.
Lakoff, G. and R. Nuñez (2001). *Where Mathematics Comes From: How the Embodied Mind Brings Mathematics Into Being*. New York: Basic Books.
Lakoff, G. and M. Turner (1989). *More than Cool Reason: A Field Guide to Poetic Metaphor*. Chicago, IL: University of Chicago Press.
Langacker, R. (1987). *Foundations of Cognitive Grammar. Vol. 1: Theoretical Prerequisites*. Stanford: Stanford University Press.
Langacker, R. (1990). *Concept, Image, and Symbol: The Cognitive Basis of Grammar*. Berlin and New York: Mouton de Guyter.
Langacker, R. (1991). *Foundations of Cognitive Grammar, Vol. 2: Descriptive Application*. Stanford: Stanford University Press.
Langacker, R. (1999). *Grammar and Conceptualisation*. Berlin and New York: Mouton De Gruyter.
Lantolf, J. P. (2002). 'Sociocultural theory and second language acquisition'. In R. Kaplan (ed.) *The Oxford Handbook of Applied Linguistics*. Oxford: Oxford University Press, pp. 104–14.

Lantolf, J. P. and M. P. Poehner (2005). 'Dynamic assessment in the language classroom'. *Language Teaching Research*, 9 (3): 233–65.

Larsen-Freeman, D. (1997). 'Chaos/complexity: science and second language acquisition'. *Applied Linguistics*, 18, 2: 141–65.

Larsen-Freeman, D. and L. Cameron (2007). *Complex Systems and Applied Linguistics*. Cambridge: Cambridge University Press.

Lévi-Strauss, C. (1969). *The Raw and the Cooked*. Chieago: University of Chieago Press.

Lewis, M. (1993). *The Lexical Approach: The State of ELT and the Way Forward*. Hove: Language Teaching Publications.

Lewis, M. (1997). *Implementing the Lexical Approach: Putting Theory into Practice*. Hove: Language Teaching Publications.

Lieberman, E, J-B. Michel, J. Jackson, T. Tang and M. A. Nowak (2007). 'Quantifying the evolutionary dynamics of language'. *Nature*. (www.nature.com/nature,/journal/v449/n7163/abs/nature06137.html. [accessed in April 2008]).

Lindner, S. (1981). 'A lexico-semantic analysis of English verb particle constructions with up and out'. Ph.D thesis, University of California, San Diego.

Lindstromberg, S. (1991). 'Metaphor in ESP: a ghost in the machine'. *English For Specific Purposes*, 10, 3: 207–26.

Lindstromberg, S. (1997). *English Prepositions Explained*. Amsterdam and Philadelphia: John Benjamins.

Lindstromberg S. and F. Boers (2005). 'From movement to metaphor with manner-of-movement verbs'. *Applied Linguistics*, 26, 2: 241–61.

Littlemore, J. and G. Low, (2006). *Figurative Thinking and Foreign Language Learning*. Basingstoke: Palgrave Macmillan.

Lorenz, K. (1957). 'The nature of instincts'. In C. H. Schiller (ed.) *Instinctive Behavior*. New York: International University Press, pp. 129–75.

Low, G. (1988). 'On teaching metaphor'. *Applied Linguistics*, 27, 2: 268–94.

Low, G. (1999). 'Validating metaphor research projects'. In L. Cameron and G. Low (eds.) *Researching and Applying Metaphor*. Cambridge: Cambridge University Press.

Lucy, J. and S. Gaskins (2001). 'Grammatical categories and the development of classification preferences'. In M. Bowerman and S. Levinson (eds.) *Language Acquisition and Conceptual Development*. Cambridge: Cambridge University Press, pp. 475–511.

Lucy, J. and R. Shweder (1979). 'Whorf and his critics: linguistic and nonlinguistic influences on color memory'. *American Anthropologist*, 81: 581–615.

Lyons, J. (1981). *Language and Linguistics: An Introduction*. Cambridge: Cambridge University Press.

Maley, A. and A. Duff (1982). *Drama Techniques in Language Learning*. New York: Cambridge University Press.

Malt, B. C. (1995). 'Category coherence in cross-cultural perspective'. *Cognitive Psychology*, 16: 1–27.

Marcos, L. R. (1979). 'Hand movements and nondominant fluency in bilinguals'. *Perceptual and Motor Skills*, 48: 207–14.

Martinez-Conde, S., S. L. Macknik and D. H. Hubel (2000). 'Microsaccadic eye movements and firing of single cells in the striate cortex of macaque monkeys'. *Nature Neuroscience*, 3, 3: 251-8.

Master, P. (1994). 'The effect of systematic instruction on learning the English article system'. In T. Odlin (ed.) *Perspectives on Pedagogical Grammar*. Cambridge: Cambridge University Press.

Maxwell, M. (2004). 'AIM', The Canadian Association for Language Teachers. http://www.caslt.org/about/about-history-past-awards_wmaxwell_en.php. [accessed in June 2008 ].

McCarthy, M. (1991). *Discourse Analysis for Language Teachers*. Cambridge: Cambridge University Press.

McNeill, D. (1992). *Hand and Mind: What Gestures Reveal About Thought*. Chicago: University of Chicago Press.

McNeill, D. and S. Duncan (2000). 'Growth points in thinking-for-speaking'. In D. McNeill (ed.) *Language and Gesture*. New York: Cambridge University Press, pp. 141-61.

Meltzoff, A. and M. K. Moore (1977). 'Imitation of facial and manual gestures by human neonates'. *Science*, 198: 75-8.

Merleau-Ponty, M. (1945/1962). *Phenomenologie de la Perception*. Paris: Gallimard. Trans. (1962) by C. Smith as *Phenomenology of Perception*. London: Routledge and Kegan Paul.

Mitchell, R. and F. Myles (1998). *Second Language Learning Theories*. London: Arnold.

Mittins, B. (1991). *Language Awareness for Teachers*. Buckingham: Open University Press.

Moon, R. (1998). 'Frequencies and forms of phrasal lexemes in English'. In A. P. Cowie (ed.) *Phraseology: Theory, Analysis and Applications*. Oxford: Oxford University Press, pp. 79-100.

Moskowitz, G. (1978). *Caring and Sharing in the Language Class*. Rowley, MA: Newbury House.

Munk, H. (1890). *Über die Functionen der Grosshirnrinde*. Berlin: Hirschwald.

Murata, A., L. Fadiga, L. Fogassi, V. Gallese, V. Raos and G. Rizzolatti (1997). 'Object representation in the ventral premotor cortex (area F5) of the monkey'. *Journal of Neurophysiology*, 78: 2226-30.

Nakajima, H. (2002). 'Considering the basic assumptions of construction grammar'. *The Rising Generation*, CXLV, 11: 34-7.

Nakamura, R. and M. Mishkin (1980). 'Chronic blindness following non-visual cortical lesions'. *Brain Research*, 188: 572-7.

Nattinger, J. R. and J. S. DeCarrico (1992). *Lexical Phrases and Language Teaching*. Oxford: Oxford University Press.

Negueruela, E. J and J. P. Lantolf (2004). 'The private function of gesture in second language communicative activity: a study on motion verbs and gesturing in English and Spanish'. *International Journal of Applied Linguistics*, 14: 113-47.

Novick, L. R. and K. J. Holyoak (1991). 'Mathematical problem solving by analogy'. *Journal of Experimental Psychology: Learning, Memory, and Cognition*, 17: 398-415.

Núñez, R. E., L. D. Edwards and J. F. Matos (1999). 'Embodied cognition as grounding for situatedness and context in mathematics education'. *Educational Studies in Mathematics*, 39(1) 3: 45-64.

Oberman, L., E. Hubbard, J. P. McCleery, E. L. Altschuler, S. Vilayanur, S. Ramachandran and J. A. Pineda (2005). 'EEG evidence for mirror neuron dysfunction in autism spectrum disorders'. *Cognitive Brain Research*, 24, 2: 190–8.

Ong, W. (2002). *Orality and Literacy*. London and New York: Routledge.

Orwell, G. (1945). *Animal Farm*. London: Secker and Warburg.

Oxford, R., S. Tomlinson, A. Barcelos, C. Harrington, R. Z. Lavine, A. Saleh and A. Longhini (1998). 'Clashing metaphors about classroom teachers: toward a systematic typology for the language teaching field'. *System*, 26: 3–50.

Özyürek, A. and S. Kita (1999). 'Expressing manner and path in English and Turkish: differences in speech, gesture and conceptualization'. In M. Hahn and S. C. Stoness (eds.) *Proceedings of the 21st Annual Meeting of the Cognitive Science Society*. Mahwah, NJ: Lawrence Erlbaum, pp. 507–12.

Özyürek, A. and S. Kita (2000). 'Attention manipulation in the situational use of Turkish and Japanese demonstratives'. Chicago: Linguistic Society of America Conference.

Panther, K-U. and L. L. Thornburg (2001). 'A conceptual analysis of English -er nominals.' In M. Putz, S. Niemeier and R. Dirven (eds.) *Applied Cognitive Linguistics*, Volume II: *Language Pedagogy*, pp. 151–200 (Berlin and New York: Mouton de Grutyer).

Peirce, C. S. (1931–58). *The Collected Papers of Charles Saunders Peirce*, ed. by C. Hartshorne and P. Weiss. Vols I–IV, ed. by A. Burks. Cambridge, MA: Harvard University Press.

Piaget, J. B. (1962). *Play, Dreams and Imitation in Childhood*. New York: Norton.

Piaget, J., B. Inhelder and A. Szeminska (1960). *The Child's Conception of Geometry*. London: Routledge & Kegan Paul.

Pinker, S. (1994). *The Language Instinct*. London: Penguin Books.

Poeck, K. (1964). 'Phantoms following amputation in early childhood and incongenital absence of limbs'. *Cortex*, 1: 269–75.

Pourcel, S. (2005). 'Relativism in the linguistic representation and cognitive conceptualisation of motion events across verb-framed and satellite-framed languages'. Ph.D thesis, University of Durham, UK.

Queller, K. (2001). 'A usage-based approach to modeling and teaching the phrasal lexicon'. In M. Putz, S. Niemeier, R. Dirven (eds), *Applied Cognitive Linguistics* 11 (Berlin and New York: Mouton de Grutyer), pp. 55–83.

Radden, G. and R. Dirven (2007). *Cognitive English Grammar*. Amsterdam and Philadelphia: John Benjamins.

Ramachandran, V. (2005). *The Emerging Mind*. London: BBC with Profile Books.

Reddy, M. (1993). 'The conduit metaphor: a case of frame conflict in our language about language'. In A. Ortony (ed.) *Metaphor and Thought*. Cambridge: Cambridge University Press.

Richards, I. A. (1936). *The Philosophy of Rhetoric*. London: Oxford University Press.

Richland, L., K. Holyoak and J. W. Stigler (2004). 'Analogy use in eighth-grade mathematics classrooms'. *Cognition and Instruction*, 22, 1: 37–60.

Ricoeur, P. (1975). *Le Métaphor Qui Vive*. Paris: Editions de Seuil.

Rizzolatti, G., L. Fadiga, V. Gallese and L. Fogassi (1998). 'Premotor cortex and the recognition of motor actions'. *Trends in Cognitive Sciences*, 2, 12: 493–501.

Rizzolatti, G., L. Fogassi and V. Gallese, (2000). 'Cortical mechanisms subserving object grasping and action recognition. A new view on the cortical motor functions'. In M. S. Gazzaniga (ed.) *The New Cognitive Neurosciences*. Cambridge, MA: MIT Press, pp. 539–52.

Robinson, P. (1995). 'Attention, memory, and the "Noticing" hypothesis'. *Language Learning*, 45: 283–331.

Robinson, P. (1996). 'Learning simple and complex second language rules under implicit, incidental, rule-search. *Studies in second Language Acquesition*, 18(1): 27–67.

Robinson, P. J. and M. A. Ha (1993). 'Instance theory and second language rule learning under explicit conditions'. *Studies in Second Language Acquisition*, 15: 413–38.

Rosch, E. (1975). 'Cognitive representations of semantic categories'. *Journal of Experimental Psychology (General)*, 104: 192–233.

Rosch, E. (1978). 'Principles of categorisation'. In E. Rosch and B. Lloyd (eds.) *Cognition and Categorisation*. Hillsdale, NJ: Lawrence Erlbaum, pp. 27–48.

Roth, W.-M. and D. Lawless (2002). 'Scientific investigations, metaphorical gestures, and the emergence of abstract scientific concepts'. *Learning and Instruction*, 2: 285–304.

Roth, W.-M. and M. Welzel (2001). 'From activity to gestures and scientific language'. *Journal of Research in Science Teaching*, 38: 103–36.

Rousseau, Jean-Jacques (1911 [first published 1762]). *Emile or On Education*. Trans. by Barbara Foxley. London: J.M. Dent and Sons.

Rudzka-Ostyn, B. (2003). *Word Power: Phrasal Verbs and Compounds: A Cognitive Approach*. Berlin and New York: Mouton de Gruyter.

Safran, J., R. Aslin and E. Newport (1996). 'Statistical learning by 8 month old infants'. *Science*, 274: 1926–8.

Sag, I. and T. Wasow (1999). *Syntactic Theory: A Formal Introduction*. Stanford, CA: Center for the Study of Language and Information.

Sapir, E. (1949). *The Selected Writings of Edward Sapir*. Berkeley: University of California Press.

Saunders, B. and J. Van Brakel (1997). 'Are there nontrivial constraints on colour categorization?'. *Behavioral and Brain Sciences*, 20: 167–228.

Saussure, F. (1974). *Course in General Linguistics*. London: Fontana.

Savignon, S. J. (1983). *Communicative Competence: Theory and Practice*. Reading, MA: Addison-Wesley.

Saville-Troike, M. (1988). 'Private speech: evidence for second language learing strategies during the 'Silent Period'. *Journal of Child Language*, 15: 567–90.

Schwarz, B. D. (1986). 'The epistemological status of second langauge acquisition'. *Second Language Research*, 2: 120–59.

Schwarz, B. D. (1987). 'The modular basis of second language acquisition'. Ph.D thesis, University of Southern California.

Schwarz, B. D. (1999) 'Let's make up your mind'. *Studies in Second Language Acquisition*, 21, 4: 133–59.

Scott, V. (1989). 'An empirical study of implicit and explicit teaching'. *Modern Language Journal*, 73: 14–22.

Scott, V. and S. A. Randall (1992). 'Can students apply grammar rules after reading textbook explanations?'. *Foreign Language Annals, 25*: 357–67.

Seliger, H.W. (1975). 'Inductive method and deductive method in language teaching: a re-examination'. *IRAL*, 13: 1–18.

Sharwood Smith, M. (2004). 'In two minds about grammar: on the interaction of linguistic and metalingistic knowledge in performance'. *Transactions of the Philological Society*, 102, 2: 255–80.

Skinner, B. F. (1957). *Verbal Behavior*. New York: Appleton-Century-Crofts.

Slobin, D. (1985). *Cross Linguistic Study of Language Acquisition*. Hillsdale, NJ: Lawrence Erlbaum Associates.

Slobin, D. (1996). 'From "Thought and Language" to "Thinking for Speaking"'. In J. J. Gumperz and S. C. Levinson (eds.) *Rethinking Linguistic Relativity. Studies in the Social and Cultural Foundations of Language*, vol. 1. Cambridge: Cambridge University Press, pp. 70–96.

Stafford, B. M. (2007). *Echo Objects: The Cognitive Work of Images*. Chicago: University of Chicago Press.

Streeck, J. (1996). 'How to do things with things. Objets trouvés and symbolisation'. *Human Studies*, 19: 365–84.

Stryker, S. B. and B. L. Leaver (1997). *Content-Based Instruction in Foreign Language Teaching*. Georgetown: University of Georgetown Press.

Swales, J. (1990). *Genre Analysis: English in Academic and Research Settings*. Cambridge: Cambridge University Press.

Talmy, L. (1978). 'Figure and ground in complex sentences'. In J. H. Greenberg (ed.) *Universals of Human Language. Volume 4: Syntax*. Stanford, CA; Stanford University Press, pp. 624–9.

Talmy, L. (1983). 'How language structures space'. In H. L. Pick and L. Pr. Acredolo (eds.) *Spatial Orientation: Theory, Research and Application*. New York: Plenum, pp. 225–82.

Talmy, L. (1985). 'Lexicalisation patterns. Semantic structure in lexical forms'. In T. Schopen (ed.) *Language Typology and Lexical Description. Volume 3: Grammatical Categories and the Lexicon*. Cambridge: Cambridge University Press, pp. 36–149.

Talmy, L. (1991). 'Path to realisation. A typology of event conflation'. *Berkeley Linguistics Society*, 17: 480–519.

Talmy, L. (2000). *Towards a Cognitive Semantics, Volumes 1 and 2*. Cambridge, MA: MIT Press.

Tarski, A. (1956). *Logic, Semantics and Metamathematics*. Oxford: the Clarendon Press.

Taylor, J. R. (2002). *Cognitive Grammar*. Oxford: Oxford University Press.

Taylor, J. R. and T. G. Mbense (1998). 'Red dogs and rotten mealies: how Zulus talk about anger'. In A. Athanasiadou and E. Tabakowska (eds.) *Speaking of Emotions: Conceptualisation and Expression*. Berlin: Mouton de Gruyter, pp. 191–226.

Thompson, E., A. Palacios and F. Varela (1992). 'Ways of coloring. Comparative color vision as a case study for cognitive science'. *Behavioral and Brain Sciences*, 19: 1–74.

Thorndike, E. L. (1932). *The Fundamentals of Learning*. New York: Columbia University, Teachers College.

Tomasello, M. (2003). *Constructing a Language: A Usage-Based Theory of Language Acquisition*. Cambridge, MA: Harvard University Press.

Tomasello, M. and C. Herron (1988). 'Down the garden path: inducing and correcting overgeneralization errors in the foreign language classroom'. *Applied Psycholinguistics*, 9: 237–46.

Tourelle, L. (1997). *Performance: A Practical Approach to Drama*. Port Melbourne: Port Melbourne Press.

Traugott, E. and B. Heine (1991). *Approaches to Grammaticalisation*. Amsterdam and Philadelphia: John Benjamins.

Ungerer, F. and H. J. Schmid (1996). *An Introduction to Cognitive Linguistics*. London: Longman, New York: Addison & Wesley.

Valenzeno, L., M. W. Alibali and R. L. Klatzky (2003). 'Teachers' gestures facilitate students' learning: a lesson in symmetry'. *Contemporary Educational Psychology*, 28: 187–204.

Watson, J. L. (1997). 'Mcdonald's in Hong Kong: Consumerism, dietary change and the rise of a children's culture'. In J. L. Watson (ed.) *Golden Arches East: Mcdonald's in Asia*. Stanford: Stanford University Press.

Watson, J. L. (2004). 'Globalization in Asia: anthropological perspectives'. In M. M. Suárez-Orozco and D. B. Qin-Hilliard (eds.) *Globalization: Culture and Education in The New Millenium*. Los Angeles: University of California Press.

Wernicke, C. (1900). *Grundriss der Psychiatrie in klinischen Vorleshungen*. Leipzig. Thieme.

Whorf, B. L. (1956). *Language, Thought and Reality*. Cambridge, MA: MIT Press.

Widdowson, H. G. (1973). 'An applied linguistic approach to discourse analysis', unpublished Ph.D thesis, Department of Linguistics, University of Edinburgh.

Widdowson, H. G. (1979). *Explorations in Applied Linguistics 2*. Oxford: Oxford University Press.

Wilkins, D. (1976). *Notional Syllabuses: A Taxonomy and its Relevance to Foreign Language Curriculum Development*. London: Oxford University Press.

Wittgenstein, L. (1953). *The Philosophical Investigations*. New York: Macmillan.

Wong-Fillmore, L. (1976). 'The second time around: cognitive and social strategies in second language acquisition'. Doctoral dissertation, Stanford University, CA.

Yu, N. (1998). *The Contemporary Theory of Metaphor: A Perspective from Chinese*. Amsterdam and Philadelphia: John Benjamins.

Zipf, G. K. (1935). *The Psycho-Biology of Human Language*. Boston, MA: Houghton Mifflin.

# Index

Accelerated Integrated Method (AIM), 58
action chains, 143–7
Adger, C., 98
adjectives, 84, 98–9, 145, 172, 175, 188, 192–5, 198–9
agent, 11, 39, 83, 115, 137, 143–4, 146, 184, 189, 190, 202, 222
alliteration, 43, 171–2
Altenberg, B., 6
analogy
 and education, 136–7
 and gesture, 55
 and second language learning, 12, 82–4, 88, 134, 212, 223
analytic syllabus, 217–18
Anderson, J. R., 217
Andrews, L., 98
antonym, 105, 106, 130, 142, 202
aplasic phantoms, 34–5
applied linguistics (AL) approaches, 2
argument structures, 169
Argyle, M., 54
Aristotle, 19
Asher, J., 48
Aske, J., 90
attention/salience, 112, 113–20
Austin, T. Y., 51
autism, 36
automaticity in language use, 34–5
auxiliary verbs, 179, 197, 222

Bates, E., 54
behaviourism, behaviourist linguistics, 1–2, 99
Benson, J., 82
Bergen, B. K., 173
bilingualism, 88
Black Death, 128
blends, 72–3, 82, 167, 224
Bley-Vroman, R., 3
Block, D., 135
Bloomfield, L., 1, 172

Boers, F., 28, 43, 44, 45, 58, 139, 140, 171, 186,
Boswell, J., 121
Brag, M., 141, 142
Brinton, D. 51
Broca's area, 35
Brown corpus, 175
Brumfit, C., 4, 226
Buczowska, E., 213
Burke, Edmund, 121
Butcher, C., 55
Byram, M., 95

Cameron, L., 11, 135, 220, 224,
Cardelle, M., 213
Carlson, R., 52
Carroll, S., 213, 214
Cartesian thought, 29, 37
Cary, M., 52
Casaubon in *Middlemarch*, 118
case, 188–9
categories, radial, 130, 133
categorisation, 8, 9, 11, 17, 20–5, 65, 66, 68, 74, 77, 79, 81, 82, 112, 117, 119, 120, 122, 128–38
Chagga, 76
chain stories, 108, 127
Charles River analogy, 2–3
Chen, Z., 137
Chinese, 18, 19, 76, 78, 86, 97, 114, 135, 223
Chomsky, N., 2, 4, 6, 48, 228
chunking, 212, 223,
Church, R., 56
cloze procedures/tests, 124–5, 213
cognate, 83, 84, 88, 175, 223
cognition schema, 194
cognitive code learning, 28
cognitive linguistics (CL), 6–9, 20–1, 69–74, 111–12, 161–4, 177–80
cognitive linguistic syllabus, 217–44
communicative competence, 4–5
communities of practice, 93, 95–6, 110

comparative construction, 188, 193-4
competence, 4, 181, 183, 224
complementation patterns, 202
complex transitive, 202; *see also* resultative construction
conceptual independence, 206, 208
conceptual metaphor theory (CMT), 2, 8-10, 18-19, 22, 23, 26, 28, 36-8, 45, 56, 58, 70-2, 75, 76, 97-102, 108, 112-13, 117-18, 122, 129
conceptual metaphor:
  beginnings are beneath, 141,
  causation, 202
  conduit, 8
  connection and linkage, 207
  course, 225
  deduction, 56
  emotions are temperatures, 9
  fictive motion, 40
  happiness is up, 37
  ideas are plants, 141
  knowledge is sight, 141
  people are plants, 9
  progress is forward motion, 200
  sadness is down, 37
  sexual desire is heat, 75
  society is a heap, 141
  spatial relations, 58-60, 70, 200
  the teacher is a conduit, 135
  time is money, 99
  unconscious is down, 37
  writing is thinking, 141
conceptual projection, 25
conceptualisations:
  bounded/unbounded, 74, 78, 81, 89, 106, 117, 128, 143, 152, 154
  shape and substance, 33, 74, 78-9, 81, 87, 89, 117, 152, 157, 168, 220
Conrad, J., 126
constitution; *see* gestalt
construal, 13-14, 106, 109, 111-57, 161, 189
construction:
  adjective+of+complement, 198-9
  angry with..., 199
  comparative, 192-4
  conditional, 12, 72

ditransitive, 187, 195, 201-3, 208, 222, 226
do one thing just to get another/exchange, 204
gerund, 91
hours a day, 207, 208-9
I've got, 180-1
incapable/capable of, 198-9
it-is-used-for, 169
link between one thing and another, 206, 209
partitive, 208
ready for, 198-9
resultative, 202-3, 226
said something, 207
the study shows..., 206-7, 209
way, 200
you drive me crazy, 203
you drive me up the wall, 203
constructions:
  and conceptualisation, 157
  and construction grammar, 7, 10-11, 14, 58, 84, 103, 123, 177-83
  and prepositions, 157, 180, 184, 188, 190, 196-9, 196, 197, 198, 199, 200, 203
  filled, 185-6
  partially filled, 186-201
  partially filled, bound morphemes, 187-92
  partially filled, inflectional morphemes, 192-7
  partially filled, lexis, 197-201
  the teaching and learning of, 170, 184-206
  unfilled, 201-5
construction teaching for advanced students, 205-12
Cooper, D., 19
copula, 202
Corno, L., 213
corpus linguistics, language corpus, 6, 58, 175
Cortazzi, M., 135
countable and uncountable nouns, 81, 114, 117, 120, 152
counter-factuals, 72

Croft, W., 112, 117, 123, 150, 165, 177, 181, 199, 210
Cruse, D. A., 112, 117, 123, 150, 155, 165, 199
Culicover, P., 7
culture and conventionalisation, 10–11, 70–1, 199
culture and language teaching, 47, 67, 92–108, 132, 142, 220
cultures and conceptualisation, 13, 18, 19, 34, 65–108, 117, 129, 161, 162, 186, 219

de Bot, K., 224
De Guerrero, M., 135
Deacon, T., 71
DeCarrico, J.S, 6, 212
definite article, 17, 60–1, 74, 89, 180
definition exercises, 116
Deignan, A., 135
deixis, 150–2
Derrida, J., 8
Descartes, R., 29
determiners, 60–2, 73–4, 86–7, 89, 114, 120, 178–80, 185, 206, 222, 223
Dewey, J. 39, 40
Dirven, R., 58, 73, 85, 113, 170, 190, 194
discourse in teaching and learning, 48, 72, 93, 95, 110, 119, 120–2, 126–8, 132, 134, 139, 141–2, 149, 150, 166
Donald, M., 44
drama, in language teaching, 42, 46–7, 50, 53, 58, 227, 229
Dudley-Evans, T., 139
Duff, A., 46
duodecimal systems, 37
Dutch, 91–2
dynamic assessment, 224–5
dynamic attention, 125–8
dynamic systems, 224–5, 229–30

Eckman, F. R., 214
Edelman, G., 7
education and embodiment; see embodiment and education
education, formal, 41

Eeg-Olofsson, M., 6
Eliot, George, 118
Ellis, N. 224
Ellis, R., 205
embodied cognition, 9, 13, 28, 29–38, 52–3, 56, 62, 179, 218
embodiment:
  and education, 39–41, 53, 56, 62
  and language teaching, 41–53, 55, 87, 220, 227–8
enactive cognition, 30, 39, 48, 52, 70, 77, 112, 113–17, 157, 218–19
enactment and movement (E&M), 28, 44–8, 58, 60, 118, 138, 229
encyclopaedic meaning, 14, 89, 161, 163, 164, 168–9, 174, 183, 194, 195, 203, 226
English as an international language, 67–8, 95, 109
English for Academic Purposes (EAP) 123, 140, 143, 170, 229
English for Specific Purposes (ESP); see Language for Specific Purposes
entrench, entrenchment, 181, 182, 183
envisioning, 108
errors in language learning, 6, 57, 80–9, 115, 193, 204–5, 213, 229
Evans, V., 72, 139

Fadiga, L., 35
Fauconnier, G., 37, 72, 82
figure and ground, 10, 90, 105–6, 107, 108, 112, 129, 142–5
Fillmore, C. K., 169, 170
Fillmore, L. W., 98
Finneran, L. R. K., 53
first language acquisition, 7, 36, 48, 81–2, 183, 220, 222
Fleming, M., 95
Fodor, J., 3
force dynamics, 142–6
formal approaches to meaning, formal semantics, 7, 18, 27, 112, 162
frames, semantic frames, 120–1, 131, 132, 136, 142, 162, 170, 184, 219
French, 20, 58, 76, 84, 86, 88, 90–2, 114, 172
Fried, M., 183

Gallagher, S., 30–4, 55
Gallese, V., 33, 35
Gaskins, S., 78–9
Gass, S., 214
Gattegno, C., 57
generative linguistics, 2–4, 6–7, 68, 88, 115, 161, 180, 212, 220, 224
genitive, 188, 189
Gentner, D. R., 137
Gentner, D., 79, 82, 137
geometry, 155–7
German, 172, 188
Germanic, 90, 91, 182
gestalt, 112, 152–5, 164, 179
gesture:
   and language acquisition, 54, 90–2
   in communication, 54–6, 71, 73, 80, 219
   in education, 56–8, 220
   in language teaching, 58–62, 96, 110, 114, 124, 173, 221, 228, 229
Gibbs, R., 9, 21, 22, 33, 39, 40, 71, 117
Goldberg, A. E., 169, 177, 181, 183–4, 195, 201–2
Goldin-Meadow, S., 54, 55, 56
Goldman, A., 35
Goldsmith, J., 153–4
Gómez-Pinilla, F., 53
Goswami, U., 137
Grady, J., 38
Graham, C., 42–3
grammatical categories, 115
Green, M., 72, 139
grounding, 60, 74, 78, 83, 86, 120, 150–1, 178

Ha, M. A., 214
Haith, M., 82
Hall, H. M., 51
Halliday, M. A. K., 1, 5
Heathfield, D., 46
Heider, E. Rosch 77, 129–30
Heine, B., 38, 70
Henderson, W., 139
Herron, C., 214
Hispanic, 55, 92
Hoard, J.E., 145
Hodges Nelson, L. R., 53

Holme, R., 5, 133, 141, 143, 186,
Holyoak, J., 82, 137
homunculus, homunculus metaphor, 32
Hong Kong, 46, 97, 132, 206, 210
Hopi, 68
Hymes, D., 4
hyponymy, 130–2, 163–5, 167, 194–6

idiom, 7, 27, 43, 88, 97, 140, 185–6, 200, 227
image schema, 22–3, 25, 27, 28, 36–8, 74–6, 103, 113, 152, 154, 156, 179, 184
Imai, M., 79
imitative behaviour, 32
indefinite article, 45, 74, 89, 180
infant cognitive development, 22, 30, 32, 33–4, 37–8, 39, 54, 74, 82–3, 136–7, 219–20, 221, 222
inflections, 103, 114, 187–9
inheritance hierarchy, 195–6
inheritance, 89, 90, 163, 164–5, 177, 180–1, 195–6, 199, 201
internal syllabus, 225
intransitives, verbs, processes and constructions, 7, 115, 190, 200, 202, 204
Inuit, 68
irregularity, irregular verbs, 9, 170–1, 179, 182–3, 189
Islamic culture, 132

Jackendoff, R., 7
Japanese, 11, 44, 74, 78, 79, 91, 96
Jaques-Dalcroze, E., 41
jazz chants, 42, 43
Jeannerod, M., 236, 33
Jenkins, P., 93
Jin, L., 135
Johnson, K., 4, 226
Johnson, M. E., 53
Johnson, M., 8–9, 37–8, 56, 65, 99, 126, 141
judgment and comparison, 112, 129

Kachru, B. B., 97
Kahnemann, D., 35
Kay, P., 77

*Index* 247

Kellerman, E., 55, 91
Kelly Hall, J., 98
Kempton, W., 77
Kennedy, J., 33
King, J., 133
Kirsh, D., 40
Kita, S., 55, 72, 91
Kosslyn, S. M., 126
Kövecses, Z., 75–6
Krashen, S. D., 48
Kurtyka, A., 58

Labov, W., 47
Lakoff, G., 8–9, 25, 37, 56, 78, 99, 100, 117, 118, 120, 129, 130, 141, 177, 199, 200
landmark, 91, 105, 143–5, 148
Langacker, R., 9, 59–60, 73, 74, 105, 106, 111–12, 115, 117, 120, 142–3, 144, 145, 152, 162, 168, 177
Language for Specific Purposes (LSP), 51, 138, 166
Lantolf, J. P., 44, 91–2, 224
Larsen Freeman, D., 11, 220, 222, 224
Latin, 39, 56, 88, 91, 172–3
Lawless, D., 56
Leaver., B. L., 51
Lego, 51
Lévi-Strauss, C., 69
Lewis, M., 6, 145
lexical approach to language teaching, 145
lexical maps, 174
lexicon, the, 6, 161, 78, 180
Lieberman, A. P., 182
Lindner, S., 48
Lindstromberg, S., 28, 43, 44, 45, 139, 171
linguistic modularity, language module, 3–4, 7, 11, 34
linguistic relativity, 65–109, 219
linguistic symbolism; *see* symbolism
linguistics applied (LA) approaches, 2
Littlemore, J., 58, 136
Lorenz, K., 181
Low, G. D., 58, 136
Lucy, J., 77, 78–9

Macdonald's restaurants, 62, 97
Maley, A., 46
Malt, B. C., 79
mapping, cognitive process of, 32, 33, 35, 37–8, 58, 72, 90, 103, 229
Marcos, L. R., 92
Markman, A., 82
Martinez-Conde, S., 33
Master, P., 85
mathematics education, 40, 52, 137
mathematics, nature of, 37
Matthiessen, C., 5
Maxwell, M., 58
McCarthy, M., 98
Mcintosh, A., 1
McNeil, D., 54, 55
Meltzoff, A., 32
Meno's problem, 29–31
mental spaces, 72–3
Merleau-Ponty, M., 9, 30, 31, 94
meronymy, 163, 165–7
metaphor:
  analysis, 135–6
  and language teaching, 134–42
  and learning lexis, 13, 138–42
  formal approaches to, 19
  in Chinese, 76
  in education, 40
  in Zulu, 76
  processing, problems with, 32
metaphorical competence, 136
metaphors:
  department store, 134,
  hour glass, 122
  mother of all battles, 18–19
  of education, 39, 225, 227
  of language, 229
  of learning, 135
  of sport, 76
  of time, 9, 27, 68, 71, 75, 85–6, 92–3, 94, 98–9, 109, 110, 132–3, 134, 137–8, 198
metatext, 141, 170
metonymy, 9–10, 101, 112–13, 116, 117–20, 165, 172, 200
  function for form, 118
  path of movement is movement, 200

mime, 41–2, 44–8, 50, 53, 54, 57, 103, 108, 220
mind maps, 140
minimalism in linguistics, 6
mirror neurons, 35–6, 44, 54, 66
Mishkin, M., 33
Mittins, B., 98
modal verbs, 51, 191
Moon, R., 6
Moore, M. K., 32
morpheme, 114–17, 138, 173, 182, 188–97, 222
morphemes:
 -ed, 88, 117, 197
 -ee, 115
 -er, comparative, 188, 193
 -er, nominal, 115
 -est, 188, 193
 -s, plural, 114–5, 188
 -'s, genitive, 188–9
 -ing, 138
motion paths, 91, 102–7, 127–8
Munk, H., 31
Murata, A., 33

Nakajima, H., 201
Nakamura, R., 33
Native American, 67, 68
Nattinger, J. R., 6, 212
Negueruela, E. J., 91–2
neonates, 32
noticing, 205, 213
Novick, L. R., 137
Núñez, R. E., 40

Oberman, L., 36
object perception, 31–4
objectification, 112, 146
Ong, W., 122
ontogeny, 44, 75
Orwell, G., 193
Ostman, J-O., 183
Oxford , R., 135
Özyürek, A., 73, 91

Panther, K. U., 115
particle, 91, 92
partitive construction, 208
passive construction, 144–5

pattern-finding in second language acquisition, 81–3, 88
Peirce, C. S., 70, 219
perceptual event schema, 190
perspective and situatedness, 147–50,
phantom limbs; *see* aplasic phantoms
phonaesthemes, 171–4
phonics teaching, 43
phonology, 113, 163, 171–6, 182, 188, 220, 223
phrasal verbs, phrasal verb constructions, 58, 92, 103
phylogeny, 44
Piaget, J., B., 32, 75
picaresque novel, 126
Pinker, S., 68–9
plural, 74, 114–15, 120, 154, 188
Poeck, K., 34
Polish, 188
Portuguese, 88
post-syllabus, 225
Pourcel, S., 68, 78, 101
prepositions, 26–7, 38, 58–60, 70, 91, 92, 103–8, 123, 124, 145, 148, 155, 155, 157, 163, 171, 178–9, 180, 184, 188, 190, 196–9, 200, 203
pre-syllabus, 225
private speech, 44, 48, 52, 221
proceduralisation of language knowledge, 11–12, 35, 187–8, 196, 217, 222, 225
process syllabus, 217–18
productivity (in grammar), 179–80, 182, 183, 204, 210, 228
proform, 210
proprioception, 30, 31–3, 34, 35, 55, 165
proprioceptors, 32
prototype charts, 211
prototype, category prototype, 129–30, 187, 205, 211

Queller, K., 58
question and answer routines, 118, 120–1, 168

Radden, G., 58, 73, 85, 87, 170, 290, 191, 194
radical construction grammar, 212
Ramachandran, S. 7, 54
Randall, S.A., 214
reading intentions, 81–2
Reddy, M., 8
rehearsal strategies, 44
rhyme, 171
rhythm and movement, 41–4
Richards, I.A., 8
Richland, L., 137
Ricoeur, P., 8, 9
Rizzolatti, G., 33
Robinson, P. J, 214
Romance (language), 88, 90
Rosch, E., *see* Heider, E. Rosch
Roth, W.-M., 56
Rousseau, Jean-Jacques, 39–40
Rudzka-Ostyn, B., 58

Saddam Hussein, 18–19
Saffran, J., 82
Sag, I., 195
Sapir, E., 67–9, 92, 93
Satellite-framed languages, 90–2, 100
Saunders, B., 77
Saussure, F., 7
Savignon, S. J., 4
Saville-Troike, M., 44
scalar adjustment, 112, 123–30
schematic meaning, 38, 51, 60, 61, 62, 79, 85, 90, 114, 115, 116, 118, 136, 163, 164–5, 170, 172, 174, 176, 179–81, 183–4, 193, 197, 200, 201, 204, 207, 208, 209, 222, 226, 229
Schmid, H.J., 152
Schwarz, B., 3
science education, 137, 160
scope, 112, 119–23, 126, 154
Scott, V. M., 214
second language acquisition (SLA) theory, 2–3, 11, 55, 56, 113–17, 205–6, 212, 224
Seliger, H.W., 214
semantic maps, 211
semiotic material, 219

sense relation, 163, 171–6, 174, 201, 222
*ser* v *estar*, 80–1
Shweder, R., 77
Silent Period, 48
Silent Way, 57
situational approach, 137–8
Skinner, B. F., 1
Slobin, D. I., 79
Snow, C., 98
Snow, M. A., 98
social practices, 93, 95, 96, 110
Socrates, 29, 31
source domain, 37, 75, 186
space builders, 73
Spanish, 80–1, 88, 90, 91, 82, 144
spatial perception, 31–4, 143
sports coaching, 51
St John, M. J., 139
Stafford, B. M., 164
Stelma, J., 135
Stevens, P., 1
Streeck, J., 55
structuralism, structuralist linguistics, 1, 5, 68, 69, 92, 161, 172
Stryker, S. B., 51
substitution table, 207, 209, 211
Swain, M., 213
Swales, J., 93
symbolic complexes, 11, 177, 180
symbolism, linguistic symbolism, 10–11, 14, 52, 69, 70–1, 94–5, 115, 161, 178, 183, 185, 187, 212, 218–23
syntax, 6–7, 120, 185, 186–7, 201
synthetic syllabus, 217–18
systemic functional linguistics (SFL), 2, 5–6

Talmy, L., 10, 90, 123, 142, 179, 184
target domain, 37, 76
Taylor, J. R., 76, 115, 182, 200, 206

tense and aspect:
  future, 57
  future perfect, 86
  past continuous, 138, 155
  past perfect, 85–6
  past simple, 49, 57, 85–6, 102–3, 108, 137–8, 152–5, 164, 182, 188–9, 191–2, 197
  present continuous, 49, 228
  present perfect, 57, 86, 197–8
  present simple, 42, 108, 115, 164
Terrell, T., 48
Thagard, P., 82
*The Soldier's Return*, 141
Thompson, E., 78
Thornburg, L. L., 115
Thorndike, E. L., 1
time lines, 137, 197
token, 179–83, 212, 213, 219, 227, 228
Tomasello, M., 11, 35, 81–2, 136, 170, 214
total physical response (TPR), 48–52, 229
Tourelle, L., 243
transformational generative grammar, 6
transitive, transitive construction, 7, 11, 115, 143–4, 184, 200, 202, 206, 207, 222, 227
Traugott, E., 38
Treisman, A., 35
truth-conditional semantics, 18–19
Turkish, 73, 91
Turner, M. 37, 72, 82
type, 179–83, 212, 213, 219, 227, 228

Ungerer, F., 152
universal grammar (UG), 2–3

usage, 12, 14, 46, 57, 116, 136, 138, 175, 177, 181–3, 185, 195, 204, 205, 213, 219, 221, 222, 224, 226–7, 228, 229

valency, 169
Valenzeno, L., 56
Van Brakel, J., 77
Van Hoof, A-M., 91
verb-framed languages, 90–2, 100
verbs of manner, 100–1, 102, 229
Vilamil, O. S., 135
visual perception, 31, 32–3
vocabulary teaching and learning, 6, 44, 45, 58, 116, 119–21, 140, 162, 163, 165, 174, 211

Waletzky, J., 47
Wasow, T., 195
Waterman, Ian, 55
Watson, J. L., 93, 97
Weist, R. M., 213
Welzel, M., 56
Wernicke, C., 32
Whorf, B. L., 67–9, 75, 78, 89, 92, 93
Whorfian determinism, 110
Widdowson, H. G., 1, 2
Wilkins, D., 217
Wittgenstein, L., 8
Woisetschlaeger, E., 153–4
Wong-Fillmore, L., 212

young learners, 42, 88, 137, 173
Yu, N., 76
Yucatec, 78–9

Zipf, G. K., 222–3
Zipf's law, 222–3